DAISY DIES

AND

SEES NAPLES

DAVID LAMB

BELLISMEDIA

Published by Bellismedia Ltd
1 Beresford Avenue Twickenham TW1 2PY England

www.bellismedia.com

ISBN: 0-9538334-0-2

A catalogue record for this title is available from the British Library

Cover design: Julia Midgley

Printed in Great Britain by The Cromwell Press Ltd

Contents

To Jack of course

YEAR ONE

Daisy Dies and Sees Naples

WE journalists make it a point to know very little about an extremely wide variety of topics: this is how we stay objective.

DAVE BARRY, *Dave Barry Does Japan*

1

Bagshot - Montacute - Torquay - Lower Yalberton - Coleton Fishacre - Dartmeet - Princetown - Burrator - Ponsworthy - Buckland-in-the-Moor - Haytor - Liverton - Shaldon - Lyme Regis - Seatown - Dorchester - Camberley - Bloxham - Charlecote

THUNDER thundered, lightning lightned, bungee-jump rain double-glazed the surgery window and we wept as we watched the vet put Daisy, our beloved cat, to sleep.

It was too simple as he neatly shaved a tiny tuft of fur from her leg and efficiently ended her 18 years of life with just a pinprick.

We told each other we were daft to cry, then we told each other we couldn't help it.

Since she'd been a kitten she'd played her full part in making ours a happy family. Now, with typical unselfishness, she'd succumbed to crippling old age at the same time as I'd managed to extricate myself from 31 years of tabloid journalism.

(The first 30 were a pleasure, then the novelty wore off).

Our two sons were old enough to look after themselves so Daisy, having needed months of constant attention, had given me the freedom I needed to go with the time I now had for travel.

I vowed to keep her memory alive.

My first priority on becoming an ex-journalist (apart from making a belated bid to become a scratch golfer) was to try to forget the names of all The Spice Girls, The Teletubbies and, if at all possible, The Royal Family.

Getting older helps, of course, and I'm pleased to report considerable success (although I do keep thinking there's a Victoria in there somewhere).

But then, as my mate Jim Harding says, brain cells are like sperms: It only takes one.

And I'm better off than another pal, Fergus Linnane, who told me he once found himself in one of those embarrassing situations where he had to introduce his wife to someone at a party and no matter how hard he tried he just couldn't remember the name... of his wife.

My second priority was to try to make enough money to pay for a loft conversion like the one they've got next door, to use as a study.

(That bit's up to you).

So it was that one damp April afternoon The Chauffeur drove me to Bagshot. Yes, Bagshot: It's one of those places you've heard of but you've never been to. (Well, not willingly, anyway). And it's one of those names that the more you think about it the dafter it gets. (Who was the bag? Why was she shot?)

We were there to visit Southern Cross Motorhomes, purveyors to the Early Retired, where we'd planned to spend about £10,000 of my redundancy money on a modest secondhand camper van.

In the event, and with surprising suddenness, we fell for a gleaming new motor caravan (not to mention manager Mike Graves's gleaming sales talk).

It wasn't just the van's handsome looks that seduced us, it was the enticing smell. As soon as we slid open the big butch side door it hit us: That pungent waft of unadulterated newness.

Maybe it's something they spray on, like the stuff you read about in men's magazines that makes you irresistible to women.

Mike cleverly made us feel we knew what we were doing by assuring us we were asking him all the right questions. Then he reeled off a list of the extras we'd be getting with his Special Bargain Deal: A heater. A battery. An engine. Seats. Etc.

We went for a test drive, with Mike watching our every move from the back seat like a vigilant L-test examiner, and we were hooked. Soon, The Chauffeur was excitedly writing out a large cheque. Or trying to.

First she wrote:

TWENTY THREE POUNDS. (That's wrong. Crumple, crumple).

Then she wrote:

TWENTY THREE THOUSAND POUNDS. (No. Crumple, crumple).

Finally she wrote:

TWENTY THREE THOUSAND NINE HUNDRED AND NINETY POUNDS ONLY.

And once she'd got it right, Mike offered us a cup of coffee. Each. For free.

For those of you who need to know these things, we'd bought a Volkswagen Auto-Sleepers T4 Trident with 2.4 diesel engine and five cylinders (whatever they do).

At least, we thought, we wouldn't have to worry about any mechanical problems.

Ten days later we were back, by train and acting like a couple of kids on Christmas morning, to grab our new toy.

We signed a number of important-looking documents without reading them. Then we were given a weighty plastic wallet stuffed with manuals and handbooks which we'd probably never read either.

Just as well then that the appropriately named Richard Yule was there to play Santa Claus and explain to us how to make everything work, while we pretended we understood.

He showed us the way to fill up with diesel, gas, electricity, drinking water etc. (You could run the clever little fridge off gas or electricity, to taste).

Displaying my extensive mechanical knowledge I said I understood it could be awkward if you put diesel in a petrol engine by mistake and asked whether it would be a problem the other way round.

Oh yes, Richard replied cheerfully.

After 35 years of filling cars with petrol it was going to be a good memory test for us.

As well as the fridge we got two tables, a bed and a bit, a cooker, a sink, half a wardrobe, numerous cupboards and drawers, a ladder leading to a roof rack, and an awning to help keep the sun off us during the cocktail hour.

Under the sink there was cutlery and crockery for four, neatly slotted into smart plastic containers.

The crockery looked as if it might be unbreakable, but we expected we'd find that out as we went along.

Finally, Richard went through the motions of demonstrating the amazing Porta-Potti. (No, not literally).

A cunning little gadget of pumps and pipes and chemicals, it tucked away snugly in one of the bottom cupboards.

The Chauffeur was quite taken with the thing, although I swore I'd never use it. No matter how desperate I was.

So, with much handshaking, we left Bagshot and drove loftily away on our high front seats which give you a far better view of the world than you get from a car.

We didn't feel we had much more width than a car though, but that could just mean our judgment was faulty. (Time would tell).

We proudly returned home to show off our toy to the neighbours. Little Eve from across the road put us in our place straight away: "Where's the dishwasher?" she asked.

But Joyce from next door humoured us wonderfully and said all the nice complimentary things we wanted to hear. She even agreed (after being asked only three times) to come for a ride round the block. In her slippers.

That night, over a couple of glasses of bubbly, we agreed to call our new pride and joy Daisy.

LOGOS. You can't get away from them, can you? Whatever you do, wherever you go, there they are. Especially on clothes. All I wanted was some nice plain casual gear to wear on my travels, but everything I looked at was smothered in the darned things.

It's all right if you're Tiger Woods and you're being bundled bunkers-full of dollars to display them, but why should I donate my left breast free of charge as an advertising site for companies who've already got far more money than I'll ever see?

Actually, it's amazing what labels people are prepared to wear, particularly on holiday. I noticed this on our last trip to Blackpool. There, hats used to say: KISS ME QUICK SQUEEZE ME SLOWLY (never QUICKLY or SLOW).

Not any more: I couldn't find one of those anywhere. Instead, they all bore more basic messages such as the one I saw a grey-haired granny wearing with pride as she brought up the rear along the Golden Mile behind Mum, Dad and two kids:
WINE ME DINE ME 69 ME

I often wonder if she understood the invitation she was broadcasting to the world. Not to mention what she got for afters.

(I tell you someone else whose worldly wisdom I worry about: The Times writer who trades under the name of Roger Boyes).

Anyway, I finally managed to track down a natty matching yellow shirt and shorts at the Marks & Sparks near us in the Kew Retail Park.

(No relation to the nearby botanic park, although that too had been going in for the hard commercial sell with a campaign of radio adverts by the Texas rose Ms Jerry Hall).

Totally untainted by unsightly logos, these sartorial gems looked just the thing to enable me to grace the most fashionable resorts of Europe.

Unfortunately the only shorts they had were a bit on the tight side, but I decided to buy them anyway: To hold hostage, as it were, with a view to swapping them for something more suited to my maturer figure at Marks & Sparks, Richmond.

When I got to the Richmond branch I was delighted to find they had just one pair left in my size. I eagerly presented both pairs, old and new, at the Refunds And Exchanges counter and asked to swap one for the other.

And that was when (not for the first time in my life) I ran into Computer Trouble: I had unerringly picked The Shorts That Didn't Exist.

Nothing is simple in shopping: Try as she might, while a daunting queue of increasingly fidgety women began to lengthen behind me, the salesgirl couldn't get the details of the new shorts to come up on her screen.

As far as her stock list was concerned, they just weren't there.

Another girl was dispatched to the rail I'd got them from to try to find a pair in my size that did exist, but (as I'd anticipated) to no avail.

By this time the women in the queue were starting to turn, well, quite ugly. I was beginning to wonder whether sexual equality didn't really exist after all, and whether clothes shops and other war zones should be left to the more belligerent half of the species.

Next, disks were fed into another terminal (a two-girl operation, this) and a record of the new shorts was finally found.

They weren't in Existing Stock, they were in Old Stock.

This meant they did exist after all and I was allowed to have them but only if I was prepared to accept a £6 refund, the difference between the new (old) shorts and the old (new) shorts.

I said the deal would be OK by me, and imagined the proud smile that would light up The Chauffeur's face when I took them home and told her I'd got a bargain (for once).

In fact, it didn't turn out quite like that: She took one look at my smart new outfit, announced it was the naffest thing she'd ever seen and said there was no way I'd be wearing it if I was to appear in public with her.

Undaunted, I decided to continue my shopping attempts and took the train to London to visit my favourite map shop, Stanfords in Long Acre. Here, I felt much easier in the more man-friendly surroundings.

(As is well known, women don't even know how to fold maps, let alone read them).

The Chauffeur isn't The Chauffeur because she's a better driver than me (although I do admit I find it to my advantage to assure her as often as possible that she is).

No, she's The Chauffeur because if our marriage is to last more than another ten minutes it's vital when we're travelling that she keeps her hands on the wheel and off the map.

(Most couples can fall out over most things, but never more so than over a woman's futile attempts at map reading).

I spent a happy half hour in Stanfords browsing, buying, and wishing I was richer. If I had a lot more money than I have, I'd spend nearly all of it collecting maps and guides (even if I knew I'd never have time to read them).

On to a nearby camping shop, which was equally man-friendly, where I seemed to be the only customer wearing long trousers. Here, I enquired of a bearded, middle-aged salesperson about mosquito repellants.

By Long-Haired Professor out of Saloon Bar Know-All, there was nothing this guy couldn't tell me about such substances, and he enthusiastically described the dangers of them to me.

One particularly scary one, he claimed, could cause some people's skin to erupt in mountainous red lumps. On no account should it be used by anyone who hadn't tried it before.

(Pity those poor innocents who might make the painful discovery that there was a first time for everything).

One luckless user, he said, had even had his glasses melted by it. Before his very eyes.

By the time he'd finished his lurid tales quite a crowd had gathered round us, presumably thanking heaven Saddam Hussein had never got his hands on the stuff.

I decided that all in all I'd be better off taking my chances with the mosquitoes.

Actually, I'm quite safe from them as long as I've got The Chauffeur with me. The best (of many) reasons for having married her is that she's the perfect Mosquito Decoy.

They clearly find her the world's most succulent dish: A sort of Parma Ham And Melon on the mosquito menu. And they avoid me altogether for the sheer gastronomic delight of getting their teeth into her.

I briefly considered the idea (in this image-conscious age) of buying a pair of Malibu surfboards or maybe even a couple of snowboards to stick on Daisy's roof rack, just for show.

I'd have to be careful, though, to take the snowboards to the Atlantic and the surfboards to the Alps.

This would have two benefits:

1. I would appear to be more widely travelled and athletically versatile.

2. There would be no danger of my having to display my sporting inadequacies.

My shopping expedition complete, I walked across Waterloo Bridge and in the late spring sunshine, from the Houses of Parliament to Saint Paul's Cathedral and beyond, London looked as beautiful as any city in the world.

I caught the train home to Richmond, sat on a warmly welcoming bench by the willowy riverside, and asked myself whether any further travels were really necessary.

THE Chauffeur's sister and her husband have a campsite: Lower Yalberton Farm, near Paignton in Devon. What's more it's where the original Daisy was born, to Honey the farmhouse cat.

So we decided that was where we should go for our new Daisy's Maiden Voyage.

We were up at seven to get everything ready and had hoped to leave by ten. In fact we set off just after one, having given ourselves ample time to demonstrate the unholy matrimonial formula:
OVER-EXCITEMENT + GROSS INEPTITUDE = A LOAD OF GRIEF

Despite our Southern Cross teach-in we struggled with the water hose, which wouldn't unwind. We struggled with the power cable, which wouldn't plug in. And we struggled with the instructions for turning on the fridge:

1.   Set the rocker switch marked with the site lead symbol to the on position.
2.   Turn on 230 volt RCD (which is in the up position).
3.   Turn on 6 amp MCB (which is in the up position).

Panic. Try to remember. What's the RCD? Where's the MCB?

Next we disagreed about what we should take with us while each of us accused the other of being the more bad-tempered, which made matters even worse.

The journey itself was fine. Our first stop was elegant Montacute House in sloping green Somerset: One of the stars of Emma Thompson's lovely film adaptation of Jane Austen's Sense and Sensibility.

Here, we had tea and walked in the gorgeous gardens with their big dark lumpily eccentric hedges of Imagine-It-Yourself topiary, in which we made out the shapes of rabbits, pheasants, teddy bears and big busty naked women.

Next, we stopped for petrol (sorry, diesel) but when we set off again we couldn't get the radio to work. Help. Is it us? Or is it it? It's all right: It's just got a mind of its own. It comes on eventually if you try it often enough. It must be some sort of security device.

(There couldn't possibly be anything wrong with our German Supervan).

Daisy trundled along at a fair lick. She reached 90 with ease on the motorway, although The Chauffeur had to make some nifty gear changes going up Telegraph Hill near Exeter to spare us the indignity of slowing to less than 30.

We called on The Chauffeur's Mum in Torquay to show her our new toy, then we drove along the seafront towards Paignton. The bay looked beautiful on a perfect early May evening: The tide was in and a full moon was waiting its turn to be the star of the night.

I wondered (again) if our travels with Daisy really needed to go any further.

We reached the camp at eight to be fondly welcomed by The Brother and Sister in Law. It wasn't officially open for the summer yet but they had some toilet facilities ready for us, so we wouldn't have to rely on the dreaded Porta-Potti.

What struck me most when we arrived was the noise, or rather the lack of it. The first sound we heard was a cuckoo, closely followed by a couple of pheasants then a wood pigeon. And that was about it.

With only minor skirmishing, we succeeded in switching the fridge from battery to gas while The Brother in Law happily regaled us with tales of domestic camping disputes.

One couple, he said, had arrived as lovey-dovey honeymooners, but were well on their way to divorce when the only thing they'd managed to get erect was their caravan awning.

After 30 years of contempt-breeding familiarity, what chance did The Chauffeur and I have?

Sunday morning: A light plane droned lazily overhead, a tractor drove past (twice) and distant church bells summoned the faithful to matins. We weren't missing the traffic, the trains, or the jets shrieking past our house on the flightpath to Heathrow.

There wasn't much room for sleeping in Daisy, or for getting out of bed. But for once it was The Chauffeur who was the first to bang her head.

(This is something that happens to me at least five times a day on holiday. As a rule, the prettier the place the more likely it is to happen: Especially in ye olde pubbes with ye olde beames).

After we'd won our fight to convert Daisy's bed back into a seat (it kept getting caught up in the rear seatbelts) we managed to get the cooker going and skilfully created bacon butties for breakfast.

Later, we drove through hedgerows spring-tide high with bluebells, red and white campion, wild garlic, buttercups, dandelions and (of course) daisies to the wonderful Coleton Fishacre Gardens near Kingswear.

Unfortunately, The Chauffeur managed to park Daisy with the passenger door about one and a quarter inches from a particularly impenetrable shrubbery.

But I battled to make it (garnished with greenery) to the pretty little outdoor café where greedy great tits and cheeky chaffinches menaced us as we sat in the sun over our morning coffee and cakes.

Coleton Fishacre is a beauty. It started life as a small stream running down a gentle valley to the sea. Now it flows with a torrent of floral colour through paths, ponds and stone walls which proudly proclaim its 1930s charm.

We saw blowzy azaleas, rhododendrons, camellias and magnolias merge with their more demure green country cousins while stern Mum and Dad Duck tried to hide their parental pride as their brood of half a dozen youngsters splashed playfully among the lily pads (especially the naughty one).

As we left, The Chauffeur had to make her first tricky driving manoeuvre: Reversing 50 yards up a narrow country lane after we found ourselves face to face with a posh Range Rover.

Despite all her generous efforts, the tweedy twit at the wheel never thanked her. In such low regard do the self-satisfied unadventurous locals hold us free-spirited go-anywhere travelling folk.

BEFORE leaving home, we'd sent out Daisy Christening Party cards to The Chauffeur's relatives (inviting them to wet our baby's cylinder head, as it were).

So on the way back to camp we called at Sainsbury's to buy fizzy drinks (alcoholic and non), crisps and other unmentionable munchables. And, of course, a cake.

On our return, we let battle commence with the awed awning. It proved an unexpectedly peaceful exercise, although I was briefly tempted to find out whether it understood violence when it refused at first to open.

The Chauffeur got a nasty nip when her hand got caught in the winding handle, but she cheered up quickly enough after she'd managed to give me a good bang on the head with it as she withdrew it. (Accidentally?)

The party was a big success, attended by 15 people aged from one to 81. I like The Chauffeur's family because, although somewhat tonsorially challenged myself, most of them make me look quite hirsute.

Christening prezzies included a pair of furry dice to hang over Daisy's rear view mirror and a towrope and ON TOW sign.

Nephew Johnny, a garage owner, opened the bonnet and gave the engine his approval, and we appointed him The Godfather (with his shaved head he looked the part) so he could put Daisy back on the right road should she ever stray from the straight and narrow.

Naturally, the younger guests found Daisy's ladder and roof far more enticing than the camp play area and climbing frame just a few yards away.

But we all drank and chatted happily until the sun went down in an evening mist and an alcoholic haze over the hills of the South Hams rolling languidly away behind us.

By then, five alcohol-drinking adults had swigged nine bottles of wine before The Brother in Law invited us for free pints of beer at the camp bar.

That night we slept with Daisy's side door wide open so we could feel we were nearer to nature, while our awning protected us from a dramatic thunderstorm.

Monday morning: Back to reality as our rural idyll was shattered at seven o'clock sharp by the clatter and thump of six heavy mechanical diggers busily beginning the task of turning a pleasant nearby field into the new headquarters for Suttons Seeds: Another corner of the countryside captured in the name of progress.

Don't get me wrong: I love the countryside, but I'm not so deviant as to want to actually live in it.

After all, it's just a theme park peopled by folk less fortunate than me, whose rôle is to keep it in good trim so we more civilised townies can enjoy visiting it now and again.

For myself, I'd much rather have the benefit of daily access to theatres, cinemas, bars, restaurants, public transport etc.

Mr Jones, who lives round the corner from us, spent all his working life in Abergavenny beneath the beautiful Brecon Beacons in South Wales. But when he retired he decided to move to London because he thought there'd be more for him to do. (And he's right of course).

Anyway, as I returned, hungover, from the toilet block The Chauffeur announced the Big News: She'd initiated the Porta-Potti. And she appeared to be none the worse for the experience.

Next, we returned to Torquay to collect The Chauffeur's Mum and take her, via Newton Abbot and Ashburton, to fetch up (no, not medically) at the Badger's Holt Café, Dartmeet, where the excellent food included a giant-sized ploughman's lunch with three local cheeses and a soggily scrummy sponge pudding with massive dollop of rich Devonshire cream.

Dartmeet is the lovely Dartmoor beauty spot where, according to family lore, The Chauffeur spent much of her childhood slipping off mossy rocks into the whirly waters of the river.

On one famous occasion she was allowed to have her first pair of jeans, bought in emergency in Tavistock, after another of her many immersions.

She and Daisy both coped well with the steep hills and the narrow lanes as her Mum sat in the front passenger seat and I sat like Royalty on the high back seat six feet to the rear.

Past Two Bridges and on through moorland bleakness to the desperate HM Prison at Princetown: A grim grey place, although the guests would have the benefit of some spectacular views if ever the mist lifted.

The prison was quite an attraction for gawpers and, we discovered, even had its own recently opened museum: Open every day that is except Monday, the day we were there, when it was securely barred and bolted behind heavy-duty padlocks.

I didn't feel too bad about it being closed because I wasn't at all sure I really wanted to see inside it anyway. But I managed to apprehend an off-duty warder, a short burly man with close-cropped grey hair, who cheerfully told me what it contained: Illegal weapons made by the inmates, old uniforms, and a mock-up of a cell.

It must do good business because while we were talking three packed cars pulled up beside us and asked us if it was open.

When I suggested to my warder that the museum seemed a bit of a ghoulish idea he told me it was OK because it was in a good cause: All its profits were given to charity once the curator's wages had been paid.

It set me wondering just how convincing an argument that was. What other barbarities could be justified in the name of charity? Floggings? Hangings? Boxing matches?

From Princetown we drove to Burrator Reservoir, surrounded by trees in every shade of green between splashes of bright yellow gorse and azalea.

For once it looked quite full: Enough to keep South West Water customers (or local people as they used to be called) free from rationing and restrictions for, well, several days.

Through forests of gorse and floods of bluebells to Yelverton before returning via Ponsworthy with its village shop boasting BRANDY TO BOOTLACES to Buckland-in-the-Moor where the clock on pretty Saint Peter's Church bears the words MY DEAR MOTHER in place of numerals, and chimes All Things Bright and Beautiful on the quarter hour as tunefully as the bells (set in the key of A sharp) will allow.

The directions for regulating the clock state fiercely:
WARNING: NO EXPERIMENTING OR DABBLING BY INEXPE-RIENCED MEN WITH PUBLIC CLOCKS SHOULD BE ALLOWED

Past haughty Haytor, standing rock-hard guard over sweeping South Devon and where a couple of coachloads of flimsily-clad foreign schoolkids battled with the fierce moorland wind, to Liverton to call on our old pal Dave Thomas: Gentleman, sportsman, but no longer bachelor since he married (for the first time) at 47 and became a father (for the first time) at 48.

Over homemade scones, we talked contentedly with him and his wife Emma about good times on and off the cricket field while Proud Dad oversaw some serious circuit training as his Boy George toddled unsteadily in his little red wellies from kitchen to hall, hall to lounge, lounge to conservatory, conservatory to garden, garden to shed (etc).

Back by the coast road which runs beside Britain's most scenic stretch of railway, past imposing Powderham Castle (where Dave and Emma were stylishly married two years before) to Starcross, Dawlish, and Teignmouth.

At Shaldon (another of The Chauffeur's favourite places) we sat on sheltered sunlit benches at high water, with the rest of the non-paying audience, and watched the evening performance as boats of many sizes passed between the spits of shingle which mark the narrow mouth of the broad Teign estuary. The fast-flowing tide made it so easy to row in, so hard to row out.

That night we were too sober and too scared to sleep with Daisy's door open after The Chauffeur raised the possibility that foxes or other uninvited creatures might jump in and join us.

Next morning we were up again at seven, thanks to the punctually noisy building workers, to take part in a brief headbutting session with the awning before we left.

(Should it carry a Government Health Awning?)

To Torquay again, this time to visit The Chauffeur's Aunty Alice at the slickly-named Choice old folks home (or whatever the politically correct term for such places is at the moment), incongruously situated within earshot of the raucous sounds of the livelier clientèle of Plainmoor, Torquay United's football ground, where a younger Alice used to serve pasties and Bovril in the refreshments hut on match days.

Despite having many of the physical and mental frailties of a 90-year-old, her face lit up as we entered the lounge where she and the other old girls were parked against the walls.

And as we chatted, she was still able to raise the odd chuckle we associated with her from years gone by.

Proudly, she opened her handbag to show us the magnificent collection of birthday cards she'd received.

Unfortunately, though, she hadn't got as many as she thought. A lot of them weren't for her: They belonged to another of the old girls, and one of them had put them in the wrong bag by mistake.

IT was time to take Daisy for her first visit to Hardy Country. We drove to Lyme Regis where a handful of early season visitors strolled the sunny prom as the seaside traders painted, polished and prepared their shops and stalls for the ebb and flow of the summer season ahead.

We trod The Cobb in the steps of Meryl Streep, The French Lieutenant's Woman, but for us (unlike her) the sea stood soothed.

We took on board the salty seaweedy scent which wafted at us from the 1950s, and bought pastel-shaded period postcards to match (six for a quid) at the beachside antiques centre with its hilarious display of plates commemorating such diverse events as the Life of Thomas Hardy, the Birth of Prince William and the Premiership of John Major.

(Not forgetting the wonderful pair of slippers immortalising arch-enemies Maggie Thatcher and Neil Kinnock as twin bed-mates).

Outside, we watched the timeless scene as a family played a game of beach cricket and we wondered why it's always Dad who's batting and the barefoot kids who must scamper to retrieve the ball painfully from distant barnacle-covered rocks.

As we left, we bought the world's two tallest iced Chelsea buns (six inches from cherry top to crust bottom) at a no-nonsense baker's among the foothills of the mountainously-inclined main street.

Next stop: Seatown where The Chauffeur bravely, but briefly, had her first swim of the year. (I reckon she managed all of four strokes).

Then we got stickily stuck into our high-rise buns as we watched an astonished angler land mackerel from the sea as fast as he could unhook them from his line.

So to Dorchester and the fascinating Thomas Hardy section of the Dorset County Museum, complete with reconstruction of the Great Man's handsome study at his last home, Max Gate, which he designed himself and where he created Tess of the d'Urbervilles, Jude the Obscure and The Mayor of Casterbridge, not to mention much of the finest poetry ever penned.

To his example may my loft conversion, if not my writing, aspire.

I REGRET to report that the day after we got home we discovered Daisy had disgraced herself by soiling our front driveway, and we had to arrange to take her in for emergency treatment to staunch an acute oil leak.

Of course Joyce and the other neighbours found it highly amusing, but I have to admit The Chauffeur and I didn't immediately see the funny side.

I rang Volkswagen dealers Whites of Camberley to explain the problem and to my surprise they told me I could bring Daisy in at seven the next morning, when I was to ask for Matt.

The Chauffeur had to go to work so I decided to take Daisy myself. I got up at six and drove down the misty-wet M3 wishing I knew how to turn my lights on like everybody else.

I got to Whites at 7.05, expecting to find a stubbly bleary-eyed Matt smoking a fag and drinking tea from a chipped mug before sliding open a battered old garage door to let in the day's work.

Instead, I walked into a spacious modern office containing about a dozen desks and 30 staff, half of them in smart blue shirts and ties (but no jackets) and half in equally smart blue overalls.

Matt turned out to be Matthew Tomlin, Team Leader no less, who took down Daisy's and my details with great courtesy and efficiency (although if I was being really picky I'd say he didn't quite allow himself enough time to laugh at all my jokes) and said his Team would give me their prognosis in 20 minutes.

I was ushered to a plush little waiting area with Big Breakfast TV, hi-tech coffee machine offering half a dozen different blends, and as many glossy Volkswagen sales brochures as you could read at a sitting.

This was VW Land, and it was easy to see why the Germans were over-running our car industry. (Shame about my £24,000 motor though).

Precisely 20 minutes later, Matt called me through to the service area where poor Daisy lay stricken on a ramp, bleeding oil profusely.

The mechanic assigned to her case shook his head in what I'm afraid I can only describe as a rather old-fashioned way and proceeded to tell me what was wrong.

I can't say I understood many of the details but it all sounded Very Nasty. I gathered transplant surgery would be required.

After two days Daisy was declared fit enough to be discharged and The Chauffeur nursed her tenderly to Bloxham, near Banbury in Oxfordshire, where we eased my creaky Aunty Muriel up on to the back seat and went for a cloudless Cotswold drive as summer exploded about us.

Sometimes our green and pleasant land shone sunshine yellow, raped beneath imported oceans of oil seed. Sometimes it glistened winter white under flurries of cow parsley, drifts of may and blizzards of candled horse chestnut.

The three of us nattered over doorstep sandwiches in the country garden of the nearby Mason's Arms and swallowed coffee from brim-full cups carried out to us one at a time, with solemn care and concentration, by the landlord's small son.

By country roads to Charlecote Park with its spreadeagling historic house where we examined the crafty eel trap, sat beside the sparkling water cascade and listened in admiration as a Brum Mum made a praise-worthy attempt to explain the origins of phaeton and brougham to her inquiring kids in the Coach House Museum.

Then we drank tea and ate flapjack on the lawn outside the Orangery, and drove home as the shadows grew and a pair of hot air balloons drifted gently across the still evening sky.

Daisy seemed none the worse for her indisposition. But surely such frailty, at just 600 miles old, didn't bode well for her future.

The nagging fear kept recurring: Was our new Wunderkind just a sickly Freitag Afternoon Job?

WE were nearly ready to set off on our foreign travels. We'd decided not to take loads of supplies with us (unlike the traditional English traveller abroad) as for once the exchange rate would be in our favour and we'd be able to buy stuff cheaply as we went along.

Not only that, but we were confident that, although foreigners, our continental cousins should by now know how to provide us with such products of civilization as pasta, wine, coffee etc.

We'd agreed, though, to buy a large jar of pickled onions and a big white Cheshire cheese for our pal Norman Rowson who lives in France where, it seems, worthwhile examples of such delicacies are in short supply.

Then there were the things we had to equip ourselves with whether we liked it or not: A spare set of bulbs for Daisy, compulsory for Spain (even if we didn't know how to fit them) and a first aid kit, obligatory if we should find ourselves in Austria (even if we didn't know how to use it).

Next, I had to fit in a trip to the dentist for some urgent repairs. Of course it's nothing like the ordeal it used to be in the painful days before they started giving you injections, but then again it's not exactly a treat to look forward to like an outing to Alton Towers.

Actually, I've been very lucky with my dentists. One, in Torquay, was most obliging: I drank and he smoked. I'd see him in the afternoon after I'd got well tanked up at lunchtime to steady my nerves, and he'd drag away while doing the business.

It was the perfect arrangement: I breathed my Watneys Red Barrel fumes at him and he gave me a mouthful of his Player's Medium Navy Cut nicotined fingers.

(Dentists weren't sophisticated enough to think of wearing gloves in those days).

My current dentist doesn't smoke (well, not on duty anyway) and I don't drink (well, not on the way to my appointment) but one thing hasn't changed: When it comes to tossing the medicine ball of conversation about, the dentist's still the man in possession.

No matter how strongly I disagree with his views (and, let's face it, you wouldn't become a dentist in the first place if you weren't going to be disagreeable) there's nothing I can do to contradict him once he gets to opining on the job.

Then, by the time he's taken all his things out of my mouth and I'm able to speak again, what I wanted to say no longer seems relevant. So I have to let him get away with it.

I've given a lot of thought to this problem over the years. And as I was sitting in the chair, the solution suddenly struck me: I needed a computer voicebox thingy like Professor Stephen Hawking's got. That would do it.

But I quickly realised the flaw: The Dentist's Revenge. (Have you seen the state of the Prof's teeth? They're awful).

Before we could finally leave, we had an anxious wait for Daisy's registration and insurance documents to arrive.

The trouble is you can no longer trust the reliability of the post. As an elderly neighbour put it to me: It's so erotic these days.

I know what she means: A short while ago I was sent some important material by Recorded Delivery. We were out when it arrived but the postman had delivered it anyway, and had written on the envelope:
RANG NO ANSWER HAVE SIGNED FOR YOU OK POSTMAN

I don't know how highly they'd trained him, but I think they'd failed to convey the Recorded Delivery concept to him.

On the eve of our departure we started to load Daisy with everything we thought we'd need, and I'm pleased to say our trial run had served its purpose: This time it was all achieved in relative harmony.

The only serious argument we had was over how many clothes we should take, and who should be allowed the more space in the little wardrobe.

It looked as if it might all turn nasty when we each started not only putting our own stuff in but also chucking the other's stuff out.

Things calmed down eventually, though, when I agreed to a compromise: I said The Chauffeur could have the whole of it.

Oh, and Next door brought round a good-luck goodie bag containing crisps, baked beans, lavatory paper, a candle, a bar of soap acquired from the Hôtel Montaigne, Paris, and an emergency sewing kit from the Hôtel du Palais, Biarritz.

So, on a dingy late May morning, The Chauffeur pointed Daisy's nose in the direction of the M25 and the Dover Road.

2

Dover - Calais - Le Touquet - Cucq - Dieppe - Rouen - Igoville -
Les Andelys - Giverny - Versailles

HINDSIGHT is a powerful weapon. I know that from being beaten
about the head with it for years by bosses of varying degrees of competence.

But I admit it: The Chauffeur and I should have made more of an effort
to avoid the rush hour.

What I'd like to know, though, is this: Who causes traffic jams? I don't
mean the sort that are the result of mass pile-ups. They're fair enough:
You come across the charred and twisted remains of a dozen vehicles.
You accept that a few more poor souls have been sacrificed at the altar of
progress. And you feel you've got your money's worth.

No, I mean the sort of jams described in those cheery radio reports as
being the result of "sheer weight of traffic." The ones where you get stuck
for hours, but when you finally reach the front of the queue you feel
cheated because you don't even get the satisfaction of seeing any evidence to tell you what happened.

What I don't understand is: Why should they bring everything to a
halt? All right, so some drivers might drive less quickly than others and
the rest of us might have to slow down to, say, 50 or maybe even 40. But
why do we all have to stop completely?

What it comes down to is this: Who's the jerk who goes out in the
mornings and causes the "sheer weight of traffic" to come to a standstill
by stopping his car in the middle of the motorway?

Anyway, despite failing to come up with any good reason for our
lengthy delay, we made it round the M25 eventually and drove through
a murky Garden of England in conditions very different from the ones
we'd enjoyed in the sunny Cotswolds just a week before.

As roadside snow quickly becomes dirty, so the may which had shone
pure white last week was now a dull pinky brown. And although may
had been well and truly out, we felt the need to put on clouts, not cast
them.

For the first time, as Daisy clocked up 1,000 miles, we turned her heater
on.

Near Folkestone, we saw a colony of genuine gipsies camped by the roadside in half a dozen vehicles not dissimilar to Daisy.

It was a strange sensation: My immediate temptation as a suburban householder was to feel superior to them.

But wasn't it they who should have been feeling superior to us? We were just playing at fleeing the constraints of a conventional lifestyle. They were doing it for real.

When we reached Dover we presented ourselves at the Eastern Docks, taking the lane signed WITHOUT TICKETS.

Everybody there seemed to be in a great rush but an unflappable policeman was on hand to tell us what to do, and set The Chauffeur the tricky test of parking Daisy in a small space behind a large coach.

Meanwhile, I headed for the Travel Centre to sort out a sailing. The man at the P & O desk said he could fit us in in five hours' time, at 15.15. I said that if that was the best he could do we'd settle for it provided the opposition couldn't do any better.

I went off to see what the woman at the Sea France desk had to offer. Answer: 16.15.

So I returned to the P & O man, established there was nobody else I could pass myself off as so as to obtain a discount and swapped him £89 for a one-way ticket to Calais.

(Yes, I know we could have booked in advance. It might have saved us money and it would certainly have saved us the wait. But it wouldn't have been in keeping with our nomadic aspirations. We'd made it a rule we wouldn't book anything in advance. We wanted to be completely flexible).

With five hours to kill, we drove into town and sat down to a lukewarm breakfast at Chaplins Restaurant and Coffee Bar where The Chauffeur marvelled (with what I hope wasn't a hint of envy) at the explicit sexual knowledge displayed by our old chum Hilary Bonner in her latest crime thriller.

Then, as light rain fell and I shivered in a thin T-shirt, we walked the prom and watched wistfully as half a dozen ferries took everyone except us away towards the sun.

We passed a line of adolescent anglers on the Prince of Wales Pier boastfully comparing the size of their pollocks, and went for coffee and cakes at the welcoming Lighthouse Café and Tearoom ("The closest café to France").

Next, we watched the free end-of-the-pier show as the Hoverspeed Princess Margaret lifted up her skirts, slipped off her apron, and swept away to sea like a secondhand vacuum cleaner.

It was odd how dated she looked, so recently does it seem that she and her like were the very newest technology: She must have been about as ancient as that other pensioner of a transport contraption, Concorde.

There was still time for us to offload some silly old sterling on a series of bargains at the De Bradelei Wharf factory outlet centre. And we consumed yet more food and drink, carefully guarding against the off chance that we might suddenly be struck down by acute attacks of anorexia.

Eventually we were able to report to the ferry terminal, this time joining the WITH TICKETS queue where a cheerful red-haired P & O lady checked us in and sent us to join our fellow passengers in Lane 17.

There, we had a minor squabble (as more experienced Channel-crossing carloads looked on with thinly-disguised interest) over the positioning on Daisy's headlamps of our Beam Bender stickers, necessary so as not to dazzle oncoming traffic when driving on the right.

(This despite the reassuring introductory words of the accompanying leaflet which described fitting them as: "A simple operation which requires no technical knowledge").

After placing them in a position more or less approximating to the instructions and expressing the hope that they would stay there, we slapped our nifty little magnetic GB sign on Daisy's behind and a few minutes later we were all aboard the Pride of Kent.

ROLL-ON roll-off ferries are widely regarded as among the most lethal inventions yet devised by man. But, credit where it's due, I can honestly say ours never keeled over and sank once during our entire crossing.

Seventy-five minutes after a punctual departure we had yet more anorexia-defeating food inside us and we were safely entering Calais having seen the White Cliffs merge into the white mist, the Gris Nez emerge out of the gris sky, and not much else.

The sea had been as flat as a sea can reasonably be expected to be.

If Calais was easy to get into, it was a lot harder to get out of. We went round in several circles, happily without straying too far on to the wrong side of the road, before we finally managed to spin off in the direction of Boulogne.

And in answer to your next question: Yes, I was the one who was dyslexically grappling with the map reading. A major problem was that we wanted to avoid the toll-charging autoroutes, but we weren't sure whether they were the ones indicated by the green signs or the blue ones.

We finally found the coast road and drove past the industrial backside of Boulogne, which was farting a crude oily stench, to Le Touquet. And the first thing we saw was a madly busy McDonalds.

After that it was all too grand for us romanies and we searched in vain for a campsite, seeing signs only to posh hotels, restaurants and golf courses.

We didn't exactly panic, but as daylight began to fade we were relieved to stumble across the Camping Municipal at nearby Cucq where a jolly (but not jolie) dame with a bulbous neck gave us the friendliest of receptions, told us to park Daisy wherever we liked and wouldn't hear of us handing over any identification or parting with so much as a franc before the morning.

And the nicest thing was that there wasn't an English voice to be heard. Everyone else on the site was French including the tracksuited single mum busily putting up a tent for herself and her three kids: Evidence (like the McDonalds invasion) that even in the land of the extended family the old social fabric is becoming irreparably frayed.

In the morning things were a bit more businesslike, although just as friendly, with a smart young man from the Mairie, in collar and tie, to deal with at reception.

There was a form to be filled in, identification to be shown (a bit late surely?) and money to be paid. But less than 30 francs (about £3) for hot showers, clean lavatories and a good night's sleep.

We decided to drive back to Le Touquet, to give ourselves another chance to like it, only to find it wasn't posh at all: It just thought it was.

The seafront with its Aqualud indoor swimming pool complex reminded us of Rhyl, except that the North Wales resort's equivalent Suncentre is more impressive.

But the beach was well up to Welsh standards, and the big sport was sand-yachting.

Across the flatlands, past delightful sculptures of birds keeping watch over every roundabout, to Le Tréport (a bigger version of Brixham in Devon) and then Dieppe.

We drove past Dieppe racecourse, which looked a bit down at hoof and whose ground staff appeared to consist of about 100 sheep, to Centre Ville where we parked in a pretty little square beneath a shady chestnut tree and scored a surprisingly comprehensive victory over the Pay-et-Display machine.

The main street was pedestrianised, in the modern manner, with coloured paving. But unfortunately that just had the effect of making it look the same as many of our town centres back home.

We headed for the dominant Café des Tribunaux where we drank coffee and cognac with more gaiety than the sad Oscar Wilde did when he was there in exile.

It was a huge characterful old barn of a place in every shade of brown from nicotine to Great Western to unmentionable, with a first-floor gallery from which to view everything going on below.

An implacably-faced madame did the same from her high stool behind the bar, watching every move made by both her customers and her staff.

From there we strolled to the unattractive harbour, lined with restaurants and antiques shops, and across the layered beach which had no sand, only pebbles.

Then we set off south on the Road To Rouen and did the naffest thing we'd done so far, but something every English middle-aged motorhome couple must do: We pulled up in a lay-by just five metres from the noisy N27 and, as the slipstreams created by EU-sized lorries shook Daisy to her axles, we brewed a cup of tea in the back. (It tasted wonderful).

Rouen was a beautiful little old bit surrounded by an ugly big new bit. We headed for the beautiful old bit, and played the world's favourite game: Hunt The Parking Space.

Eventually, The Chauffeur managed to squeeze Daisy into a little gap right in the middle of town. But here we had less luck with the Pay-et-Display, allowing ourselves to be robbed of 10 francs before we managed to sort out a satisfactory deal.

We walked round the corner to the Place du Vieux Marché. A colourful bed of dwarf azaleas marked the spot where the heroine Joan of Arc met her fiery end, and a group of lads were using the nearby wall which salutes her memory (in letters as big as her courage) as a goal for their game of football.

To the cathedral, whose façade was famously painted by Monet many times over in different lights and moods. (Its moods, not his).

I'd always assumed he'd cheated and painted it from a load of photographs, but now I've been there and tried to photograph it myself I realise that would have been tricky.

Even if he'd stood right back by the cosmetics counter of the chemist's opposite, he'd still have had trouble getting it all in.

The façade didn't look too healthy when we were there, except as a conservation area for several varieties of birds and a thicket of green foliage growing vigorously from the top of its central arch. Work was in hand to restore it, though.

The rest of the building looked somewhat eccentric: It appeared to have sprouted a mini Eiffel Tower from its roof.

The pedestrianised parts nearby reeked of history. But yes, there was a McDonalds in the oldest street in town, the Rue du Gros Horloge. Next to C & A.

ON attempting to leave Rouen we ran into more navigational problems, recognising the same landmarks several times over as we followed those signs that are so unhelpful but so loved by the French: TOUTES DIRECTIONS.

The more you think about them the sillier they get, especially as they usually do just what they say: Point in All Directions.

Not only that, but there are also signs saying: AUTRES DIREC-TIONS. Other Directions. But what other directions? Other directions from what?

Often the only respite for the confused motorist comes from the trees, always plentiful beside French roads, which have the useful habit of hiding the roadsigns from view.

Still, we cracked it in the end and headed on south beside the magnificently wide River Seine.

We stopped at a Carrefour hypermarket, having to exercise our brains before we'd even left the car park as to how to pay the 10 franc ransom to liberate a shopping trolley.

We succeeded eventually, and pushed it into a massive hangar of a store which made our English equivalents look puny.

It was like B & Q, MFI, Tesco, Smithfield, Billingsgate and Covent Garden all in one. And we only wanted some bread, milk, cheese, fruit and wine.

Although my French is a little better than The Chauffeur's I felt panicky and out of my depth in such overwhelming surroundings. But she immediately knew her way around, instantly understanding every notice and every label.

(I suppose shopping is an instinct in women. Like homing in pigeons).

Impressive though the place was, it didn't have automatic doors as we'd have had back home. But the wheels of our trolley reassuringly had minds of their own just like the ones I'm used to.

And we managed to recoup our 10 francs all right when we handcuffed it up again in the car park.

We spent our second night in France at Camping Les Terrasses in the Seine-side village of Igoville. The site lived up to its name, being cut into a hillside and having fine views across the valley, marred only (in typically messy French fashion) by an absolute eyesore of a gravel quarry.

This was a far posher site, with individual pitches divided by hedges. Here, too, the management were extremely friendly. But they did ask us to hand over identification, in the form of our Camping Card.

It wasn't quite as quiet as the last place, with traffic noise from the nearby N15 and trains rushing through the valley below. But we both got another good night's kip.

Campsite toilet facilities can be a little unnerving if you're more used to the privacy of your own bathroom, as I discovered the next morning.

I went to the men's toilet block and entered one of the doors marked DOUCHE, singing heartily and feeling full of the vigour of the outdoor life.

Slowly, I became aware I wasn't alone: Someone was surreptitiously Doing Things behind a door marked LAVABO just the other side of the thin three-quarter height partition separating us.

Gradually my singing became quieter, then stopped altogether as I began to feel more self-conscious and carried out my showering and towelling in silence.

Meanwhile I got to wondering what clandestine acts my neighbour was furtively perpetrating, interpreting each little sound as some bizarre personal practice, and all the time trying to remember what a lavabo was.

I left the block as quickly as I could so he wouldn't see me, just in case he'd been wondering what unsavoury activities a singing Englishman might get up to in the shower.

I returned to Daisy and looked up lavabo in our small travelling French dictionary. It said: Washbasin. I think my camping comrade may have been having a shave.

We had breakfast, paid our dues of 50 francs, and set off... three times: First we had to drive back to return their shower key, then we realised we'd forgotten to reclaim our Camping Card.

For once (twice, in fact) the words Au Revoir turned out to be the mots justes.

On to Les Andelys where we climbed up to Richard the Lionheart's rock-top Château Gaillard and were rewarded with wonderful views of the Seine Valley, white-cliffed and green-wooded, and the fertile plains beyond.

The only snag: The castle was closed the day we called. But we were able to walk round it and got a good idea of the place.

One of its points of interest is that it was built in less than a year. I wasn't a bit surprised: It was in a dreadful state.

Afterwards we walked down into the pretty little town, bought pains au raisin at a pâtisserie which had croissant-shaped door handles and sat on a bench beside the peacefully green river.

As we ate, a greedy cormorant caught a big fish right in front of us with ease but then found it hard to swallow. And a wide flat barge laboured past us, weighed down to within just a few centimetres of danger level by its heavy cargo of gravel.

MY appreciation of art more or less begins and ends with the Impressionists, so we headed next for Monet's house and garden at Giverny.

As we approached, we had to make a rapid calculation whether to turn left across the busy road and try to fit Daisy into the car park under a height restriction barrier saying 2.2 metres. (Southern Cross had told us she measured 8 feet 6 inches).

Mental arithmetic not being one of our strong points and time not being in our favour, we agreed to make a dive for the verge on our side of the road and park there.

I still haven't worked out if it was the right decision. But at least Daisy remained unscathed.

We joined a sizeable queue of fellow grockles to get in, including an uncomfortably large number of Brits and, worse still, Yanks. (Don't their voices carry?)

By now, we'd accumulated a lot of little French coins and decided this would be a good opportunity to get rid of some of them. So we added them all up while we queued, and tried to pay 20 francs of our 70 francs entrance fee in small change.

But it wasn't as easy as we'd expected: The frigid femme at the cash desk would have none of it. She grabbed our notes but scornfully shoved our coins back across the counter towards us, and gave us our tickets stamped: TARIF RÉDUIT.

(Could this be a tactic to remember?)

The lily pond lived up to every one of my expectations, but was bigger than I'd imagined: More like a lake. Willow, wisteria, azalea, lupin, rose and iris were foremost among the forest of flowers, trees and shrubs leading the eye to the world-famous Japanese bridge, which attracted as many cameras as any other international megastar and appeared just as vulnerable as the crush of eager fans crammed the water's edge to try to get the best view.

In the midst of all this adulation a gardener aboard a squat green punt calmly scooped up weeds from among the lily pads with a fishing net.

We certainly timed our visit right: During the afternoon we were there the light changed constantly as the colour of the sky shifted between blue and white and grey, just as Monet would have wanted us to see it.

And surely there can't be a better month than May to admire his garden at its splendid peak.

As ever, of course, there was a snag: The place was cut in half by the main road, with the lily pond on one side and the house and formal flower garden on the other. (A pedestrian subway linked the two parts).

The flower garden was laid out with surprising regimentation, in straight lines and rectangles. Perhaps in the end the ageing Claude needed to put some reality back into his life after doing all those impressions.

But the effect was lovely, with roses, pansies, cornflowers, wallflowers and much more. And the old man didn't half love his iris.

There was quite a wait to get into the house: A long low green-shuttered building with a red-sea foreground of geraniums. And we witnessed an International Incident when a middle-aged American couple objected as two young Frenchwomen jumped the queue (the locals clearly thinking, with some justification, that they had a prior claim to the place over all us presumptuous foreigners).

The irate Yankee hubby raced off to grab an attendant. But French Officialdom wasn't impressed, finding in favour of its own and adopting a laissez-faire attitude towards the two méchantes.

Inside, the walls were smothered in the Japanese prints Monet admired so much. But of course they aren't a patch on his own masterpieces, which are now expensively dispersed elsewhere.

Only the yellow dining room and the blue kitchen gave a hint that anyone with any artistic taste had ever lived here.

Afterwards we went to the Salon de Thé, and even that had a prettier garden than most you've ever seen. The flower-patterned crockery, too, was beautiful.

And The Chauffeur learned one thing: Japanese women must be the most honest people in the world, because when she went to the Dames she watched a whole party of them each shut the lavatory door in the next one's face so they could all have the satisfaction of paying their two francs to get in.

On up the scenic Seine to Versailles where we stopped for more supplies at a supermarket, and I experienced the worst moment of the trip so far: I'd decided before we set off to carry my most important belongings in a straw shoulder bag but somehow, in the process of reclaiming our 10 franc trolley deposit in the car park, I managed to leave the bag in the trolley.

It contained all our valuables: Cash, credit cards, passports and my notes for every word of this book you've read so far.

(Well I considered those notes valuable then, even if you don't consider them valuable now).

When we got back to Daisy, I assumed the bag must have been nicked (not thinking for a moment I could have been so stupid as to have actually abandoned it) and the chances of finding it, let alone its contents, were minute.

So merci mille fois to the most magnifique little garçon in the whole of France who, while dutifully helping his maman do her shopping, handed it in at the supermarket office which was where I found it when I raced back (in the early throes of a heart attack) a few minutes later.

I was in too deep a state of shock to think straight away about setting up camp for the night, so instead The Chauffeur took me for a couple of steadying cognacs and a crash course in handbag management. (Rule No 1: Don't leave it in the car park).

The bar we went in was like French bars are meant to be. It had a long stainless steel counter and, despite the best efforts of about a hectare of mirrors, it was funeral-parlour dark.

It contained a dozen drinkers (all men) who obviously had better things to do than to keep abreast of the latest developments at their nation's famous fashion houses.

Their conversation was conspiratorial and important, too serious to contain too many jokes.

The place smelt tobacco brown and the floor beside the base of the bar was ankle deep in the smoker's debris of packets, butts and ash.

Pastis was popular and was served in chunky glasses together with attractive little flat-sided bottles of water taken, full, from one of the many wooden-doored fridges which lined the bar's back wall.

None of the regulars arrived or left without giving each of the others a handshake. Nobody, apart from le patron, took any notice of us. Which is as it should be. (Well, would you want to be a regular in a bar where they wasted valuable gossip time on strangers? I wouldn't).

France may be being overrun by McDonalds and the mobile phone, but the rank and file of bar-room resistance doesn't seem ready to capitulate just yet.

My heart beating a little more evenly, we made for the tree-covered Camping Versailles and checked in for the night. A more officious operation this time, with barriers, passcards and even a computer.

Our bill: 102 francs (more than £10) even though we had a hard job finding a piece of ground flat enough to park Daisy on.

WHEN you've seen inside one stately building you've seen inside them all (apart from Brighton's Royal Pavilion, which is both fascinating and funny).

Old buildings aren't like gardens (which offer infinite permutations of pleasure).

But we had to go inside the Palace of Versailles because it was pouring with rain and, to be fair, I admit the Hall of Mirrors, where they signed the treaty to end the First World War, was more impressive than the one you'll see on your average pier.

We didn't get in without a struggle, though, because at the cash desk I had to fight my first Language Duel.

I'm not saying my French is fluent. Far from it: Brackish would be a more accurate word for it. But I do feel that if I've invested the time and money to travel to their country I should be permitted at least to try to communicate with the natives in their language, if I wish to.

On this occasion I (being English) was determined to speak French, and the efficient lady with unsynchronised eyes sitting behind the cash desk (being French) was determined to speak English.

Sometimes such confrontations can end in humiliation for one side if they can see they're hopelessly outgunned by their opponent's superior linguistic firepower. The game's up and there's nothing for it but to back down.

This time, though, it was a dashed close run thing and no quarter was given by either protagonist throughout a lengthy battle during which tickets were bought and entry instructions were issued.

I went into the palace feeling that in her latest hostile encounter with the French I had upheld the honour of my nation.

Obviously, a good many of the visitors were wearing logos. And as they soaked up the gloire of French history they demonstrated to the world that they'd also sampled the less cultural delights of Disneyland and The Warner Brothers Store.

(I suppose France always did embrace catholic tastes.)

As we walked round, we couldn't help noticing that all the nice helpful signs describing points of interest were in French only, whereas all the nasty bossy signs telling you what you mustn't do, smoking, touching, flashing (cameras, that is) were in English as well.

The lavatories cost a rip-off 2.50 francs a go, and we wondered whether to fetch Daisy's Porta-Potti and use it to stage a public sit-down demonstration against such blatant piss-taking.

(The French have a lot of time for such protest movements).

The cheerful cloakroom attendant couldn't be persuaded to accept a tip for looking after my umbrella, though.

Outside, the gardens were as stilted and formal as you'd expect them to be. In one section there were about 1,000 trees each in its own square pale-green wooden container. (The Chauffeur told me they were called Versailles containers at home, too).

We speculated about what a huge task it would have been to keep them all watered (although not on the soggy day we were there).

As the grounds geometrically progressed further from the palace, they tried to throw off their inhibitions. But for our money Monet (despite his late conversion to straight lines) left us a far more attractive horticultural composition than all Louis XIV's vast armies of gardeners.

The whole time we were there we could hear the sound of heavy gunfire, and wondered if another Revolution might have started. But we were told it was La Police (ruthlessly feminine in French) practising on a nearby firing range.

It sounded as if she'd be ready to deal with some pretty desperate customers.

Versailles is well worth a visit (as they say) but we ended up wondering if the only really remarkable thing about the old place, inside and out, was the massive scale of it all.

It's like painting: A Monet or a Van Gogh can be impressive no matter what size it is. But all those old dark religious and battle scenes (of which there are plenty at Versailles) are much better appreciated by the yard.

Afterwards we went to the Brasserie du Musée next door for tea, but unfortunately when we got there the customers' needs were taking second place to Plant Manoeuvres.

Amid much animated chatter and gesticulation, and some ill-temper, the shrubs beside the pavement seating area, in their heavy cement containers, were being repositioned.

It seemed to be some kind of border dispute with the neighbours, and the entire staff had to have their say.

It was some time before we could persuade them to get us our tea. When it finally arrived it was served, whether through ignorance or lack of concentration, with hot milk.

(Don't they know anything, these French?)

3

Le Perray-en-Yvelines - Rambouillet - Orléans - Sancerre - Pouilly - La
Charité - Vézelay - Villy-en-Auxois - Dijon - Beaune

GREAT Barkeepers of the World: No 1: Mad George, late of The
Douglas Hotel, Corporation Street, Manchester. No 2: Norman Rowson,
of Le Volet Vert, Le Perray-en-Yvelines, France.

George (aka The Barmy Greek) was a one-off among one-offs who
always kept his customers on their toes and never let his less than perfect
English get in the way of a good joke.

One winter lunchtime a couple of unsuspecting strangers, sitting quiet-
ly beside The Douglas's dimly flickering fire, were bold enough to complain they were cold.

Immediately, George came racing out from behind the bar brandishing a large hammer and launched a ferocious attack. . . not on them,
but on their wooden table and chairs.

They leapt to safety, and George hurled the splintered fragments of furniture on to the fire. As it blazed into life he yelled at them triumphant-
ly: "You no cold now."

Some of George's funniest moments came as a result of his language
problems.

A senior newspaper executive who used the place was known as Biffo.
But this wasn't quite the cuddly term of endearment it sounded, having
been coined by his less-than-admiring subordinates and secretly standing
for Big Ignorant Fucker From Oldham.

When George discovered this he thought it was hilarious and gleefully
shared the joke with all his customers for days afterwards, delighted to
find it got a good laugh every time even from those who'd already heard
it.

Biffo, he chuckled, got his name because he was a Big Thick Bastard
From Rochdale.

Eventually, The Douglas was demolished (not by George) and he
moved around the corner to Hanging Ditch where he helped open The
Moonraker Club ("A Touch of Class").

Here, when he wasn't busy serving drinks to upwards of a dozen customers at the same time, with the utmost speed and efficiency, he liked

to sit and peep through the little window beside the entrance door and grant admission only to the "Happy Smile Faces."

One of his finest coups came when he managed, late one night, to persuade two drunks from opposite ends of the bar that each was the other's taxi driver.

The two, although somewhat unsteady on their feet, almost came to blows as they accused each other of all manner of irresponsibility and anti-social behaviour before they finally realised they'd been had.

Another of his tricks was to select the biggest burliest ugliest-looking brute in the place, point out another customer to him (usually me) and tell him: "He say you queer."

I often had to use all my diplomatic skills to wriggle out of such testing situations.

For all that, George is one of the warmest, sharpest, most generous and certainly funniest people I've ever met, and it's an honour to have known him.

By chance, and without having had any contact with him for 10 years, I got a letter from him just as I was starting to write this book.

It began: MY RED SHIRT FRIEND THIS A SURPRISES FOR YOU TO WRITE A LETTER. It then went on to give news of old friends, and ended: ALL THE BEST GEORGE THE GREEK BARMAN.

And that's what really creased me up: That he thought it necessary to remind me he was The Greek Barman.

George, nobody who had the privilege of being served a drink by you will ever forget you.

I'VE known Barkeeper No 2, Norman Rowson, since he had nothing (except two women and three children) and we started playing cricket together for the Richmond Nomads 25 years earlier.

Originally from Yorkshire, the only drink he knew in those days was Light And Bitter In A Straight Glass (pronounced as in lass).   But now he and his second wife Josette run Le Volet Vert, and that's where The Chauffeur drove Daisy and me next.

(His first wife, Saga, a psychiatrist, couldn't cope with him any longer and ran off to Canada where she married again and became a llama farmer).

Norman has adapted well to the rôle of Le Patron in the nine years he's been doing it. He's acquired all the shrugs and gestures of Gallic body language, not to mention a magnificent nose that any Frenchman would be proud of.

36

The bar's clientèle are mainly young (Norman says he prefers the company of young people) and come in to play pool at the six tables he's installed in the big extension he built on the back of the bar himself.

In the early days the drink orders used to be more varied: Beer, pastis and wine were all popular. Now, his young customers nearly all drink beer: Fizzy Amstel on draught, or one of the growing number of flashy bottled beers, Desperado (with tequila), Adelscott (with whisky), Kingston (with rum) etc.

Having something of a fondness for drink himself, he'd recently decided he couldn't be bothered wasting his time making pointless cups of coffee like other French bars do. So he put the price up from the going rate in the town of 4.50 francs to six francs.

The result: More people come in to drink coffee at his place, but only so they can have the additional pleasure of complaining to him about the extra cost.

When I first knew Norman I'd have said he'd be just about the last person who'd have chosen to leave England. Now he says there's no way he'd return. I asked him why and he cited, among other things, the standard of service. He gave me some examples:

POST OFFICE (France):

Go to cashier who takes parcel, weighs it, sticks appropriate stamp on it and posts it.

POST OFFICE (England):

1. Go to cashier who points to scales where you can weigh parcel.

2. Cashier gives you about 20 stamps to lick and stick on.

3. Cashier tells you to take parcel to other end of counter where you have to push it through hatch.

ESTATE AGENTS (France):

Go to agents and you are driven to address you want to see.

ESTATE AGENTS (England):

1. You are given address where you can meet agent.

2. Impossible to find it unless you know area.

3. When you do find it you can't park.

4. Agent is late.

BANK (France):

You want to transfer money abroad but aren't sure what to do. Explain to cashier who fills form in and describes clearly how everything will happen.

BANK (England):

1. Same situation as above.

2. Cashier greets you with a grunt.

3. Ask your question.

4. Cashier throws complicated form at you and orders you to fill it in.
5. Say you've forgotten your glasses.
6. Cashier begrudgingly fills in form for you.

WE stayed with Norman and Josette for two nights, not in Daisy but on a spare mattress on the floor of one of their upstairs rooms.

We drank a little too much, but we also discovered the peace and beauty of the surrounding Forêt de Rambouillet, an out-of-town favourite with Parisian walkers and cyclists, on a day when it kept trying not to drizzle but never quite succeeded.

We explored the pretty town of Rambouillet with its businesslike château, and had a snack lunch at the Café le Celtique: One gruyère sandwich and one rillette sandwich. Plural spelling, logically enough: Sandwichs, without the e.

(Well if you think about it, the e doesn't matter, does it? Because they don't bother to pronounce the last syllable anyway, do they?)

I'm not sure quite what we were expecting when we ordered them but when we got them they were made from two enormous sticks of French bread, each at least half a metre long, precariously served on not two but just one tiny saucer (not even a plate) measuring all of 10 centimetres in diameter.

Nobody seemed too bothered about crumbs in these parts.

As is normal in France, nearly all the shops in the town were closed at lunchtime: Another hint of resistance to the onset of a less enlightened age.

Norman and Josette had appeared welcoming enough when we arrived but at night, and especially whenever I tried to roll over and give The Chauffeur a cuddle, I became aware of a sharp stinging pain in my right thigh.

It gradually dawned on me that there was no doubt about it: The bedding they'd given us had been booby-trapped (or else fitted with some sort of anti-sex device).

And on the morning we left, I finally discovered the culprit: A three-inch needle sticking, point upwards, out of the centre of the mattress.

For a fortnight afterwards I bore thin red scars as a reminder of it.

Sadly, Norman and Josette said they were planning to close Le Volet Vert (it means The Green Shutter) and convert the building into flats. Norman reckons he's been in the same spot long enough, and he wants to spend some time travelling.

But Josette gave us a nice souvenir of the place as a late christening present for Daisy: A lovely little straw-coloured traditional French café teapot.

We accepted it gratefully, said our Au Revoirs and set off (in unaccustomed sun) for Orléans and the Loire.

We followed a French van man who, despite some enthusiastic early competition, put in a spirited bid for our MAD (Most Awful Driver) award.

He drove his clapped-out old red wreck all over the N20, right in front of us. Now on the verge. Now over the white line in the middle of the road.

Just as well he didn't have a WELL DRIVEN? CALL THIS NUMBER sign on the back: The switchboard would have been jammed for days.

Come to think of it, you don't see many of those in France. (I wonder why).

The Chauffeur's driving was as tidy as ever, though, and she kept Daisy on a true course south.

In Orléans she parked with ease (and for free) beside the river. We walked the short distance up to the city centre. And that's when life got complicated.

We went to a café where, in an attempt to order coffees to our taste, we did what Josette had taught us: Asked for Grandes Noisettes (which we hoped would contain a lot of coffee and a little milk) as opposed to Grands Cafés au Lait (which come with too little coffee and too much milk) or just plain Cafés (which have too little coffee and even less milk, ie none at all).

In the event we got Cafés Crèmes (which contained the right amounts of coffee and milk, but the wrong sort of milk).

It all began to make me realise that there aren't too many bureaucrats in Brussels after all. In fact I reckon they probably need a lot more if we Europeans are going to understand just what it is we're eating and drinking.

After that we stepped out into the main square, and crossed paths with Joan again. This time she was sitting in the middle of a roundabout, larger than life, armour and copper plated, astride a charger.

(She evidently didn't have any hang-ups about it being more ladylike to ride side-saddle in the old days).

The centre of Orléans wasn't a patch on the centre of Rouen, nor was the cathedral. So at least Joan finished her days in the prettier place.

Not only that, but she must have been glad to get away from all the dogshit which seemed to be spread even deeper in Orléans than elsewhere in France. And the millions of little midges which were plaguing the city (although presumably the fire would have got rid of them for her).

We drove on east up the Loire, passing a particularly French piece of traffic management: Lights were in operation for roadworks being carried out on the other side of the road from us. But the works were far too close to a bus stop on our side, and the bus stop hadn't been temporarily moved further along, as it would have been in England.

As a result, when the bus in front of us stopped it caused most of the oncoming drivers to miss their turn at the lights.

Needless to say, this caused all kinds of hooting and hubbub.

Of course, use of the horn isn't taken as seriously, as personally, in France as it is in England, where it can be an instant cue for road rage.

Obviously road rage exists in France (it must do, the way they drive) but hooting is regarded as just part of the fun of the road.

Up the Loire as The Chauffeur told me off for contentedly crying THIS IS THE LIFE "for the hundredth time." She's somehow got the idea that I'm prone to repeating myself.

(I suppose it must be true because she keeps on telling me so. Repeatedly).

We stopped for a picnic lunch on the banks of the Loire. But we didn't make as much of a meal of it as two middle-aged German couples who rolled up in one of Daisy's close relations and laboriously humped tables, chairs, coolboxes and food down the steep slope to the river's edge.

As we ate, a laughing armada of green and orange canoes lurched downstream in the sun under the paddles of a couple of dozen schoolkids. And we were engulfed in a snowstorm of small dandeliony seeds carried toward us on the wind.

Next stop: Wine-famous Sancerre, proud on a hilltop, where we sat at a café table in the sun at the town's highest point right in the middle of the old square.

Here we rediscovered that if ordering a suitable cup of coffee is a linguistic challenge then ordering a proper cup of tea is an inter-racial improbability.

This time we stressed we wanted cold milk, which we got. But the tea turned out to be Earl Grey, and everyone in the civilized world knows you don't drink any milk at all with that.

We fought our way through clichéed crews of Wine Hunt TV programme makers and, as a single evening church bell tolled, we drank in the view of the ordered vineyards and corkscrewing Loire beneath us, and the flat green fields and calm blue hills beyond.

From Sancerre to Pouilly (Fumé in wine terms as opposed to Fuissé, which is Burgundy).

Here, we wanted to buy a bottle of the local brew to drink with our evening meal. But it was a story of Wine Wine Everywhere when we pulled into town just after all the shops had shut.

We eventually ran a bottle to earth in a cellar behind one of the village bars. Congratulating ourselves on our achievement, we drove to the local campsite, invitingly plonked at the river's edge. Unfortunately, its gates were padlocked shut.

The Chauffeur reversed Daisy out and, as the light faded, we headed further up river to La Charité. There, we found another site and drove in past an empty reception office where a welcoming hand-written notice said:

LE GARDIEN EST ABSENT INSTALLEZ-VOUS MERCI

And, on a Loireside patch of grass prettily patterned with daisies, we did as we were told.

This was our best campsite so far. The facilities were new and clean (it even had lavatory paper) and it was situated just a bridge-length from the tinnily-chiming church clock in the town centre.

Later, the pleasant young gardien came over to introduce himself, but insisted we get on with the more important business of eating before helping him with his paperwork.

After our meal of tuna and bean salad followed by French bread and cheese (and the Fumé, which tasted all the better for being from just a few miles downstream) we made our latest contribution to French bureaucracy, then walked over the old bridge into the historic little town.

And the first thing to catch our eye was a gleaming new Guinness sign proclaiming the Lansdowne Road-Pub. (They're gluttons for punctuation, the French).

Like the Irish theme pubs that have taken over Britain, it was doing a better trade than most of its rivals. The barman hadn't a clue how to pour a proper pint of Guinness, though.

(You don't see many English theme pubs on the Continent: flat lukewarm beer, exorbitant prices and uncivil service must be acquired tastes I suppose).

In the morning we interrupted the gardien's conscientious camp cleaning to pay our night's rent and walked over the bridge again, this time to visit the busy market in the sunny main square, where fruit, veg, flowers, bread, cheese, fish, meat and clothing of all kinds were being sold from a variety of stalls and vehicles, large and small, old and new.

Not one of the traders was noisy or pushy or tried to give us a hard sell, as you might expect of their English counterparts. They were all smiling, helpful and polite with beaucoup de Bonjours and Au Revoirs, even for us grockles.

We asked for Grandes Noisettes at a nearby café, but that just brought blank looks from the waitress. So, instead, we ordered the coffees we wanted the long way round, with detailed descriptions of how much coffee and how much milk, of which type. And that way we got it right at last.

We left La Charité with regret, and drove east until our route was blocked by the lofty barricade of hill town Vézelay.

Here, we ate a picnic lunch then walked up the Hovis-steep main street, past half a dozen tastefully tempting shops filled with paintings and photographs, to meet the star of the show, the church of La Madeleine.

The Chauffeur's always said she'd like a tomb with a view, and she could have one here all right in the proudly pretty little cemetery with its neat family graves overlooking the rippling beginnings of woody-sloped Burgundy.

WE drove into the centre of the little Burgundy village of Villy-en-Auxois, and there it was: A cricket match. We parked Daisy at deep long leg and went to investigate.

On a sporting pitch, more hacked than mown out of the village football field, the Strasbourg Strollers were playing a team of ex-pat "locals."

And what's more they were a man short. In fact they were three men short. And would I please pad up immediately and go in at the fall of the next wicket, as their ninth and last man?

So I did. And I amassed four, not out, as I shared in a last wicket stand of 14 which took our (well, the Strollers') total to 104.

Then we all went over the road for tea in a nearby barn. The tea to eat was excellent, but I regret to report that the tea to drink, even at a cricket match, was of the French washing-up water variety.

In all, including me, there were 19 of us: 18 Englishmen and one Frenchman, a young lad from the village. And we were all fully and properly dressed in whites, except me: Cricket lover though I am, I'd been short-sighted enough to leave my cricket trousers at home, and was able to wear white only from the waist upwards.

After tea, as upper-crust cries of "Yours, Hugo" and "Good show, Adrian" pierced the evening air, amid the russet-roofed houses of a little Burgundian village, we Strollers set about showing the chaps of Villy what for.

And we jolly well did: We bowled the bounders out for 75.

The Chauffeur was very good about it all, as she sat reading Hilary Bonner's book behind the lbw-high boundary of newly-cut fever-inducing hay.

But I could tell from her body language what she was thinking. No, not: How come my pal Hil knows so much about sex? But: How come I drove all this way to spend yet another afternoon of my life watching him play cricket?

(Blonde Hilary, six foot and some and handsome, and like me a former Daily Mirror journalist, was once informed by a diminutive colleague in the office local, The Stab in the Back, that he fancied giving her one. She replied: "If you do, and I get to hear about it, you'll be in Big Trouble." Her little chum was left muttering something about whether she ought to consider doing children's portions).

After the match we carried on eastwards to Dijon and the Camping du Lac where, unfortunately, we got off on the wrong foot: The entrance barrier was locked shut so we rang the bell beside the reception office, and made the mistake of interrupting dinner. A serious offence in France.

The gardien shouted to us (none too welcomingly) from an upstairs window that we'd have to wait until he'd finished.

And it must have been a good dinner because he made us wait about 20 minutes, along with a young Dutch couple with babe in arms who'd hauled their caravan all the way from Holland that day.

He finally came down, relieved us of 52 francs, and checked us in to Pitch 115.

It was the biggest bossiest site we'd been on so far. There were numerous notices telling us how to behave.

But we soon saw why the gardien was feeling a little harassed: It was busy. Very busy.

We'd arrived just in time to collide with a children's cycling championship which was being held nearby.

And if there's one thing the French take even more seriously than dinner, it's cycling.

Everywhere there were bikes, bikes and more bikes. With kids on. Whizzing and wheeling all over the camp. Proudly displaying their competition numbers on their handlebars.

As you've probably gathered by now, we hadn't exactly been spending fortunes on posh nosh on our travels. That was never the object of our exercise.

But as Dijon is supposed to be something of a gastronomic centre we treated ourselves to a couple of portions of French fries from the happy but hard-pressed husband and wife team running the camp snack bar.

And very gastronomic they were too.

As darkness fell, we took a stroll round the camp before going to bed. And the bike kids were still going through their paces. But by now even more frenziedly. And two to a bike instead of one.

When we're on the Thames towpath back home in Richmond and cyclists come zooming along, showing no consideration for us walkers, The Chauffeur has a simple method of teaching them a lesson: She pushes me in front of them.

But I'm pleased to say she didn't resort to that tactic here, and as far as I know all campers, young and old, ended the night unscathed.

For the first time on our trip the lavatories were squatters, not sitters. These may be more hygienic but they're much harder exercise for the legs (perhaps it's why the locals are better skiers than us, said The Chauffeur) and when you've finished it can be quite a challenge trying to leap out of the way of their ferocious flush without getting your feet soaked.

In the morning it was chilly, it was wet, and I was starting a cold. We wondered how much further south we'd have to go before we could count on some sunny weather. And we set off to find out.

I may be doing Dijon an injustice (and then again I may not) but as we drove through it that miserable wet morning I could see very little to recommend it.

So we headed for the bit that Burgundy's really all about: The Côte d'Or, and the richest little vein of arable land in the world.

It wasn't so much an itinerary, more a wine list as we drove through a dozen places, some barely big enough even to be called villages but all regarded as full-bodied superstars the world over. It's best if I let them speak for themselves:

Gevrey-Chambertin
Vougeot
Vosne-Romanée
Nuits-Saint-Georges
Aloxe-Corton
Pommard
Volnay
Auxey-Duresses
Meursault
Puligny-Montrachet
Chassagne-Montrachet
Santenay

So strongly does the sight of their names bring to your mouth the raspberry-sharp taste of the Pinot Noir grape and the buttery smoothness of the Chardonnay that it makes you wonder whether it's safe for you to drive through them at all, without so much as a single glass inside you, for fear of being over the drink-drive limit.

The young vines sparkled a crisp banknote green. And the only things important enough to compete with them for a share of this valuable land were the little walled cemeteries beside each village.

We parked (with difficulty) in Beaune, the main town of the Côte d'Or, after The Chauffeur had squeezed Daisy through the narrow car-strewn streets, and went to visit the Hôtel-Dieu, the ancient hospice where the sick and the poor of the town used to be cared for.

It's an amazing sight with its red, black, yellow and green tile-patterned roof. And even in the rain (which noisily splattered the courtyard below as it gushed from the gargoyled downspouts) it retained its sparkle, like the vines whose rich juice helped to fund it.

If you're going to get a cold, the centre of the world's finest wine region isn't the place to do it. I felt unable to do justice to any of the numerous wine tasting offers being made all about us, so I treated myself to a take-away from a posh-looking wine shop, Moillard, opposite the Hôtel-Dieu: A bottle of their fins de lots Chassagne-Montrachet '94 for about seven quid.

To encourage business the shop's madame had put up a notice trans-lating her offers into English, and fins de lots was interpreted as ODD BINS. I told her I thought BIN ENDS would be a better translation, and explained that she was in danger of giving free publicity to one of her retailing rivals.

She said she'd been told it was right by a group of Australians. I said I couldn't be responsible for the damage Aussies had done to my lan-guage, but assured her I was correct. I left her still wondering what she should believe.

Everywhere in the area sold wine, even the garage where we coura-geously filled Daisy from the pump marked GAZOLE, having sought confirmation from a mere four fellow customers that that was the same as diesel. (Most garages call it diesel anyway these days).

Once we'd inspected enough of the vines to assure ourselves that Burgundy looked set for another good year, we drove on south to con-tinue our quest for that elusive sun.

4

Tain-l'Hermitage - Montelimar - Avignon - Les Baux-de-Provence - Arles - Apt - Aix-en-Provence - Saint-Maximin-la-Sainte-Beaume

WE'D begun to notice by now that some of our fellow motor caravanners, coming the other way, liked to give us a friendly flash of their headlights.

I took quite a shine to this happy act of campers' cameraderie and tried to persuade The Chauffeur to reciprocate.

But she firmly refused, saying it was quite naff enough of us to have bought a mobile home in the first place without making total tits of ourselves.

(For good measure, she also went on to give me the benefit of her opinion that I was becoming naffer every day as this whole middle-aged motor caravanning business began to tighten its grip on me).

If the centres of French towns tended to be attractive, the same couldn't be said for their outskirts.

Their entrances and their exits and their ring roads were usually a raucous cacophony of huge, screeching signs, posters and hoardings, and even huger, more screeching depots, warehouses and stores, discordantly painted in lurid clashes of colours.

We passed plenty of these eyesores as The Chauffeur gave Daisy a good workout and we cruised beside the Rhône.

The sun tried hard to come out, as friendly white clouds clung, snow-like, to the hills. But it was clear from the swampy fields and the standing water beside the road that they'd had more than just a couple of light showers that afternoon.

French allotments, we noticed, were all beautifully kept, with none of the poor, neglected, overgrown, weedy ones you so often see in England.

On a gantry above the autoroute near Lyon we saw a typically no-nonsense French idea of a traffic warning sign: An electronic, flashing picture of a car lying, cartoon-style, on its side.

I don't think it actually had dents in it but sure enough, a couple of kilometres further on, we came across the battered remains of a little white car surrounded by members of the emergency services trying to assist its stricken driver.

We stopped for the night in the midst of another famous wine region, at Tain-l'Hermitage, where the real blockbuster Rhône reds come from, the ones made with the full-fat Syrah grape rather than the semi-skimmed Grenache, which fights a losing battle to compete at Châteauneuf-du-Pape further south.

We checked in at Camping Municipal les Lucs: A lengthy process because both we and the German couple in front of us, who couldn't (or wouldn't) speak either French or English, had to have all our details, including dates of birth, fed into the computer.

I've had my doubts about computers for some time. And now I've seen the potential for chaos in their clash with the petty minds of the Mairie I've got even more doubts about them.

(Perhaps the French should never have been allowed to get their hands on them in the first place).

The inputting was done by a very pretty, very pleasant, very capable jeune fille. And she did her best. She did very well in fact.

But it would have been a lot quicker if she'd been allowed just to jot down our names and addresses on a piece of paper instead of laborious-ly having to key in information they couldn't possibly need again.

(Her screen did reveal less than usefully, though, that another Lamb, AJ, from just round the corner from us in Isleworth, so presumably not the former Northants and England cricketer, also slept here).

We parked Daisy and walked beneath terraced vineyards beside the dark Rhône. A lone sculler glided past and as heavy raindrops returned to pockmark the river a rainbow did its best to form a bridge from the far bank.

Once again, I was glad of my cricket sweater and my golf umbrella, the only items I'd brought with me to combat either cold or wet weather.

A game of boules was being played on a patch of rapidly-dampening, sandy gravel, but the rain didn't impede its lively progress.

Along with babyfoot table football, alive and kicking in many bars and cafés, boules can still excite a little joie de vivre in a fast-changing France.

And it's amazing how many places it can be played in: On nearly every street corner there seems to be the perfect spot.

The next morning, I got the only sitter in the toilet block to the obvi-ous envy of all my fellow campers who tried my locked door before hav-ing to settle for a squatter.

I'm sorry to report that The Chauffeur was already suffering from the dreaded mosquito bites, a tormenting rash of them menacing her right foot.

Needless to say, with her as my decoy, I remained uneaten.

We checked out of the camp for 75 francs: Above the average price so far, partly because we had to have a mains electricity hook-up included in the price even though we'd said we didn't need one.

We carried on south as the weather grew sunnier and the surrounding hills more serious. We reckoned we saw the remains of some snow on one of them as a TGV high-speed train hurtled past us going twice as fast as we were, about 240k.

Power station towers are ugly everywhere, and nowhere more so than in France where they're usually positioned to cause maximum unsightliness. But, south of Valence, we were cheered to see one joyfully decorated with a colourful 30-metre-high mural of a child at play.

Next, to Montelimar, delight of sweet-lovers, where the gaudy cluster of signs at the entrance for once sang the same chorus: NOUGAT NOUGAT NOUGAT.

So we bought a box of it in the town centre as a present for Next door.

We had lunch at the Café de l'Ardèche where we ordered meat salads at 60 francs a head. As ever, we weren't quite sure what we'd get (or what we got).

We knew from the menu that they contained gésiers. But what were gésiers? The Chauffeur roughly translated them as "the foul bits of fowl we'd throw away."

But what fowl? And what bits? We decided to look it up later in the dictionary.

(The Chauffeur said it reminded her of the time we had a French boy to stay on an exchange visit, and she'd asked him when he arrived if there was any food he didn't like. "Brains," he'd replied).

From Montelimar to Orange (of William fame) as our journey threatened to turn from a list of wines into a list of chocolate centres.

Past poppy-peppered fields which looked just like Monet's Poppy Field at Argenteuil, to Avignon, in Provence, and Camping Bagatelle where we arrived at teatime to be checked in by a friendly blonde receptionist.

But this time it was so much easier: No computer, no palaver, no fuss. Just: Name? Shaded or unshaded? Merci... And 90 seconds later we were heading for Pitch 54.

OUR campsite was on the Île de la Barthelasse opposite the famous Pont d'Avignon, or Demi Pont as it should really be called.

We made a proper cup of tea and walked over the bridge (a whole one) into the city, passing The Irish Shop which sold Irish linen, books, booze etc. I was starting to wonder whether the French might like the Irish rather more than they liked us English.

By now the locals, as well as our fellow tourists, were beginning their evening's promenading, on foot and by car, up and down the main streets, stopping here and there for a drink seated at one of the many pavement cafés.

The pedestrianised main square, the Place de l'Horloge, was ideal for promenaders. It had pavement tables and chairs by the hundred, street performers including musicians, puppeteers and mime artists, a lovely old riding-horse roundabout, beautifully decorated and illuminated, and, of course, other people (who are always the most interesting sight of all to watch).

Only the ubiquitous French dogshit threatened to spoil the idyll.

The place was dominated by the formidable Palais des Papes, where the Popes lived for a while (when they weren't guzzling Grenache juice at their nearby Châteauneuf) before they sent out change of address cards and moved back to The Vatican.

We climbed up to the public gardens hanging spectacularly above the river and the poor old demi pont.

Further away, a massive new bridge was in the course of construction, set to dwarf all its rivals.

I hope they got it finished, and it hasn't been left cut off in mid-air like its famous predecessor.

In the gardens was a horseshoe-shaped table-top panoramic map. Beautifully crafted in ceramic tiles, it indicated the direction and distance of all the surrounding landmarks, near and far.

And although it was nearly 25 years old it hadn't been vandalised, damaged or defaced. At all. In the slightest.

The pont and the palais looked even more beautiful after dark, stunningly floodlit against the black Provençal sky.

That night we had a near-outbreak of World War III thanks to two groups of Germans, camped on either side of us, who invaded our territory and gutturalled away until all hours right outside Daisy's back door, causing me to make a mental note to bring on future trips a bloody big notice, and a bloody big mallet to hammer it home with, saying:
ACHTUNG NOISY GERMANS VERBOTEN

In the morning we were woken by the bossy cries of the camp cleaner, a whole-hearted worker who enthusiastically turned his high-pressure hose on anything in the toilet block that didn't heed his shouts to get out of the way.

In the block there were notices in several languages alerting us to the danger of flooding. The English one warned:
IT IS POSSIBLE THAT ALL OR PART OF THE CAMPING MAY BECOME FLOODED MORE OR LESS QUICKLY

(It couldn't be anything to do with the cleaner, then: There was no chance of his flooding the place less quickly).

While we were there, I'm sorry to say I got involved in a brief but ferocious new outbreak of Language Duelling during which I intemperately accused a polite, pleasant, friendly, helpful jeune fille serving in the camp café of not knowing how to speak her own language.

Despite these hiccups we decided we liked both Avignon and the campsite enough to stay a second day, and I got all dressed up for another visit to the city in my smart new matching Marks & Sparks shirt and shorts.

But The Chauffeur stuck to her word: To my great irritation, she refused to come into town with me wearing them.

A tense half-hour stand-off ensued during which not many words were spoken, but Daisy's doors got slammed a couple of times.

Eventually, I decided to change. Not because I'm a weak-willed wimp or anything, but because I'm such a much more reasonable sort of human being than some people.

So we went into Avignon again. And we found a bookshop containing dictionaries with bigger vocabularies than our travelling one, which hadn't been able to help us, and looked up our unknown ingredient, gésier.

It meant: Gizzard. But our problem had only been partially solved because we still didn't know what creature it was from.

Next, we discovered the station. It may not have been in the same league as Huddersfield (which is magnifique) but, framed by the city wall's Porte de la République, it was a stunner as provincial stations go.

It had a 100-metre symmetrical façade and, above the main entrance, an important-looking clock and proudly-displayed SNCF French national railways logo. None of your fragmented Connex, Virgin, South-West, North-East nonsense.

(Come to think of it, most of those are French too, aren't they? Or is that just our water?)

As troop movements of tourists entered the station to overrun Paris and the north and Marseille and the south, The Chauffeur took great delight in pointing out to me that most of the men felt obliged to prove their strength by sweatily struggling to carry their suitcases (even the ones which had wheels) while all the women coolly pulled theirs along behind them.

She said that was just like us when we go through airports.

We had a drink in the cheerily-cluttered Place des Corps Saints, where every bit of ground not consumed by greed for the car was devoured by appetite for the table.

From there to the fascinating, shade-cool Rue des Teinturiers, consisting half of cobble-swirled street, half of fish-swirling stream.

And that's where we returned later, crossing the stream to one of the little restaurants for an evening meal.

The décor, with bare wood and green and brown floor tiles, was paysan-style and so was the food.

The new owners of the place had taken it over so recently that they hadn't had time to give it a name yet.

We more or less understood what we'd eaten: Courgette and pepper stuffed with tomato and basil for her and slices of roast pork with onion and apple for me. We also shared a carafe of house Côtes du Rhône and some goat's cheese.

It was all good and, as they weren't too busy, we were able to tell the chef so and wish him luck with his new venture.

We also asked him what animal he thought our gésiers might have come from. "More than 50 francs, duck. Less than 50 francs, chicken," he said.

Problem solved: It was 60 francs, so it must have been duck.

On our way back, we called at a café near the Porte de l'Oulle, where I meticulously and painstakingly ordered Deux Grands Cafés Noirs avec un Tout Petit Peu de Lait.

The waiter listened to me in a long-suffering sort of way before replying somewhat impatiently: "Oui, Monsieur, Deux Grandes Noisettes."
Help, bring me a bureaucrat.

NEXT morning we left early. A little too early in fact, because the camp office was still closed. We hung about for a while waiting in vain for it to open before we twigged we could check out at the café, where we handed over 118 francs for our two-night stay in exchange for the return of our Camping Card.

As usual, we had trouble finding the right way out of town. It's not just the TOUTES DIRECTIONS and AUTRES DIRECTIONS signs that are confusing in France: All the signs are, because they don't actually point the correct way, firmly, at right angles.

Instead they point, indecisively, at 45 degrees. And that's how we came to miss the main road to Arles.

As so often happens in these situations, though, it turned out to be for the best, because we accidentally discovered Les Baux-de-Provence and the unlikely, unexpected and unrealistic Alpilles Hills, which look like the badly constructed backdrop for a Moorish action adventure B-movie.

(So badly constructed, in fact, that a large section of them had come sliding down, destroying the livelihood of the restaurant beneath).

Les Baux is an equally improbable cliff-top village and (give the B-movie makers their due) it was hard to see where the papier-mâché rock ended and the cardboard citadel began.

We eventually found Arles (for ever to be known as the place where the daft-as-a-brush Sweet Genius Vincent did his head in) and parked Daisy beside the Rhône near where he painted his Starry Night.

Before we'd even got into the town, we were stopped, stunned, in our tracks by the astonishing street market which ran along the outside of the old walls. A living larder of Provençal plenty:

Trailers of spuds, armfuls of garlic, fat tomatoes, shiny aubergines, raspberries, strawberries, cherries, olives, bread made with olives and without, cake, honey, jam, nuts, green melons, yellow melons, green and yellow melons, apples, pears, peaches, carrots, beans broad and long, radishes, cucumbers, asparagus, artichokes, courgettes, peppers red and green, fat and thin, round and square, lettuce, celery, peas fat and flat, herbs, spices, pâtés, meats, fish and shellfish, cheese, sausages, cheese sausages, sausage cheeses, chicken and egg, egg and chicken, rabbit, quail dead and alive, cooked and uncooked, hot and cold, wine, lard and rice. (Yes, locally-grown rice).

Next, as the market wound on round the town walls: Clothes for young and old, the means to make clothes for young and old, shoes and socks, hats and caps, ribbons and bows, baskets and bags, household goods, leather goods, watches, jewellery and toys. And fabrics, fabrics, fabrics: Printed, patterned and dyed Provence-bright with whirls and twirls and stars and stripes and spots and checks and waves and clouds and fish and fruit and flowers and Michael Jackson and Elvis Presley.

Then came the antiques: China and brass, wood and glass, silver and gold, art and craft and clay. And we hadn't got into the town yet.

Exhausted by our market marathon we flopped down in a pavement café and asked the waiter for two Grandes Noisettes. "Oui, Monsieur, Deux Cafés au Lait."

Well, not exactly…

We lugged a couple of sackfuls of fruit and veg back to Daisy, then we finally made it into town.

We walked round the Roman amphitheatre, spattered with the blood of centuries and where they still hold bullfights but not always to the death, past the McDonalds sign, to the Place du Forum and Vincent's Café la Nuit where we toasted his memory in vin rouge.

Mind you, we've often passed the spot where he preached in Kew Road, Richmond. (Yes, honestly).

When we walked out of town, less than two hours later, every market stall had gone and a lone water truck was spraying the last leaves, pips and juices away.

We left Arles and drove past silver-blown olive groves, blind-you-bright yellow broom and a puce patch of lurid larkspur. We headed north up the craggily wooded Montagne du Lubéron, and down across its slopes of vineyard and cherry orchard.

I don't want to sound hard to please, but after the unseasonable weather we'd had so far, as we entered June, it was starting to get hot. A bit too hot. So an iced tea was apt at Apt, as we watched some more-than-usually serious boules matches.

There's a rule of the road in France which is particularly daft even by French standards. It's called PRIORITÉ À DROITE, and it means you're supposed to give way at junctions to traffic coming in from your right. Or at least it used to.

It came into force when roads were a lot smaller and a lot less busy than they are now.

Today, as in most sensible countries, the major road tends to have priority over the minor road. But not always, because some traditional French folk, being by nature conservative like the rest of us, enjoy trying to uphold the ways of the good old days.

And it was one of these types we bumped into (well, nearly) as we were leaving Apt. He came hurtling out of a side road, and all but smashed into Daisy's side.

In the event no physical harm was done, although The Chauffeur was treated to a good Gallic tongue lashing and some angry Anglophobic gestures.

But the point is this: Who was in the right and who was in the wrong?

Maybe French road junctions should be equipped with a Third Umpire and slow-motion replay camera to help dissenting drivers decide.

We recovered our composure and drove south again by steeply overhanging turns and through villages isolated enough for old locals to give Daisy stares of disapproving curiosity.

But a wild boar showed neither disapproval nor curiosity when we stopped to watch her foraging for food for her eight young.

WE checked in at Camping Arc en Ciel, Aix-en-Provence. The price for the night, demanded in advance: 95 francs, the second most expensive so far.

It certainly wasn't our quietest site, with a network of main roads nearby and a marauding mob of ducks who raced round the camp more menacingly and more noisily then the bike kids at Dijon.

(And at least none of the bike kids bit The Chauffeur on the leg).

The best thing about the place was that the toilet block had separate little cubicles, each with its own basin, shower and lavatory (not just a sitter but a sitter with a seat).

Unfortunately, though, someone with a massive and moulting overabundance of pubic hair had been in the one I used before I had.

We had a moment's anxiety when Daisy's bed refused to open out and we had visions of having to sleep in our seats or on the floor, but the problem was resolved with a little semi-controlled violence.

Rain drummed on Daisy's roof during the night (again) but the sun we'd come so far to find shone strongly in the morning.

We drove straight out of camp, having completed all our financial dealing when we arrived, and straight into traffic-troubled, pedestrian-packed Aix.

Here we visited the atmospheric Atélier Cézanne, atop terracotta-coloured shutters among a tall dense clump of trees on a hillside above the city centre.

Cézanne had it purpose built as his studio with one huge north-facing window, two smaller south-facing ones, and a giant vertical letterbox in the wall to slot his biggest canvases through.

His table along with his easels, stools, chairs, jars, bottles and other artist's equipment was exhibited to help paint us a picture of his working life.

Hopefully the trees weren't as intrusive in Paul's day as they are now: He'd never have seen the light. Or the view.

As we were leaving, a large group of Japanese men each held out their ticket for me to inspect as they entered, but all I was doing was waiting for them to come in through the door so I could get out.

We found Aix attractive and pleasingly scaled, with smart spacious boulevards and squares and calm cooling trees and fountains. The traffic, though...

East, through more vineyards and rocky bits, to Saint-Maximin-la-Sainte-Beaume. (Not bad that, even for the French: Two saints and four hyphens in one name).

We had lunch at the Restaurant la Renaissance in the sunny central square, under shades which clacked like football rattles in the stiff wind.

There were no Plats du Jour left, so we had Salades du Berger: Lettuce of the variety most commonly found in these parts and known (I should imagine) as Tonsil Tickler, cucumber, peppers, olives, tomatoes, eggs, goat's cheese and mushrooms. But no gésiers.

It was all attractively served on big scallop-shaped plates. The cost: 48 francs each.

Then we drove south over a massif or two where, at times, the white lines indicated two lanes coming downhill and one going up.

Non-French logic suggested things might have been better arranged the other way round, but it didn't cause anybody any problems because nobody took any notice anyway.

There's another difference between us and the French: Overtaking.

Normally we wait for a straight stretch of road before we do it. But they're just the opposite: They wait until there's a corner coming up, then go for it.

And another thing: They don't half get close to you when they drive up behind you.

Something that was beginning to impress us was the astonishing energy of the people we saw cycling, walking and even running up impossible slopes in unsurvivable sun.

For all those who spend their leisure hours slumped in front of the telly getting pig-roll fat, there are an admirable few who devote that same time to becoming ribcage thin.

Next, we went to the seaside.

5

Hyères - Bormes-les-Mimosas - Cavalaire-sur-Mer - Saint-Tropez - Cannes - Juan-les-Pins - Antibes - Cagnes-sur-Mer - Nice - Menton - Sospel - Monte Carlo - Cap Ferrat

ORANGES were ripening on the trees in the streets as we entered the lovely old Côte d'Azur resort of Hyères. And there were as many palm trees as cars. (Oh, all right then, maybe not quite that many).

On to the beautifully named Bormes-les-Mimosas, although when we were there the only yellow flowers on view were cacti, and Le Lavandou, where we stopped at a supermarket called Casino. (Well, everything's a gamble in France).

We stocked up with bread, cheese, ham, pâté, yoghurt, milk, fruit juice, beer and wine to accompany our Arles harvest of fruit and veg.

Next, amid sunbathers of both sexes stripped to the waist for inaction, three weeks and nearly 2,000 miles on from Dorset, The Chauffeur went in for her second swim of the year and I went in for my first, off the pretty little Plage de la Fossette.

And to me the water still felt cold.

As we drove east along the winding coast of the Med we were struck by the speed with which the land took off from the sea, rising sharply to form dark green hillsides richly variegated with light brown villas.

We got a cheery and relaxed reception at Camping la Pinède, on the outskirts of Cavalaire-sur-Mer, and were told to park anywhere we liked.

We made a cup of tea, then The Chauffeur checked Daisy's oil. The dipstick showed minimum.

We tried to remain unconcerned as we ate our campers' supper. But, oh dear, was our delicate Freitag's Child having another of her Bad Turns? We'd have to have her checked out again.

That evening we walked into town expecting to find the little fishing port which, a few years ago, Cavalaire would have been.

Instead, we were gobsmacked to see a huge harbour containing so many yachts that it was almost impossible to detect the sky through their masts.

And some of them were so posh that... Well, you didn't need to be a forensic scientist to detect that the quayside dogshit was composed largely of foie gras.

And no matter how many of you buy this book, I'll never be able to afford one.

We drank at a couple of bars, then walked back to the camp in darkness. And as we approached Daisy we heard what sounded like a loud dripping noise. We feared the worst: Her lifeblood was draining away.

But it turned out to be the fridge ignition system ticking to tell us our camping gas cylinder had run out: Another problem for us to worry about, but we decided it could wait until morning.

The toilet arrangements at La Pinède, as at many sites, were unisex: A little disarming at first for the uptight English, but you soon get used to it (and the women don't have to use the urinals if they don't want to).

It's the same arrangement in a lot of cafés and bars. Also, it's common practice for men to pull up and have a pee at the side of the road. But not women.

Showers: Now there's a fertile area for camping debate. The ones at La Pinède weren't bad, but the trouble is there are so many ways in which they can make life awkward.

The most frequent problem is the cubicle that is too small. No matter where you put them, you can't keep your towel and your clothes dry and douse yourself at the same time.

Then there's the flow: Sometimes it's a paltry trickle down the wall which makes it impossible for you to wash more than a finger at a time. Sometimes it's a mighty gush which soaks everything in sight up to a height of two metres.

Next, there's the temperature which can get stuck on any one of the hundred numbers discovered by Herr Celsius, or run through the lot of them at a single standing.

Finally, there's the length of time you can get your water for. Shower taps, like pretty well every tap on campsites, are of the push-button variety.

Some give you a generous 30 seconds per push. Others (no matter how much energy you put into pushing them) give you only a miserly five seconds.

This can make life extremely awkward if you also want to use your hands to do other things at the same time. Such as washing.

In the morning we managed, between us, to swap the dead gas cylinder for the spare. It's a tricky operation, performed by fiddling about in a little cupboard just inside Daisy's back door.

It's hard to say whether it's better done by two people (who get in each other's way) or one (who, as in the showers, doesn't have enough hands).

Anyway we did it. And we reminded each other to remind each other we must get a new one.

Oh, and The Chauffeur emptied the Porta-Potti in the chemical toilet place. I still haven't used it and I don't want to talk about it, but she did.

We checked out of the shade and into the sun, and set off anxiously to look for a Volkswagen garage. And as we drove out on to the main road, incredibly, there was one right opposite us.

We parked Daisy on the forecourt, and the boss came out to meet us.

We told him our problem, and nervously waited for his reply. But it couldn't have been more reassuring: He said it was normal during running-in, and there was nothing for us to worry about.

Phew. He topped up Daisy's oil for us, and we were on our way again.

We drove, with relief, by hilly headland road, through trees and villas we'd seen from afar, to the shining Azur star, Saint-Tropez.

And it was all right. But that's all. Only all right: We weren't that impressed with it. (Honestly).

There was money there. And there were yachts. Even posher yachts than at Cavalaire. (One was so posh it came from the Isle of Man).

And it was a good place to buy chic clothes and be seen wearing them. And to buy chic food and be seen eating it.

And there were beautiful people. But not that beautiful. (I'm not just saying so because The Chauffeur and I got there about 35 years too late).

And the old town was pretty enough, with its small streets and its smaller alleyways off its small streets.

But it wasn't that different from plenty of other places on the Med and elsewhere. And it was hard to avoid thinking it was expensive and famous only because it was expensive and famous.

We sat outside a bar at the harbourside and had a beer, and looked at the rich looking at the rest of us with about as much boredom as they looked at each other.

Then we returned to Daisy, and drove on past villas and bougainvilleas and yachts and more yachts and rocks and white-horsed seas and beaches buried beneath bodies browned by the tan-assisted oven of sun and wind.

And suddenly, above us and below us, the land turned red, with rocky sandstone heights that would have been better cast in a Western movie.

We hugged the hills and we wound our way to film star-famous Cannes, already sighted from a dozen miles away. And it was as yachty dotty as the rest.

I've got a problem with yachts. And I don't mean your average bonny little sailing boat, I mean your mini-QE2 beloved by all those with more money than taste.

58

You know what the trouble is, don't you? That big, bloated, thieving, mid-European carpetbagger who gave gipsies a bad name and took over the Mirror and my life.

It's like actors and Macbeth. They can't bring themselves to say the name because it's unlucky, so they refer to it as The Scottish Play.

Oh, all right then: Maxwell. There you are, I've said it.

For seven years he trampled all over us at the Mirror like the bully he was, having us believe he had more money than we had.

And he got away with it because, within the company, he set himself up as all-powerful, hiring and firing staff as his mood of the moment took him, sometimes offering people amazingly generous deals, sometimes extremely mean ones.

Of course, as under any dictator, there were scattered outbreaks of raw courage among us subjugated suckers.

Once, he rang the composing room, where the pages were put together for printing, to find out why the paper was late. The printer at the other end of the line was brave enough to give him a dismissive reply.

"Do you know who I am?" Maxwell's gruff voice boomed.

Printer: "No. Do you know who I am?"

Maxwell (wrong-footed for once): "No."

Printer: "Well fuck off then."

Eventually Cap'n Bob did the decent thing and took a dive from his yacht off the Canary Islands. And I can picture now how straight-faced we all stayed when the then editor of the Mirror, Richard Stott, called us together in the newsroom and announced in sombre tones that The Publisher was lost at sea, presumed drowned.

A week or so later I was in charge of the Night Desk when Stott called me into his office and told me what he wanted the following morning's front page headline to say:

MILLIONS MISSING FROM MIRROR

What he went on to describe caused in me what you might call Mixed Feelings: On the one hand I was being asked to handle a Big Story. On the other hand I was being told my entire life savings had vanished.

(I've only ever had two worthwhile financial assets to my name: The first is the part of my house which isn't owned by The Halifax, the second is the cash I've paid into the Mirror Pension Fund since the 1960s. I'd just learned that the second had gone).

I'm relieved to say that enough money has since been returned (willingly and unwillingly) for me to be able to get my hands on my share of the fund when I need to. But it was definitely a Nasty Moment.

Apart from nicking all my money, Maxwell never did me any harm. He didn't lack courage and he certainly didn't lack nerve. But in the end there was one thing he couldn't face: Ridicule.

He did himself in because he was about to be exposed as a sham. The world had been on the verge of discovering that he had even less money than the rest of us.

But if you're going to be conned, it's a privilege to have been conned by the best.

LET'S be honest about it: The Côte d'Azur isn't exactly camper friendly. And it treats us motor caravanners as second-class citizens.

Most of the seafront car parks have height-restriction barriers to keep us out. And there are lots of aggressive road signs showing innocent little Daisies being towed away by big bullying tow-trucks.

Maybe it was because of this or maybe it was because of the yachts, but one way or another we didn't like Cannes.

It looked smart and prosperous enough, with its city centre streets lined by pretty petunias in neat pebble-dashed troughs. In fact it looked a bit too smart and prosperous: It lacked soul. Or if it did have soul, we weren't able to find it.

It seemed to suffer from the same problem as the yacht owners: It was too mercenary, too competitive. It had too much of today's concrete and not enough of yesterday's charm. It certainly wasn't any place for us nonconformist nomads.

One good thing did happen in Cannes (although it could have happened in any number of other places). Before we'd set off on our trip I'd got an international debit card, and I used it that afternoon at a bank-in-the-wall machine.

It was brilliant: First it asked me whether I wanted to conduct my transaction in French or English. Then it asked me for my PIN number. Then how many francs I wanted. Next, it said it was consulting my own bank. And then it paid out, just like at home.

The whole thing took less than two minutes. It almost made me feel computers were bloody marvellous and I shouldn't have been so rude about them all these years. Almost.

Near Juan-les-Pins we were held up in a huge traffic queue as police swarmed all over the road brandishing mobile phones. Fearing there must have been a serious accident, we waited patiently until we were eventually waved through.

But when we got round the corner we discovered the cause of the hold-up: Three brand-new Peugeots parked, empty, in the road and an advertising camera crew taking glamour shots of them with the Med in the background.

Most of the residents of Juan-les-Pins and the Cap d'Antibes are prob-ably wealthier than most of the residents of Cannes, but that didn't stop their towns being infinitely more inviting.

The Old Town of Antibes, although horribly overrun with tourists and virtually impassable by road, was charming: It certainly had soul.

We booked in for the night at laid-back Camping Panoramer, above Cagnes-sur-Mer, with its magnificent views over the town. What's more, we got the best view of the lot, parking Daisy on the corner pitch, the ground dropping sharply away from us on two sides.

Beyond the town to our right we could look back across the bay to the Cap d'Antibes. And to our left we could see the planes coming in to land at Nice Airport. (Just like at home, said The Chauffeur).

Then, as we sat there eating our meal beneath Daisy's awning, the whole scene started to change for the evening performance.

First, we were entertained by dozens of streamlined swifts who put on an astonishing airshow for us, divebombing our hilltop eyrie and darting between the trees beneath us, crazier than any ducks or bike kids and more skilled than The Red Arrows. After that, it was the turn of half a dozen bats to go through their paces.

Meanwhile, the night-time light show had begun: First, the Cap d'Antibes lighthouse began to flash. Next, the lights beside the bay came on, and the sea slowly started to pick up their reflections. Then, gradu-ally, the town lit up, to turn into a twinkling fairyland below us.

And all the time we could pick up the procession of the approaching headlights of the planes as they flew in across the dark waters of the Med.

We slept with Daisy's big back door and side door open, facing away from the other campers and towards the view.

In the morning we had to hand over a steep 149 francs for the return of our Camping Card. But we had no doubts it had been worth it for the view alone.

WE drove into Nice to see if we could take to it more than we'd taken to Cannes.

It had a head start because throughout her childhood The Chauffeur had been brought up with a picture (her Dad's favourite) of Nice's esplanade, the Promenade des Anglais, in her living room.

She used to look at it every day and wonder what it would be like for real. When we got there, the Promenade immediately reminded her of Torquay (as it was meant to).

But she was amazed at the forest of seafront palm trees, and the sheer size of it all. ("Torquay ten times over," she reckoned).

Nice was full of elegant squares with tall imposing buildings, balconied and shuttered. It seemed older than Cannes. And classier.

There's another thing about driving in France: Zebra crossings. They're everywhere and they look the same as the ones in England but the difference is they don't mean anything, except to mark the venue for a death-defying game of chicken between driver and pedestrian.

In Nice, The Chauffeur stopped at one to let an elderly couple cross, and the jeune français at the wheel of the car following us pulled out, whizzed round us and just missed them, albeit having calculated (correctly) that he'd reach the other side of the crossing a metre or two ahead of them.

Although we were starting to like Nice, its seafront signs were no more welcoming for us itinerants than anywhere else's. But we managed to park centrally, for free and legally (as far as we could tell), in the Avenue des Fleurs (suitable, because The Chauffeur's Dad was a florist) just a few blocks from the seafront.

The good thing about the hotter weather we were now getting was that the dogshit was drying quicker on the pavements. And there seemed to be even more dogs in Nice than elsewhere in France. If you could call them dogs: The ones I saw reminded me of the time I was out for a toddle with Son No 1, then aged two, beside the river at Richmond and we encountered a middle-aged couple deriving particular pleasure from showing off their particularly tiny Yorkshire Terrier as they took it for walkies.

Parental pride welled within me as my little lad loudly and joyfully blurted out: "Look, Daddy. Like a dog."

The Chauffeur and I sat beside the Promenade and had coffee and croque-monsieur toasted cheese and ham sandwiches. And, wonderful to relate, the gentille young waitress was happy to do business with me in French. For my benefit. Although her English was almost perfect.

Then we did the Promenade des Anglais (literally) and the sea was blue and the sun was shining and we weren't disappointed (even though, unlike Torquay, the beach was of pebbles, not sand).

But the place was bossy, with notices beside each set of seafront steps, in French and English, saying: THE FOLLOWING ARE STRICTLY FORBIDDEN, then listing 16 things including (No 4): ACCESS TO BREAKWATERS DYKES AND RIPRAPS.

(That was it. Your guess is as good as mine).

The long wide Promenade was a paradise for bladers and skaters. They were everywhere, advanced age or lack of proficiency no object.

Across the road, on the other side from the sea, there was a McDonalds (of course) and a Video X sex shop, with blacked-out windows like in

England. But right there on the seafront, not tucked away down a side street.

We joined about 30 other grockles, mainly American (although it's hard to tell because they always sound more numerous than they actually are) to take the Train Touristique, with beautiful brunette driver, through the streets to the Flower Market, the Old Town and Castle Hill.

We all sat aboard and waited patiently, like good grocks, for over half an hour. Then the bell rang and we were off, intent on causing maximum disruption to others on wheels and on foot. And feeling, in the case of The Chauffeur and me, more than a little self-conscious.

There was a commentary throughout, which must have been taped (unless our lovely train driver was really a bloke). First in French then in amusingly accented English, it consisted almost entirely of history and dates and Greeks and Romans and Napoleon and Foche and tosh.

A Japanese passenger fought a losing battle to stay awake at the back of the class, so he didn't learn much for his 30 francs.

The Flower Market had just closed, so he didn't miss much there: We saw a lot more broken leaves on the ground than fresh blooms on the stalls.

There's no longer a castle on Castle Hill but we were allowed a stop at the top, for 15 minutes we were told, so we could all visit the café, shop and viewing terrace.

Our Japanese fellow traveller just about managed to sleepwalk himself and his camcorder to the view. And a wonderful view it was: Almost as good as "our" view from the campsite.

Spread out beneath us, Nice was an impressive sight. But that's all we saw: Nice. Its streets, its houses, its shops, its apartments, its hotels.

In a heat haze which restricted visibility to about five kilometres it was hard to make out, beneath the concrete and the bricks and the tiles, any of the beautiful natural countryside which had helped to make it the ideal spot for such a popular resort in the first place.

We hurried back to the train so we wouldn't miss it. But there was no rush: We had to wait another ten minutes for the driver.

She was in the café helping to do the dishes.

ABOUT the same time as "Like a dog" we'd had a number of French students to stay while they were on summer language courses in Richmond. Our first (and favourite) was the affectionate Didier Bernard.

We'd kept in touch with him but hadn't seen him since he and his then fiancée Bernadette had visited us 20 years earlier.

Now married and parents of two themselves, they live in a pretty village just outside Nice. So when we were in Avignon we sent them a postcard (we didn't have their phone number) saying we'd be coming to visit them.

We found their village, and The Chauffeur squeezed Daisy down a narrow lane to their gate. Then Bernadette came out of their house and told us to go away: They hadn't got our postcard, she assumed we were lost and she was trying to prevent us getting any further off course.

We managed to establish our bona fides and (Take Two) we were warmly welcomed into the family home where we chatted away in a happy mixture of French and English over tea and biscuits.

And their kids squabbled over their toys just like ours had done when we last saw Didier and first met Bernadette.

Although it had been nearly 25 years since Didier had stayed with us as a student he reminisced in great detail about the happy time he'd had, even remembering the names of some of our friends we'd introduced him to all that time ago, and asking after them.

We told him how much we'd enjoyed having him and how we still spoke fondly of him.

It's rather odd: We don't have much in common. He's a tax inspector and I'm innumerate. There's a big age difference between us. We don't see each other for 20 years. But there's still this lasting bond of friendship between us.

It was good to see him and Bernadette, and to meet their children. And it will be good to see them again whether it's in another 20 years or a little sooner.

They asked us if we'd like to stay the night, but because we hadn't planned to we said no. Instead, with much kissing and embracing, we left.

But before we reached the end of their lane we both said we regretted our decision.

As we drove away, we remembered the other students we'd had, and how different they'd been. There was the dashing Daniel who'd brought friends round to visit us by the dozen, made us croques-monsieur (or should that be messieurs?) and, after midnight, climbed across the glass roof of our dining-room extension for illicit trysts with the beautiful blonde fellow student staying next door.

Then there was the one who demanded an immediate transfer from us (yes, young-thinking, broad-minded, liberal us) because, he claimed, we didn't have enough furniture. (Instead of a three-piece suite, our dead trendy 70s front room had a sunken conversation pit filled with cushions, the envy of all our friends who visited us for our oh-so-with-it parties).

We decided to camp that night at Menton, the seaside border town where French and Italian architecture and language collide.

As it was late and it was raining we took a péage toll autoroute for the first time. It cost us only 10 francs, and we wondered whether we'd been wrong not to have started using them before. (We didn't have far to travel on it though, which kept the price down).

We ended up at Camping Fleur de Mai, where we were shunted off into a small gravelled parking area at the bottom of the site near the entrance, in unwanted intimacy with a dozen other motor caravans, alongside the toilet block.

But it was late and it was wet and we couldn't be bothered to complain. So we put up with it.

It was an officious little site, with notices everywhere telling us what was FORBIDDEN, VERBOTEN, VERBODEN and VIETATO.

And I had to use a squatter because all the sitters were in use when I got to the toilet block.

The showers were fine for space, flow and temperature. But here the problem was that they were too dark: I couldn't see what I was doing.

We got away as early as we could the following morning, at a cost of 112 francs (for a night in not much more than a car park).

We set off towards town, and immediately ran into a ludicrous impasse at a mini-roundabout: Half a dozen drivers were blocking each other's progress because they all refused to give way.

You find this in France: In heavy traffic when regulations (even if they did make any sense) would be of little use, nobody ever gives way in courteous "After you" style, as can happen in England.

Instead, the French only give way when they have to, to avoid a collision (and sometimes not even then).

The Chauffeur reckoned women drivers were more reasonable than men. (Well, she would, wouldn't she?) I thought them just as unyielding, and equally accomplished hornblowers.

She found a parking space for Daisy, and we walked to the town's little street market where we bought bread and cheese. But after Arles, no other market would ever matter again.

We walked beside some flats where a disembodied voice was singing happily from the entryphone, to the amusement of a crowd of passers-by, its owner unaware that somehow he'd managed to leave the thing switched on.

We passed a flower shop which, although closed and locked behind iron bars, had its front doors wide open to give the goods some air, then strolled on to the Old Town with its pretty pedestrianised main street and shadily-inviting cafés.

Next, we drove along the seafront and into more traffic trouble: When you want to park in France it's no good driving past a space, indicating you plan to reverse into it and waiting for others to stop and let you go. No, you've got to get in there before they nip in behind you. And that's not always easy in a Daisy-sized vehicle.

Sure enough, when we found a suitable space beside the beach and tried to back into it so we could go for a swim, it was grabbed instantly be the pushy monsieur following us in his Renault Clio.

I was furious, and to The Chauffeur's amazement (she says I normally do nothing about it at the time but then go on to moan at her for ages afterwards) I leapt out and gave monsieur a real mouthful.

Whether it was my non-matching shirt and shorts or not, I don't know, but when this barmy Englishman began yelling at him in a furious attempt at his own language he scarpered.

Judging by the stunned look on his face I'm not sure who was the most surprised by what he'd done: Him, me, or The Chauffeur.

It was a sunny morning, but grey and white clouds smoked in to give the town's backdrop of lumpy hills the appearance of threatening volcanoes.

We launched ourselves into the turquoise-white sea from the steep stony shore (glad we'd brought our Brighton jellies with us to protect our feet) before the rain could reach us.

Despite the unfriendly weather, we wound Daisy up into the hills and stopped to make proper cuppas and eat juicy strawberries beside a patch of pink peaflowers near the peaceful but puddled old town of Sospel.

Then we spiralled back down to Menton and found a different campsite, the Municipal Saint-Michel. And again we managed to pinch the pitch with the best view: Over the town and the bay to Cap Martin.

Once more, over our meal, we watched the evening performance as the lights came on to be reflected on the water.

We slept with Daisy's side door open again, and in the early morning the view was even more beautiful as the pale sun spread gently across the town, painting it pastel pink and yellow.

Our stay cost us 86 francs: A sight better value than the cramped parking lot of the night before.

TO ludicrous little Monaco, with its pettily restrictive laws and sinister dark-spectacled policemen on every street corner to enforce them.

In Monte Carlo, motor caravans are directed to an underground car park to be hidden away from the gaze of the rich. Towed caravans aren't allowed in at all.

Noisy and unsightly helicopters are permitted to come and go as they please, of course. As are Rolls-Royces. (We even saw one which didn't have a poodle in the passenger seat). And yachts Robert Maxwell, pompous and preposterous like this pretentious principality, would have died for, complete with uniformed crews swabbing the decks to please their absent owners.

To help remind us what a footling place it is, most of the streets and landmarks are named after its "royal" family. You know the sort of thing:
ALBERT SQUARE.
THE GRACE GATES.
THE RAINIER WEATHER CENTRE.
But some of the wealth did filter down to benefit the likes of us: Lifts and escalators were laid on to carry us between the hilly town's different levels, and conventional flights of steps were fitted with chairlifts for the disabled.

There were sparkling-clean public lavatories every couple of hundred metres, and pedestrian crossings had electronic pictures of egg-timers to show you how long you'd got to wait until it was your turn to go.

I'd put on long trousers and a proper shirt, and The Chauffeur a dress, to increase our chances of being admitted to the snooty Casino. But I think what really swung it for us was that I hadn't shaved, which made me look the part of the serious gambler.

Anyway, for whatever reason, they were prepared to accept us and our money.

First, we had to show our passports (presumably to prove we weren't unwelcome guests who had previously run up big gambling debts) and they were photocopied for future reference.

Our entry cards (50 francs each) were handed to us with our names neatly printed on them.

It was only 1pm but gambling was already well under way in the main hall with its carved and gilded ceiling and mega-ton chandeliers.

Three of the eight tables were in use: Two for Roulette and one for cards. The tables all had seats for up to eight players (although others could play standing up).

Three croupiers wearing light grey uniforms and bow ties sat at each, while another sat in an umpire's chair at the head.

The Roulette tables (where the minimum stake was 20 francs) were the busiest.

Of course, a lot of the punters were just grocks like us. But there was a bit of serious money about, too.

Several of the more professional-looking gamblers were noting down the Roulette numbers on squared school exercise-book paper.

One kept dashing between the two tables frantically betting at both for fear he might not be able to lose his cash quickly enough at just one.

I put 50 francs on Black 17 for four consecutive spins, but how it failed to come up even once is beyond me. In my dreams of breaking the bank it always came up at least four times running.

Still, at least I'd helped to pay the wages of the 40 flunkies we'd already seen by then.

The card game was a more serious affair. The empty places all had reserved notices on them and the minimum stake was 100 francs.

The players included a couple of elderly Peter O'Sullevan lookalikes whose complexions suggested they didn't see a lot of the sun and two younger men who were far from over-dressed in surprisingly casual shirts.

They were joined by an unlikely-looking grey-haired dame in a shabby baggy cardigan who greeted them all like old comrades in arms when she sat down to join them.

The game they were playing was called Trente et Quarante. And for those of you who don't know how to play, here's what you do:

1. Smoking is compulsory.
2. A croupier deals an indeterminate number of cards.
3. Nobody takes the slightest bit of notice until the last couple of cards are dealt.
4. Then the players start to become a bit more interested in what's going on.
5. Some of them win or lose money.
6. Voices are raised and (one out, all out) the comrades angrily leave the table.
7. They gradually begin to drift back, and soon it's FAITES VOS JEUX again as usual.

On our way back to the second-class citizen's car park we ordered coffee and sandwiches at a little café near the Palais, but we had to wait while the shapely blonde waitress chatted sexily on mobile phone and six-inch platform heels.

After a while, I walked up to the counter and collected our order myself. But if my pointed display of direct action cut her to the quick, she disguised her hurt feelings admirably.

The price to get out of the car park: 62 francs for less than six hours, a good deal more than we'd paid for some of our nights' camping.

Then, safe in the hands of The Chauffeur, through the curves of high drama that killed Princess Grace, to classy Cap Ferrat, corniche cream of the Côte, with its opulent houses and succulent gardens secure behind their wrought-iron fortifications.

Back again via Nice and The Chauffeur's Promenade des Anglais to Cagnes-sur-Mer, where we stocked up with campers' supplies of bread, wine, coffee, salad, cheese and fruit.

And after four days of trying (and of trying to remember) we managed to find the right type of camping gas cylinder for Daisy.

This time we checked in at the pleasantly green Camping du Val-Fleuri, parking Daisy beside a large sweet-smelling honeysuckle bush.

And as we finished our meal and darkness fell we were treated to our most beguiling evening's entertainment yet: The Dance of the Fireflies.

First one, then another, then hundreds of flashing white lights, tiny but bright, began to dart, like so many fairylight Tinkerbelles, all around us. The trees above us were full of them, and some came within inches of our faces.

One landed on Daisy, and we were able to examine it. It was like a small ladybird, but longer and narrower, with a dark brown body and a light brown head. The flashing came from its under-carriage and, close up, its light had a green tinge.

In the morning, we went to the beach and had a cool (very cool) swim followed by coffee at a seafront bar. Then The Chauffeur left me. Not because we'd had a row. And not for good. But because she had to get back to work

I drove her to Nice Airport at lunchtime and dropped her off to catch her 670 franc easyJet flight home.

Actually I only wish it had been that simple. In fact it was a nightmare, and for the first time in my life I found myself on the receiving end of a police whistle.

It was Daisy who got me into trouble, and it was the familiar problem: She was too tall to get into most of the car parks.

There was one which was suitable but it was full, so I stopped in a no-waiting zone to offload The Chauffeur and her bags.

And instantaneously (to the considerable interest of quite a large crowd) I became the target of half a dozen shrill blasts from an excitable gendarme.

The Chauffeur bundled herself and her bags out, but there was still the problem of where to park so I could go and see her off.

Daisy and I completed the same circuit three times: Past two unsuitable (but not full) car parks, round the roundabout, past the suitable (but full) car park, round another roundabout and back to the gendarme.

With each lap, his arm movements became more exaggerated and his "Oh no, not you again" expression more accentuated.

On the fourth circuit, the equally officious attendant standing guard at the entrance to the full car park decided it wasn't full any longer and let us in.

What's more, the first half hour's parking was free and that was all I needed to make sure The Chauffeur's flight was set to leave on time and to hug her goodbye.

Later, I was to learn that she'd become involved in even bigger excitements of her own: As her plane had descended to within a few inches of the runway at Luton, the pilot had suddenly aborted the landing and roared skywards again.

Then he'd circled round and landed successfully at the second attempt, to an enthusiastic outburst of applause from his relieved passengers.

But that afternoon, happily ignorant of The Chauffeur's escapades and accompanied by a tape of The Essential Pavarotti to put me in the mood, Daisy and I took off for Italy.

6

Genoa - Chiavari - Portofino - Viaréggio - Pisa - Florence - Fiésole -
Siena - Perúgia - Assisi - Budino - Gualdo Cattaneo - Bastardo - Todi -
Orvieto - Bracciano

THE FRENCH NATION: AN APOLOGY

I DEEPLY regret that during the course of the last few chapters I may
have inadvertently given the impression that the skills of some French
drivers might leave something to be desired, and that French traffic regulations might be somewhat less than perfect. I now realise that any such
allegations are entirely without foundation and I would like to take this
opportunity to withdraw them unreservedly.

Daisy and I had been out of France for less than two minutes when we
began to discover what bad driving really was: We were confronted by
two oncoming Italian motorists who were each trying to overtake the
other. On our side of the road.

The Chauffeur and I had agreed that scooter riders could be a menace
in France, but the first one Daisy and I encountered in Italy was speeding between the white lines right in the middle of the main SS1 coast
road to Genoa. Sidesaddle.

If there were any rules of the road, they were like the rules of Trente et
Quarante: Hard to detect by observation.

I saw a driving instructor. There was no pupil in the car with him. Well
there wouldn't be any point, would there?

The most charitable way I can put it is that in France (most famous car:
The Citroën Deux-Chevaux) driving is a game. In Italy (most famous
car: The Ferrari Testosterone) driving is a sport.

The journey itself was a reeling rolling spectacular of stunning views,
close-up and long-shot, beautifully varied and unvaryingly beautiful.
Now low by beaches of stripe-show parasols, now high above rocky in-
crops and out-takes, Technicolored by blue sea, blue sky and oleander
trees in every shade of pink, the pleasure of it all amplified by Luciano's
soundtrack.

(Sorry, France, I reckon you've lost this contest already).

Oh all right then, parts of Savona and Genoa weren't exactly way out in front in the beauty stakes. Also, there were a hell of a lot of roadworks, nicely timed to coincide with the start of the summer holiday traffic and add to the sport of driving (like chicanes and pit stops). But you get the Big Picture.

So what about my own driving performance? Well, not too bad actually: For a start, I discovered how to turn on Daisy's lights for the many cliff tunnels.

Then there was Genoa in the rush hour: I used to have to drive across London every day from Richmond to Canary Wharf (because I didn't finish work until after the public transport had packed up at midnight) so I knew a thing or two about traffic. But what did amaze me was the self-inflicted nature of the Genoese wounds.

There were three lanes out of town. The inside lane was full of parked cars. The other two lanes were equally full, but of moving cars.

Or at least they should have been: Many of them kept stopping for shopping. Double parked. In the middle lane.

Pianissimo wasn't the word to describe the response of those other commuters who'd already done their shopping. Or were hoping to get home in time to do it.

Despite taking a couple of wrong turnings, Daisy and I coped pretty well. But I will admit to one small error, in Imperia, when I pulled up sharply at a red light only to realise that it didn't apply to us but to the railway running alongside.

Although admirable in the harmony of its orchestration, I'm afraid I can only describe the reaction of the drivers behind me as pathetically predictable.

The next problem in Italy was the money. In France £1 equalled 10 francs. Roughly, anyway. In Italy it was harder to work out. The easiest comparison I could make was that £2 was about 5,000 lire. So £20 was 50,000 lire, £200 was 500,000 lire and £2,000 was 5,000,000 lire.

Could that be right? If so, it's no wonder there's so much crime in Italy. Where else can you end up a multi-millionaire just by robbing your local post office?

There was some good news, though: The language. If my French is brackish, then my Italian is stagnant. Thanks to half-remembered Latin lessons 40 years before, I can understand a few words when they're written down.

But when it comes to oral expertise I'm about as much use as a Trappist monk (although what they consent to in private is their business).

As we crossed the border from France to Italy, though, I felt an immediate sense of relief. There need be no more competing. No more Language Duelling.

I could get along as the English abroad have done for years: By speaking my own language, but slightly slower, and a great deal louder.

I had hoped to stop for the night near Portofino but I couldn't find a campsite, so I drove on. And it was getting late. The views from the coast road were just as beautiful in the dusky light, but as I thrashed through Daisy's gears in an increasingly desperate search for somewhere to stay I found it harder to appreciate them.

We ended up at the Al Mare at Chiavari. It was a small campsite, it was packed, and it wasn't long before I discovered another problem: Although it had every right to its name because it was only about 100 metres from the sea, it could even more accurately have been called the Al Ferrovia, because it was only 50 metres from the railway. (Presumably the one that had caused me inadvertently to disturb the peace in Imperia).

And, like the site, the railway was busy, with a full overnight train timetable. But thanks anyway, Al, for being there for us when we needed you.

IN the morning I was up early, and first to the only sitter in the men's toilet block. I proudly dressed up in my matching shirt and shorts, and we set off back to the place that sounds more like a vintage after-dinner drink.

There was the usual difficulty: It had Daisy-discriminatory car parks. A polite policeman intercepted us with the words: "There izza problem."

He went on to explain (in entertaining English) that we must park at Paraggi, about a kilometre back, so we did and I had the pleasure of a beautiful wooded walk over the headland, high above road and sea.

A very Fine Port it was too. As good as a '77, or maybe even a '63. With its natural harbour sunk between leafy slopes, it took some beating. And despite all the thousands of tourists it attracts, it remained remarkably unspoiled.

Some of the yellow and orange harbourside houses were peeling a bit. They looked like painting-by-numbers pictures with some of the spaces still to be filled in.

But this, along with the rows of green shutters and the balconies of potted plants, only added to the mature charm of the scene.

Everything about Portofino was bellissimo. It was in a different league from over-the-top Saint-Trop.

And that reminds me: As a reformed journalist I tried but failed to avoid noticing a couple of chaps from Chelsea, Ken Bates and Gianluca Vialli, meet for a drink on one of the posh yachts.

On the walk back to Daisy I saw bright-green tongue-twisting lizards zigzag across a sunny stone wall. Some darted for cover at my appearance. Some stopped motionless, hoping they hadn't been noticed.

I went for a piccolo pizza at a beach restaurant, then took the SS1 to Chiavari again, but this time driving less frantically.

At one point I had to slow down for firemen who were clearing away the battered remains of an upside-down red scooter. (There's a surprise).

And we were getting used to a new hazard: Little three-wheelers, half truck, half motorbike, which kept pulling out right in front of us, causing us to brake suddenly to about 30k, before they turned off again as unexpectedly as they'd appeared.

But I admit I was beginning to enjoy Italian driving: It was exhilarating, with vehicles on two, three, four or more wheels coming at us from all directions. I started to enter into the spirit of it: Daisy and I began to perform a few kittenish town centre tricks of our own.

And even an Italian would have been impressed with the way I was beginning to master the art of driving and writing at the same time.

(The most nerve-racking thing about doing that is when you press too hard on the paper, hoot the horn by mistake and think it's someone warning you you're about to run into them. It startled me every time, no matter how often I did it).

We stopped at a 24-hour filling station because Daisy's diesel was running a bit low. But it was closed. So was the next, and the next (which described itself as a SELF-CENTRE).

In fact, all the filling stations on the SS1 seemed to be closed that afternoon, except the ones which dispensed fuel automatically if you put the right amount of lire into the accompanying machine and pressed the right buttons.

The instructions for these looked too complicated for me. As they didn't have automatic fuel dispensers in the days when they spoke the language I learned, and as I wasn't sure what sort of fuel I might get, or how many lire I might lose, I decided to give them a miss. Roulette looked a much easier bet.

"Our" road remained just as beautiful as before, but it began to take us further from the sea. It became hillier (and more fuel consuming).

At times we were high among birds of prey, and I could look down through wispy clouds at the poor flat dull autostrada below.

Finally, a few kilometres short of La Spézia, as the needle of Daisy's fuel gauge began to flirt with the bottom of the barrel, we found a little filling station that was open, and had yet to discover the automatic dispenser.

It was the best 90 grand I've ever spent.

74

It's funny how you begin to take things for granted: I didn't give a second look at the oranges growing in the town streets now. But I noticed there weren't any of the huge out-of-town hypermarkets we'd seen in France.

There were some pretty impressive pizzerias, though.

After La Spézia the SS1 became a bit obvious and boring. So despite the pleasure it had given me, I wasn't sorry to leave it.

I stopped at a supermarket for bachelor beer and bread, then followed the clearest campsite signs I'd seen so far to Camping Viaréggio, just outside the town of the same name.

It was quite full, but it was large and shady, with a bar, pizzeria, shop and lovely, light, spacious toilet block. All sitters. With seats. And paper.

During the night it rained, hard, with thunder and lightning. The next morning I saw a couple of bedraggled-looking tents hanging on a fence to dry, and was grateful to Daisy for having protected me.

I walked through peaceful pines to the nearby beach, where a notice told me:

THE NAVIGATION IS FORBITTEN WITHIN THE LIMIT OF 350m FROM THE NO MARKED COASTLINE

The sky was clear, and apart from a bit of a breeze and a few puddles there was no sign of the storm of the night before.

There was a bar near the sea, and I spent much of the day getting soused in one and trying to read my own writing in the other.

It seemed odd to be camping on my own: I suppose it's a strange thing to do. Women campers tended to stare at me, not because they fancied me or anything but because they were curious about me (presumably wondering why no partner would have me, and whether I'd be a danger to their kids).

The men didn't seem to take any notice of me. Maybe women are more observant, more inquisitive than men.

That's certainly the case with The Chauffeur and me. And she can tell me what flowers are called.

THE Germans are the keenest campers, followed by the Dutch. And that night I got talking to one of the many Germans on the site, Aleks J Arndt.

He was far from typical, though, with his bushy beard, pop-eyes magnified by thick glasses and the little fingernail of his left hand painted permanently red in memory of his Socialist youth.

He spoke fluent English. (He said he had to for his work, travelling the world for an international removals firm). But he confirmed the growing suspicion I had that when it comes to getting around, we campers aren't always as adventurous as we could be.

He told me this was the twentieth year running he'd come to Viaréggio, always to the same site, with the same people, for the same week.

He came by the same route, in the same old Volvo, and he stopped at the same places to get the same presents for the same recipients (who in turn would be most disappointed if he didn't).

These presents were cheese and salami, illicitly bought from peasants whose land had been invaded by the motorway he came on.

It seems the peasants put plastic bags in the trees as a secret sign to tell their regular customers when they had things to sell. And, of course, they always knew when to expect Aleks.

He also told me that every New Year the whole of Germany sits down to watch the same black and white TV sketch, in English, starring our old music hall comedian Freddie Frinton.

In it, a lady instructs her butler to serve drinks to four guests. But the guests aren't there, because (like Freddie now) they're dead.

Apparently every German roars with laughter at it every year, and even those who don't understand a word of it are able to repeat phrases from it. Example:

"The same procedures, M'Lady?"

"The same procedures, James."

Clearly, the Germans are creatures of habit. But one question still remains unanswered: Have they got a sense of humour?

After two nights, I paid £36,000 to leave Viaréggio. Yes, £. Because when I got the bill I made the alarming discovery that that's the sign for lire as well as sterling.

It had rained again overnight, though not as heavily. But this time it didn't stop, and it was still wet when we drove into Pisa. I managed to cope with the Pay-e-Display (with considerable assistance from a lovely passing signora) and once again I was glad of my umbrella as I went to see what you go to Pisa to see.

The first thing that struck me about it was just how far it leant, especially in relation to the other buildings and to the vertical flagpole on the top.

It seemed as if it could go over at any moment, and all the time I was looking at it I kept thinking I was about to get a news scoop.

The second thing I noticed was that even in its infirmity it was rather pretty, with its wedding cake decoration and detail. Now, it had a rather worn and world-weary sort of look, but in its youth it must have been a real beauty.

Unfortunately they don't let you get near enough to shelter under it from the rain, otherwise it could have made itself useful for once.

There were hundreds of other tourists there, and I thought what a great money-spinner it must have been for the town. All by mistake.

Of course, like the Bridge of Avignon, we wouldn't have allowed it to survive in our country: The Health and Safety people would have ordered it to be pulled down long ago, and written off millions at a stroke.

I found staring at it a bit disorientating. And when I left, I fancied all the other buildings had begun to lean the other way.

I went to a nearby lavatory to do a pisa, and I must confess my aim wasn't quite as true as it ought to have been.

So Daisy and I went on our autostrada-free way. By now I'd had enough of Pavarotti, so I decided to tune in to some of the local music stations. There were plenty of them: BRUNO, VERONICA, ROSA, DEEJAY, PLANET, CAPITAL. (Yes). And many more.

Nearly all the tracks they played were in English, not Italian (exactly the opposite of opera) but no matter what their style, from Heavy Metal to Middle of the Road, I'd never heard any of them before.

The news bulletins were mainly about big-money embezzlements and daring kidnaps. At least I think they were: Maybe they just seemed to be because that's what I was expecting.

I noticed that Italian allotments were usually less tidy than French ones, and many of them were given over to vines.

The trees around us were now displaying a tendency to become darker and thinner, but bright yellow broom still swept the bumpy country.

And everywhere there was the oleaginous oleander. (Sorry, I don't know what oleaginous means, but I couldn't resist the alliteration).

THE rain had eased by the time we reached Florence. A dodgy-looking local invited me to park Daisy half on and half off the road in a square near the river, about a kilometre from the city centre.

He demanded £30,000 for an authentic-looking ticket, but when I said that sounded a bit expensive he reduced it to £20,000.

I still reckon I got done, and the problem was I didn't know whether I'd parked Daisy legally or whether I'd eventually end up having to pay many thousands more in fines.

I couldn't help noticing that my Iti pal left the scene quicker than I did.

On the other hand, £20,000 seemed a reasonable down-payment for the chance to join the culture feeding frenzy of Firenze, so I deserted Daisy and walked up the riverbank to the Ponte Vecchio.

And what a wonderfully jumbly, crazy construction it was: Like London Bridge would have been if they hadn't pulled it down. (Those Health and Safety meddlers again).

It was thronged with grockles and locals looking at the posh jewellery shops on top of it, the dirty brown river beneath it and the dirty brown houses beside it.

Just one brave canoeist was sharing the murky water below with about a dozen ducks. But I wouldn't have wanted to swallow what he'd have swallowed if he'd capsized.

I joined the 20-minute wait to get into the Uffizi Gallery, and tried not to worry about whether Daisy was OK.

The queue was made up largely of unnaturally cheery, middle-aged American couples with bored teenage kids who were toothbraced and overweight.

I paid my £12,000 at the cash desk, where notices carried pictures of flags alongside the entry instructions which were given in several different languages. I was relieved to see the English words were accompanied by the Union Jack, not the Stars and Stripes.

There were no lifts, and most of the Americans (both young and old) found the long flights of stairs to the top floor quite a struggle.

I looked at the Daddis and the Gaddis and the Botticellis and the Da Vincis and all, and I wondered what they would have painted if there hadn't been religion: It must have been a real Godsend to them.

I remembered to look up at all the right ceilings, as well as noting that the fat American kids' yawns hid their toothbraces from view.

But all the paintings were too flat and too formal. They lacked life, as Latin lacks life compared with Italian.

Most of them were too dark and too small. It was still only the big ones that did anything for me.

My visit reassuringly confirmed to me my view that painting has come a long way since those days.

Through the Piazza della Signora with its magnificently butch nude statues. (Size certainly mattered here).

Past the Palazzo Vecchio, parodying a Spanish castle, and a couple of fierce-looking cops, each with fag in hand.

Along the pedestrianised Via dei Calzaiuoli (where I didn't see a McDonalds, but there was a Disney Store).

To the dominating Duomo cathedral with its surprisingly snazzy, carved and statued, pink, green and white ice-cream parlour façade, walls and belltower.

Inside, the patterned marble floor was pretty, but the breathtaking five-ringed circus fresco of The Last Judgment was... well, heavenly.

(Oh dear, was I in danger of becoming a Renaissance convert? No, it was all right: It was big. Very big).

Next, £10,000 to climb the 463 steps to the top of the dome. (Well, at least there weren't any own-the-place Americans).

I got an even better view of the Last Judgment fresco from the gallery two-thirds of the way up. And, from on top, an incomparable panorama of the old city and the sun-and-rain shafted hills all around.

Call me a wimp, but up there on the outside of that massive dome my vertigo-induced sense of self-preservation made me keep a lot nearer the inner wall than the outer railing.

Then I joined the queue (or line, as the Americans loudly insisted on calling it) to see the Michelangelo statue whose name I share.

It had started to rain again, heavily, and I hadn't brought my umbrella, but I'd always promised myself I'd see him so I didn't care how wet I got.

It was half an hour before I was able to pay my £12,000 for the privilege, but like the hordes around me I was smitten: The proud profile, the disdainful expression, aloof to admirers of no matter what nationality.

He was stocky, not slender. His hands and feet appeared out of sync with the rest of him: Bigger, older, veinier. His other parts still seemed to have a bit of growing up to do.

I got back to Daisy to find her her usual self. (No, not leaking oil all over the road, but unviolated, unticketed, unclamped and untowed away).

We drove to the attractive Camping Panoramico at nearby Fiésole, with a lovely view of Florence but temporarily a little damp.

Was I eating properly? Well that night I cooked myself pasta, sprinkled it with Parmesan cheese and ate it with cut-up green pepper, cucumber and Tonsil Tickler. And I had a couple of cans of cold beer.

Then the evening sky cleared and a weak sun went down over Florence, painting an ever-changing composition as the city paled from orange and brown to pink, and the background hills deepened from blue and green to purple.

The toilet facilities were the best yet: Lovely clean sitters with seats and paper, and lots of hot water (not push-button). The cost: £35,000 for the night.

Campsites were fewer in Italy than France, and they didn't come cheap. But I was beginning to discover that many of them had superior facilities. And they were a lot better signposted.

WE trundled through Tuscany and ambled across Umbria, to Siena, Perúgia and Assisi. The countryside was green and refreshed, the sky was cloudless, and it was wonderful.

THIS IS THE LIFE. (Oops, sorry).

In Siena, I parked Daisy near the station and walked up the steep hill to the old walled city, then by narrow, shady streets to the main square, the Campo.

And it was a cracker: The best bits of Florence had been indoors. (Not such a bad thing in that rain). But Siena's were all here, out in the open and under the sun.

The Campo, scene of the annual bareback, breakneck Palio crazy horse race, was shaped like a posh handbasin, with the curved front of the Palazzo Pubblico and its huge belltower at the bottom end and a wide semi-circle of bars and restaurants at the top.

Everything was brown, but never the same brown. The bowl of the basin was pie-charted in different patterns of brown brick. All the buildings were brown, again in brick. And the shutters and shades were brown, but not the same. And there weren't any nasty browns, nicotine browns or worse. They were friendly browns. Relaxing, restful browns.

I sat there in a brown study, drinking brown cups of coffee and topping up my brown tan. In my yellow shirt and shorts.

Next, I went to see the Duomo, and a Major Duomo it was.

The walls and belltower, in layers of black and white marble, were more liquorice allsort than ice-cream parlour, but the façade was intricately rounded, pointed, arched, carved, curved, curled, friezed, fluted, turreted, statued and muralled out of white, black and pink.

From the outside, it knocked spots, squares, circles, diamonds and gargoyles off Florence. Inside it was stunning too, with more liquorice allsort columns and pillars containing varying proportions of liquorice. But there was nothing to compare with Florence's Last Judgment fresco.

Then I got lost. If you've ever been to Siena you'll know the problem. Admit it, you got lost too, didn't you? The place doesn't need a maze, it is one.

I had half an hour's entertainment (if that's the right word) trying to get out. My map reading skills were no use to me, because the map I had was too puny for the task.

The tourist people ought to put up warning notices about it, and issue all visitors with compasses and sticks of chalk and balls of string to help them unravel their way back to where they started.

I saw anxious groups of grockles standing at every corner, scratching their heads and each pointing in a different direction. Most of the poor lost souls just hadn't realised what they were getting themselves into.

When we drove on, I saw half a dozen ladies standing in lay-bys, scantily dressed in short skirts and black stockings.

In all the glowing descriptions I'd been given of these parts, this particular aspect of the scenery had never been mentioned.

As a respectable married man, it took me a moment to work out what they were there for. But I soon realised they were more interested in liras than leerers.

It reminded me of a newspaper report I'd read, which said that ramblers in Britain were being accosted by vice girls.

I'd discussed it with a couple of pals and we'd agreed the girls should know how to give good hedge, but with our luck we'd probably be the ones to end up with Offa's Dyke.

After being flat for some time, the country became lumpier as we passed handsome islanded Lake Trasimeno and approached hilltop Perúgia.

Again, I left Daisy near the station and climbed to the summit of the town as tumbling Umbria began to spread out, yellow, green and blue beneath me.

Popular it may be, but like many large places Perúgia had more ugly bits than pretty bits.

The old part was attractive enough: I lapped up the liveliness of the much caféed main street, the pleasantly paved Corso Vannucci, and I savoured the quiet quaintness of the steep little sidestreets, steps and squares.

But I went away thinking that all in all Perúgia was probably a better spot to look from than to look at.

As I left, afternoon was turning to evening and an echo of thunder sounded through the streets. I took the road to Assisi and the easy-to-find Camping Internazionale. And again grey cloud swirled about the hills.

That night I cheated, and ate not in Daisy but at the camp pizzeria. I had ham and mushroom pizza, coffee, ice cream and a bottle of local white wine for £21,000.

The restaurant was in a large marquee, which was almost empty when I went in at 7.30. But when I left an hour or so later, it was filled with the chatter, clatter and slurp of about a hundred Itis messily and noisily eating their dinner just like they do in that TV advert for their Dolmio sauce.

But I discovered the reasons: It's a favourite for all seasons with the local Assisans.

(Sorry about that, I beg your pardon, I got a bit carried away there. I think the wine must have gone to my head).

After my meal, I was entertained to drinks (in a motor caravan just like Daisy) by Roy and Norma Freeman from Yorkshire. And the first thing

I learned from them was that Daisy's crockery must be breakable, because they'd just broken some of theirs.

Both former nurses, they told me they'd travelled the world as back-packers. They'd had their van for four years and had already taken it all over Europe, from Scandinavia to Greece. The whole point of having one, they said, was to see as many different places as possible.

But, er... they'd been to one site, at Tamarit, south of Barcelona, 13 years running.

Next day, I paid my bill (18 grand) and drove into town, leaving Daisy in one of those pay-as-you-leave car parks with an automatic barrier which opened for us when we entered as I helped myself to a ticket.

Avignon has its bridge and Pisa its tower, but Assisi owes everything to its saint. If Francis hadn't chosen to befriend the dumb animals in these parts, nobody would ever have heard of the place. But now it's us dumb tourists who flock there.

For a change, this town was built on the side of a hill rather than on top of one. It did its best to retain its saintly dignity despite all the crowds of grocks, but when I got there much of it was hidden under scaffolding.

It was very beautiful, saintly scaffolding, though, consisting of black poles and brass joints: People would have paid to see it if you'd put it up as an exhibit at The Tate.

Assisi was another attractive town with pretty sloping streets and steps, but again the view from it was the most impressive thing about it.

I drank coffee in the sunny square, and bought fruit, veg, bread and cheese in a couple of the little shops, then walked back to the car park.

And it took me 25 minutes to get out.

First, the man in front of me at the ticket kiosk was trying to buy a season ticket. Through the computer. There was bad temper and there was loud language, and the whole operation took nearly 10 minutes.

Then came the next problem: The cashier wanted to charge me £3,800 but I had only £50,000 notes, having done the local traders a favour by giving them all my smaller stuff.

Because it was still quite early in the day, he hadn't enough change. He wouldn't budge. I couldn't.

Other customers were served. I was ignored. I got angry and told him to let me out for free because I had to drive to Rome. He wouldn't.

Another customer was served. The cashier told me to change one of my notes at a nearby souvenir stall. They refused. More customers were served.

Eventually he locked up his kiosk, went to the souvenir stall himself, and managed to get some smaller notes. Our parting was less than cordiale.

NEXT, as the day grew hotter, my progress was slowed by hundreds of sweating, exhausted runners taking part in a road race.

A serious race it was too, with feeding stations and plenty of police to cause even more disruption to the rest of us than was really necessary.

Not so much a fun run, more a sun run.

Once again, I admired the amazing energy of some of my foolish fellow beings.

Although we'd avoided the autostradas up till now, we'd still stuck mainly to major roads. (My map didn't show anything else). I decided to take some of the smaller roads and see some of the more out of the way bits of Umbria.

In fact, we got lost. But deliberately.

The first thing I noticed was the state of the roads. They were terrible: Nearly as bad as most of ours back home.

We passed several serious cyclists (more crazed energy) and one less serious one with a basket at the front and a dog at the back, on a lead.

On the flat parts, the roads went quite straight, between large, open fields of sunflowers, sweetcorn and other veg. Here, the villages tended to be nondescript. Budino was boring.

The hilly parts were bittier and prettier, with olive groves and vine-yards. And here the villages, too, were more interesting. Gualdo Cattaneo was delightful, with towers and turrets atop a small peak, and a tiny, intimately appealing main square.

(Italian builders don't believe in making things easy for themselves. Show them a nice flat piece of land, and they'll ignore it. Show them a challenging hump, lump or bump, and they'll be all over it).

There weren't many signposts, but I couldn't resist following one saying BASTARDO (and, under the watchful gaze of a couple of rustic old locals, setting up my tripod in the middle of the road and taking a picture of it pointing at me).

But, as I should have realised from its name, it turned out to be an ugly place.

I took the road to Todi and soon had to stop again, this time to take a picture of a regional highways sign saying TODI - BASTARDO. (Honestly).

But I didn't put myself in it: That's one thing I've never been.

Todi certainly wasn't ugly: It was a little gem to hilltop the lot, more beautiful from both above and below than Assisi or Perúgia, with an antique market doing good business among the even more antique build-ings in the main square, the Piazza del Popolo.

Past three more roadside ladies offering their body parts for a quick lay-by, to the next hilly highlight: Wine-giving, flag-showing Orvieto, with a

Duomo to challenge (but not beat) Siena's, its façade less carved but more muralled and with the same black-and-white allsort walls.

I walked down the narrow Via del Duomo, past the Bar Duomo and the Ristorante del Duomo, which had recently changed its name to the Mauritzio (well there's always one, isn't there?) to the Palazzo del Popolo: Big on flags, but otherwise an austere glum-looking structure.

German voices may have been the most invasive on camp and American voices the most intrusive in Florence, but here in Umbria stridently clipped upper-class English tones, reminiscent of my Burgundian cricketing chums, were embarrassingly to be heard asserting themselves above the more sotto-voce locals.

I knew about Italy's magnificent northern lakes and planned to visit them later on, but I hadn't realised there were also some stunners further south. I'd already admired Lake Trasimeno from the road, and that night I camped beside a whopper, Lake Bracciano, at Camping Porticciolo.

In the morning, the toilet block was packed with German Youth, and I couldn't get near the showers.

When I finally got one I discovered that, as on some other Italian sites, I needed a token for hot water. I bought one from reception (£500) and began to wash, but how much time would I have before it ran out?

Did I have to wash quickly, or could I afford to take it easy? Would it dry up when I was still soapy, or after I'd had time to rinse myself?

You're right: I was still soapy, and the soap wouldn't rub off with a towel so I spent the rest of the day feeling uncomfortably sticky.

But I learned something: The secret is to get two tokens, one for washing and one for rinsing.

It was a day to be practical: By now, I'd worn every bit of clothing I'd brought (at least once) and my sheets were getting a bit iffy as well.

Something had to be done, so I got the captivating signora of the camp to help me work one of the washing machines, then I rigged up a washing line between two trees and hung my nice clean clothes up to dry.

Next, I went off to explore the lake. And you've guessed: It rained. We hadn't had brilliant weather on the trip so far but the day before had been hot, a bit too hot for travelling to be honest.

Wash Day had started fine, then the rain had returned.

The lake was beautiful, all the more so for the dark rainclouds sweeping dramatically across it.

But I had to suffer a sheetless night.

7

Rome - Mondragone - Naples - Vico Equense - Pompeii - Sorrento - Positano - Amalfi - Pésaro - Punta Sabbioni - Venice - Malcésine - Limone-sul-Garda - Varenna - Bellano - Luino - Arona - Stresa - Baveno

MY late great former colleague Ronnie (The Old Bowler) Gallemore once observed, after he'd been there on a boozing trip: "Rome. It's just a load of old ruins, Buster."

Mind you, I'd heard an item on the radio which had said some of the ruins weren't old at all: They were cunningly created replicas designed to fool the tourists, while the real things were stashed away somewhere safe from thieves, vandals and pollution.

But it was time to test the wisdom of The Old Bowler's words, so I left Daisy and my line of wet washing at the camp, and took the bus to town.

It was an old bus, and the journey took nearly two hours. At first we rattled and bumped along, stopping to fill up with commuters, mainly young office workers.

An older, grey-suited man came and sat in the seat in front of me, and began to read a notebook filled with important-looking scientific data and diagrams.

He must have feared I was in the espionage business, because he kept looking round nervously as if to make sure I wasn't studying his notes.

When I was asked to open a window because it was beginning to get hot in there, and it became clear from my confused reaction that I must be a foreigner, he began to fidget anxiously in his seat.

Then I produced my own notebook (to write the words you've just read).

He took a bottle of pills from his pocket, and downed a handful.

We crawled through the traffic-jammed suburbs, and people began to get off. I'm pleased to report that the scientist, like the rest of us, completed his journey safely.

The bus terminated near the Prefetura di Roma municipal offices, where about 500 scooters were parked just off the street and about 50 cars were double-parked on it.

I wondered if any of the officials inside ever nipped out to have the fun of giving their colleagues parking tickets.

I passed the Metro bar (FANTASY FOOD) and the Bellissima dress shop (PREZZI SHOCK) and walked to Saint Peter's Square, which wasn't square but round, and The Vatican, which was hidden beneath more scaffolding than Assisi but not as tastefully.

I wondered what McDonalds would have given for a bit of advertising space on it.

Six no-messing cops kept me back as a convoy of 11 cars (one of them said to contain the Secretary-General of the United Nations) raced each other, flashing and wailing, to the Pope's tradesman's entrance.

Then the rain came back. And I hadn't got my umbrella. And I was worried about my washing. Would I be trapped at Bracciano for weeks, unable to take my clothes off the line and move on until the sun finally came out again?

I walked beside the much-bridged green twisting Tiber, sheltered from the worst of the rain by handy trees, and watched two scullers dip their oars in the wake of all our histories.

I noticed the drain covers carried the letters SPQR which, in the period I learned about, stood for Senatus Populusque Romanus (the Senate and the Roman People). But they didn't look that old.

To The Coliseum (£10,000 to get in) which forms the world's most impressive traffic roundabout, but is also remarkable for its size and for the amount of it left standing. (Assuming it isn't another cunningly created Roman replica).

Here, I was enchanted by the sight of a classic Italian beauty, her hair gorgeously long and black with blonde highlights. But my fantasies were shattered when she announced to her companions: "They knew 'ow to build, them Romans." In broadest Lancashire.

Between Planet Hollywood and Blockbuster Video to the Spanish Steps, destination of flights of sightseers.

And as I sat on them, with a hundred other tourists, the steps started to sparkle in the sun. I hoped my washing would be doing the same until I could get back to it.

Next, to the grocky shores of the Trevi Fountain, flowing with well worn statues and flooded with well worn-out visitors.

Then for a properly-poured pint of Guinness at the Trinity College Irish Pub, with its dark wood panels, book-lined mantelpiece and signs saying STUDENTS UNION and BUTTERY BAR. (There's also a Tam O' Shanter Scottish Pub).

Back to the bus station past a teenage girl wearing a T-shirt saying

FUCT in the style of the Ford logo, but not the girl who kept pestering me for money at the Trevi Fountain, sticking out her stomach and crying: Bébé. It became quite embarrassing the third time. People were starting to stare at me.

I'm sure the American kids I saw aimlessly Roming the ruins of the Forum would have agreed with The Old Bowler's verdict. But then they couldn't slope off for a good pint of Guinness. (And even The Old Bowler had no complaints about the booze).

The rain hadn't returned when I got back to camp, so I was able to stow my washing aboard Daisy and was free to leave the following morning. The cost of our three-night stay: £43,200.

The site had been the friendliest I'd found yet. So thanks, Camping Porticcilio, for making my stay such a happy one. Thanks to the Romanian pizza chef. (Romanian chef, not Romanian pizza). Thanks to the beautiful signorina behind the bar, who spoke English with a lovely Irish lilt because she'd spent a year working as a barmaid in Dublin. And thanks to the Dutch students who were such good company in the evenings.

AS we left, we immediately ran into a new traffic problem: Men holding red and green bats were standing at each end of a long stretch of road while one side of it was being resurfaced.

The man at our end waved us on with his green bat, but unfortunately the man at the other end must have been waving his green bat too.

A queue of cars led by Daisy and me met the oncoming queue in the middle. In large numbers. Our queue was ordered back, but it was some time before those behind understood what was happening and were able to reverse out of the way. Not only that, but new traffic was arriving all the time.

It took a good 10 minutes to sort it out, with much predictable continental over-excitement. And the worst thing was that from the looks they gave me I could tell everybody involved was agreed on one thing: It had all been entirely my fault.

We took Rome's M25, the Grande Raccordo Anulare. And it was just like our M25: First, everybody hurtled along at more than 100k. Then we all had to brake sharply, and there was a jam. A red-haired woman in a little red car with a little red dog had had a (mercifully) minor shunt with a burly trucker driving a huge lorry towing an equally huge trailer.

The polizia were already on the scene, and negotiations were in progress as we crawled past. The dog was taking a keen interest, sitting there in the middle of the slow lane and looking up intelligently at one protagonist then the other as each in turn had their say.

Italy gets to you after a while: As we drove on south, I found myself singing out the words on the roadsigns we passed. Loudly, in outrageously exaggerated Italian accents: ROMA... NAPOLI... ATTENZIONE... RALLENTARE...

Oh, all right, it got to me anyway. Maybe it was because I had only Daisy for company.

We rejoined the coast (and the hills) near Terracina, and it was great to have them back. I stopped for a cappuccino and a cake at a little bar near Mondragone.

As I entered, three smartly-dressed men in dark glasses came out and got into a waiting car, which contained a fourth man already at the wheel.

There wasn't actually one of those stickers on the back window saying MAFIA STAFF CAR KEEPA DA HANDS OFF, but it made you wonder.

The coast now became even more beautiful, more spectacular, with bigger sticking-out bits and bigger sticking-up bits.

Driving in Naples was the most sporting so far: In England cyclists tend to ignore red lights, and in most of France and Italy all two-wheelers, motorised or not, did the same.

But here everybody did it, no matter what number of wheels they were on. I adopted a When-In-Naples approach, and joined in.

(That almost makes it sound as if they gave me a choice).

The system worked a treat, speeding up the city's traffic flow with the utmost efficiency.

Meanwhile, fearful of losing their street cred, those Neapolitans who were on two wheels forgot altogether about the rules of the road, such as riding on the right, and just went wherever they wanted.

Then there were the trams and the trolleybuses, which also did their own thing. And the cobbles, which didn't slow the locals down in the slightest. But made a hell of a mess of my writing.

The seafront was attractive to start with. There were elegant buildings and beaches and bathers and yachts (of course) and big handsome rowing boats.

Then, suddenly, it all turned ugly: In the middle of the bay there were docks and smoking factory chimneys and a gasworks.

Next came kilometre after kilometre of winding cobbled roads between tall tatty houses dripping oceans of plaster and paint, their pride salvaged only by their balconies: Many of them colourful with plants, most of them colourful with washing.

And between the humble buildings were unbelievably beautiful glimpses of the sea and the mountains.

Finally, there were more factories, with more smoking chimneys, and lots of rundown railway yards.

Petrol stations in Italy often consist of just a couple of pumps at the kerbside. But as we left Naples we came to one that formed the roundabout in the middle of a busy junction. (More useful than The Coliseum, though).

We carried on round the bay to Camping Sant' Antonio, at Vico Equense with its pretty little harbour, beaches, bars and restaurants.

I joined about 200 locals for a late-afternoon swim, and from the sea I looked back at Naples, the blue water glittering in front of it and the grey Vesuvius menacing behind it.

And it was as stunning a view as I'd ever seen. (Wharfs and all).

IN the morning I caught the train to Pompeii, its daily life freeze-framed for ever after Vesuvius suddenly overwhelmed it a couple of millenniums earlier.

I paid £12,000 for the privilege of fighting my way in through the gate with several thousand other visitors, and quickly discovered the place was sex mad: It had brothels, pornographic murals of Romans in every conceiving position and a phallus carved into one of the lumpy stones that made up the main street.

I battled my way through fellow grocks and stray dogs to see houses and shops (where the fateful day's takings had been found on the premises) and temples and public baths. And plaster casts of the contorted body language and facial expressions of locals surprised by the eruption, one a chained slave.

I strained and craned through the crowd to get a view of the world's most famous Beware of the Dog sign: CAVE CANEM written in mosaics in the porch of a wealthy merchant's house.

Traffic, as well as dogs, must have been a problem even in those days: There were road rage-sized ruts in the stone streets to prove it, caused by chariot wheels.

None of the tourists looked in the least bit cheerful as they sweatily scrummed their way from ruin to ruin. (Holidaymaking can be such a tiresome bad-tempered business).

The biggest queue was at an almost-intact villa which had belonged to two rich brothers. When we finally got inside, it was full of friezes and murals including an erotic picture of an over-endowed Roman intent (but not bent) on sexual pleasure.

Another intact, if not intacta, attraction was a brothel illustrated with more instructions on Latin loving. (The stone beds looked a bit uncomfortable, though).

But the real stars of the Pompeii show were the many tour guides, large and small, ancient and modern, each determined to be the main attraction as they noisily policed their charges beneath their rolled-umbrella batons.

One colourful old female of the species chain-smoked as she bossily barked out her instructions to her obedient class of middle-aged students, and her husky delivery spoke of a million fags dragged before.

Another, slow of movement and speech, used his umbrella more to prop himself up than to direct his followers. He bragged he was 77 and spoke five languages.

(A lot of old people are boastful in this way, as if the accident of age is in itself sufficient excuse for it).

Next I caught the train to Naples, Europe's most wanton and unredeemed city, home to rich and poor, ugly and beautiful, beggars, shoppers, bag-snatchers and pickpockets.

And I found the journey really intimidating: Through vandalised, graffiti-smothered stations, some more ruined than Pompeii, wondering all the while which of my fellow passengers would be the one to rob me.

But I made it safely to Naples Central Station, and sidestepped my way through the street traders, the shoeshiners, the kids and the firecrackers to the seafront at Santa Lucia where dozens of fishermen were outnumbered by scores of cats.

I was offered food and more food: Pizzas and pastries and corn cooked on the cob and roast peanuts and roast chickens and popcorn and candyfloss.

Then I walked the ever-changing city's streets and witnessed instant shifts from depth of squalour to height of fashion: Suddenly, tatty little shops and stalls and cafés gave way to posh designer names: GUCCI, VERSACE, ARMANI, CARTIER, PRADA.

Next: More tiny streets well shadowed, even in the afternoon heat, by high balconied buildings. And cavernous entranceways leading to murky warrens of hidden homes. And busy markets in half-shaded squares selling fruit and veg and cheese and wine and pots and pans and pasta.

And busy and excitable and fun, fun, fun and ciao and arrivederci as shoppers and scooters and bambini battled for supremacy over the paved and cobbled territory, with cars for once the outmanoeuvred losers in such confined spaces.

And hot, so hot, whenever the shade ran out. And grocks completely outnumbered by the locals (which is as it should be).

Then from narrow streets to the massive shopping hall of the Galleria Umberto I, carved and columned with monumental pride a hundred feet high from its marbled and tiled roots to its Crystal Palace roof. And alongside, bank headquarters to put royal palaces in the shade.

And buskers and young and old and big family groups parading and promenading and showing more and more contempt for cars in the packed shopping streets. And excitable middle-aged men arguing like kids on the street corners.

I took the funicular railway to the top of the city and walked past rows of parked cars, each one protected by a dustbin lid of a steering lock, big, red and armour plated.

I was struck by the variety of smells, some of delicious family meals, some more sick-making than mouth-watering.

Perhaps that's the attraction of Naples: Its contrasting sights and smells, poverty and wealth. How better to appreciate beauty than to set ugliness against it?

I drank cappuccino beside the Castel Sant'Elmo at the balcony café of the Belvedere Hotel (never was place better named) and gazed in wonder over tower and tenement, dock and dome, crane and train, finery and refinery to brooding Vesuvio, clouded with menace and wondering not whether but when to explode.

Through sad old quarters, where fine churches and mansions were falling into decay, to come upon attractive little squares, palmed and shrubbed and alive with music and diners and drinkers shielded and sheltered by pot plant and parasol.

And poor kids playing full-blooded football on cobble-pitched roads among silver seas of overflowing wheelie-bins and dark shoals of rubbish that had failed to find its way in. And bus routes too narrow to be bus routes. And little old women sitting at little old tables desperate to sell cigarettes and lighters.

A scooter sped past, and I could only look on with something like admiration as its lone rider neatly snatched the bag from the shoulder of a middle-aged Englishwoman beside me and disappeared up a side street whirling his newly-won trophy above his head as if he was a celebrating goal-scorer: Italia 1, Inghilterra 0.

That evening I felt even more threatened than before as I took the almost-empty train back to the campsite safety of Daisy. But happily Napoli, despite my fears, took mercy on both me and my possessions.

NEXT day, Daisy and I rode the crazy roller-coast that is the Amalfi peninsular. Between olives and vines and oranges and lemons and bougainvillea too bright to be real. And cacti and palms and oleander and wisteria to compete with the blue of the sea. Beneath mountains with houses and churches clinging improbably to the sides of them.

Cars weren't parked where the road was wide or straight: All that mattered, in that Campanian heat, was whether they were in the shade. Rainy Rome seemed centuries away.

Now there were even more scooters, and very few helmets. And there were usually two people to a scooter. Sometimes more, with a bambino or two wedged in front of or between adults.

Sorrento was superb, and superbly chaotic. I drove Daisy down a steep spiral to the busy little port, then on the way back we got lost.

We drove past a couple of threatening-looking signs and ended up in what seemed to be a pedestrianised street (although with all those cobbles, you couldn't really tell).

But none of the pedestrians of Sorrento seemed surprised or upset to see us as we struggled to extricate ourselves to return to the mainstreet maelstrom.

While we were in Sorrento, I managed to get my glasses fixed. The previous afternoon, to make both driving and writing even more difficult, a lens had fallen out and I'd lost the little screw that held it in place. But a friendly optician mended them for me, and waved away all my attempts to pay him.

Back on the rock and roller coast, I saw the Isle of Capri. Jagged and steep and tall and sudden and blue. And it, too, had buildings hanging off it.

I didn't think of Gracie Fields because I'm not that old, Sally. But I remembered I'd once read a report of a newspaper interview with Ian Botham which was said to have taken place at Lord's cricket ground beneath a portrait of the legendary WC Fields.

On the twisting cliff-clinging road to Positano, where every rocky promontory was prettier than any other country's prettiest, I saw a sign in four languages, the English version saying:
GIVE WAY TO OVERTAKING TRAFFIC

I couldn't think of any better advice to give you if you were planning to drive in Italy.

Positano was perfect, happily piled together among bougainvillea and no-parking signs in, on and around a steep deep wooded cleft piercing the mountains from the beach.

Amalfi, too, was amazing. It even had a bit of palmed seafront next to the harbour, although any non-Italian fool could see it was impossible to build one there.

I stopped to buy some stamps. Because I was an Italian driver, I didn't park. I just stopped.

There was a song called Turning Japanese by The Vapors. I thought (hoped) I was turning Italian.

In the night I was attacked by mosquitoes and woke with mega-bites on my left elbow and right thigh: I was missing The Chauffeur.

When we left the camp I looked at Vesuvius, smoke-ringed in grey and white cloud, and I'd have sworn she was about to blow, like she did in the year I was born.

As in Pisa, I was convinced I was about to get a scoop.

My last view of the wonderful wild west coast was from above Salerno. Then Daisy and I ran over Italy's knobbly knee, or tried to: The trouble with avoiding autostradas is that it makes it so much easier to get lost.

As in France, the town centres were the worst. In Avellino we needed signs to BENEVENTO but they all said NAPOLI, which was where we'd just come from.

(Right then, I'd have given anything for a nice friendly TOUTES DIRECTIONS or AUTRES DIRECTIONS).

Benevento was a cruel deceiver masquerading as a friend. We wanted COMPOBASSO, and to start with there were plenty of signs to it.

Then... Well, it's happened to you, hasn't it? You follow signs meticulously for miles and, all of a sudden, there aren't any more.

We finally hit the Adriatic at Térmoli, and took the SS16 coast road to Pescara and Ancona, stopping for the night at Pésaro and Camping Marinella.

I went for a pizza at the camp ristorante, and a two-man band was playing all the naffest pop songs in the world on a couple of keyboards: Not my scene, but it was impossible not to enjoy the sheer happiness of it all.

The band were happy and the half dozen Italian family groups they were playing to were happy. They weren't drunk, just happy. And happy to be happy.

Each song was loudly applauded. Then the families began to dance, adults with adults, kids with kids, adults with kids.

I thought what a shame it was that so many of us have become too sophisticated to be able to enjoy ourselves, sober, in such a simple uninhibited way.

These unspoilt Italian families still had that capacity.

A middle-aged Belgian got up to dance with his wife. She didn't seem to want to take the dancing too seriously, but he didn't know how not to.

He wore gold rings and a gold neck chain, and had a large carefully cultivated moustache: He must have spent ages trimming it and preening it.

The other dancers weren't too hot on style. They were just having a laugh. But he had to give it the full ballroom bit. Stiff and straight-faced and up on his toes. And missing the point.

But then people with moustaches do take themselves too seriously.

Look at my mate Chris Hockley. He's got a huge moustache, and he takes his tennis too seriously. He must do: He keeps beating me.

It isn't just a question of size, though. Charlie Chaplin had a tiny moustache but he took himself too seriously. (That's why he wasn't as funny as Buster Keaton).

Saddam Hussein is different, of course: Nobody without a moustache could ever be taken seriously in Iraq. And, anyway, you're not allowed to be a dictator without one.

NB: The above need not necessarily apply to beards. Some bearded people may be quite normal and may have nothing to worry about. Pipe-smokers, though…

I LEFT Pésaro after a sleep disrupted at least 20 times by the busy overnight schedule of the railway running beside the camp, and carried on up the coast. But it wasn't a patch on Italy's other side.

The beaches were sandier, the sea bluer, and the oleander more oleaginous (I must look that word up). But it was flat. And it was straight. And it was ugly.

The entire route from Térmoli was a built-up clutter and sprawl of towns and villages, pylons, adverts, factories, filling stations, restaurants and motels.

For about 400k I never got away from the sight of a building of some sort. And not one of them was attractive.

Then there were the traffic lights: There must have been at least 150 sets of them. And in Italy you're sought-after prey at traffic lights.

As in England, there are windscreen washers. But that's not all: There are beggars who hold up notices saying how many bambini they've got to support. And leafleters. And sellers of all kinds.

A favourite sales line is a six-pack of paper hankies: Daisy's glove compartment is still full of them. In the end, I got smart. Whenever a seller approached, I just held up a six-pack and that showed:
1. I was a good guy, having helped one of their buddies.
2. I didn't need any more at the moment, grazie.

Between Rimini and Ravenna there was a hold-up, and we came across the crumpled remnants of a small blue car which had come off worse in a collision with a white van about the same size as Daisy.

In the road, among the blood and the debris and some personal possessions, lay a body completely covered by a white blanket apart from its shoes. Women's.

Just a few minutes earlier she'd have kissed her husband and children goodbye and set off with a cheery won't-be-gone-long wave (not forgetting to cross herself like the good Catholic she'd have been) to meet a pal for coffee or buy a new outfit or have her hair done.

Then, in a split splintering second, someone's easy error had ended everything.

Somewhere nearby, a family would be overflowing with as much grief as I'd seen those similar families overflowing with joy just 12 hours earlier.

Police urgently waved us all through, because that's the way it is in Italy: The quick and the dead.

Suddenly, driving didn't seem so much fun any more.

VENICE has fewer miles of canals than Birmingham, is easier on the eye and harder on the nose. I got one thing right: I approached it from the sea, which is the best introduction.

I'd spent the night at Camping Miramare, at Punta Sabbioni, from where I could catch a ferry to Venice across the Lagoon (£9,000 return).

I joined about 20 other early risers aboard the 6.30am sailing, and as the morning mist slowly cleared and the sun began to slant across the approaching belltower of Saint Mark's Cathedral... Well, if you were an artist you couldn't have asked for more.

Venice may have a more refined reputation than Naples, but don't let that put you off. It's just as dotty, except it has boats instead of scooters. And not just sedate gondolas: The locals zoom about that Lagoon of theirs all day and nearly all night in every kind of high-powered craft.

We landed at Saint Mark's Square and I walked to the Rialto Bridge, its graceful glory blemished by the prominence of the bleak backboards of its many grock shops, and watched the sun slowly light up the scene as the waters of the Grand Canal waked into life: There were gondolas, of course, and bus boats and taxi boats and luggage boats and workmen's boats and police boats.

A two-way thoroughfare this, although many of the side-canals were one way, set against a background of barber's pole moorings and listing listed buildings, faded and jaded in yellow, orange, pink, brown and grey, arched, pillared, balconied and waterfront-doorstep deep in the dirty green high-tideway.

I bought a £4,500 ticket to take the No 82 bus (standing room only, thanks to arriving American tourists) down the Grand Canal past a dozen palaces and as many churches, every one a star and every one under the weather, back to Saint Mark's.

Then came the expensive bit: £10,500 for just one cappuccino in the marvellously muralled, mirrored, gilded and glazed Café Florian, favourite of Goethe, Byron, Dickens, Proust and anyone who's ever been over-endowed with a capacity for writing or loving.

That was about £4 sterling (as you'll know if you can do maths and have been paying attention). But a pee was free, and I took my financial foolhardiness on the chin by giving my white-and-braid-jacketed, black-bow-tied waiter a £1,500 tip.

Then I went to take a look at the cathedral. The façade was wide rather than tall, more railway station shaped than cathedral shaped, but magnificent: Gilded, muralled, carved, arched, angelled and arch-angelled.

I joined the 20-minute "line" to get in. The floor was prettily patterned in a colourful muddle of tiny tiles, but the domes, arches and ceiling were sticky with the sickly glare of one huge gilded mosaic: Byzantine out of Golden Syrup.

After that, I wandered the car-free, care-free streets and alleyways and got lost. Lost in the pleasure of the sights, if not the smells, of the world's most astonishing city: Veni, vidi, Venici.

For lunch, I found a little ristorante near the fish market which did a pizza for less than the price of that cup of coffee. And it did Draught Guinness.

Then, past McDonalds and The Disney Store, to the agenzia ippica (betting shop to you) near the Accademia Gallery.

My fellow punters stood shaking their heads, shrugging their shoulders and exhaling big breaths from puffed-out cheeks in the manner of punters everywhere. But there was a no-smoking room, which was unexpectedly civilised.

I managed to make myself understood sufficiently to back Belicoso in the 3.30 at Turin. A sign said the going there was BUONO. Shame the horse wasn't, but it gave me a great feeling to tear up a 25 grand betting slip and not have to worry about how I was going to explain it all to The Chauffeur.

I ended up feeling frightened for Venice. It was fantastic, but in the way that a freak show is fantastic. Its problem is that it can't evolve like other cities.

Birmingham has been able to. Its city centre is exciting and alive: The daringly modern Symphony Hall complex, Brindley Place, the newly pedestrianised, fountained and statued Victoria Square area framing the city art gallery, and more to come.

But the best Venice can hope to do is to cling on to what it's got: Its palaces and its churches and its comic-opera gondoliers serenading the gullible grockles.

Tourists were invading the place in their boatloads, but as its beautiful buildings dilapidated before their eyes, it seemed to be losing its life-and-death battle to keep its head above water.

I tried to have a lie-in the next morning, but was woken at seven by a selfish group of German neighbours noisily moving their vowels and laxatively laughing (presumably at how funny it was to be disturbing everybody so early).

This trip hadn't done much for my opinion of Germans or Americans. But in fairness I think it could just be the travelling ones who are so boorish: People who've been to America tell me they're very friendly over there. And I'm prepared to believe it's the same in Germany.

But what I'd like to know is this: Do the friendly ones stay at home while the boorish ones go travelling, or does going travelling make the friendly ones boorish?

WE checked out of Miramare (£52,000 for two nights) and headed for the Italian Lakes. I hoped I'd like them because The Chauffeur and I are fond of the English ones, especially Ullswater and Derwentwater.

The first was Lake Garda which appeared, in the heat haze, to be even larger than it was: At times, it was impossible to see across it. But it was lovely, and calming.

After the crowds of Venice and days of sweatily legging it up and down Italy's thigh, Garda's gently lapping waves said: Slow down, take it easy.

So I did, and so did everyone else. We all drove round the lake at less than 60k. And nobody overtook, even when it would have been easy to do so.

I found a non-heightist equal opportunities car park for Daisy at Malcésine, a pretty town perched on the rocky eastern shore, and had a cappuccino in the cobbled town square beneath the little castle.

The lake was narrower here and the mountains on the far shore became visible, silver-rocked in the blue-grey haze.

We drove round the head of the lake, where there was enough of a breeze to have tempted out about 200 windsurfers, and stopped beneath those same silver-rocked cliffs, among olive trees, at Camping Nanzel, near Limone sul Garda.

You've got to hand it to those Italian builders. They just don't know when they're beaten: There was a road right round that lake, even though the sides of it were sheer for much of the way.

They'd hacked dozens of tunnels through the cliffs, often with the side nearer the lake left open, supported on pillars, so you could still enjoy the view.

Another thing about Lake Garda: It was full of fish. That evening I counted more than a hundred of them, each nearly half a metre long, just off the shore beside the camp bar. Cavedano, the friendly camp boss told me they were called.

Neither of us knew what that was in English, but he drew me a diagram to show me the snag with them: They contain far too many bones.

(I've since learned that they were chub. And after talking to a couple of Thames anglers the other day, I gather that as well as having an excess of bones they also have a rather unpleasant earthy taste).

I woke to rolls of thunder, and large raindrops riddled the lake. The far shore had vanished. I could have been in Keswick.

I was glad of my golf umbrella as I walked into Limone, a pretty little Alpine town of cobbles and shutters and geraniums, crammed between the mountains and the lake. And crammed with tourists, English and German in equal numbers.

I watched a lot of them board a ferry which came alongside the café-lined waterfront and carried them off into the mist. I went for a spaghetti at one of those cafés, the Jacky Bar. And despite the mass of grockles I still felt soothed by the gently rippling calmness of the lake.

Later the weather brightened up, and my mountains returned. But I wasn't tempted to go for a swim with some of my fellow campers. And all those fish.

As daylight faded, I watched a swan preen itself in the shallows. Then, slowly, it and the lake and the mountains and the sky turned to one grey-blue-white watercolour wash, with just the flickering lights on the far shore to give perspective.

At eight the next morning, I wasn't really ready to appreciate the I-Love-To-Go-A-Wandering community singing, to accordion accompaniment, which drifted in my direction from the hotel next door. An English coach party wanted the world to know it was ready for another jolly day on the road.

I checked out of Camping Nanzel, a clean and friendly site, and left Garda for the smaller Lake d'Iseo, bendily beautiful, with tiny islands. But unfortunately the haze wasn't sufficient to blur the eyesores of a couple of large factories planted between the tunnels on the west bank.

Two-legged Lake Como didn't just have tunnels, it had tunnels on top of tunnels where the road and railway builders had vied to surpass one another in the audacious spending of their Public Sector Burrowing Requirement.

On the east bank, Varenna, a challenger to Limone for cobbles and geraniums, and Bellano, brimming with palms and hydrangeas, were delightful.

It must have been near here that my old pal Jim Warburton tried to bend the ear of one of the locals (as he would) and tell him how wonderful the view was.

The local would have none of it, sharply telling Jim (in excellent English) that he didn't know what he was talking about, and that it wasn't half as beautiful as Macclesfield: He'd been held there as a prisoner of war, and it had the best view in the world.

The scenery round the northern end of the lake was flatter and duller. But Como was still a winner.

We'd driven round three of the lakes but we didn't drive round the fourth, Maggiore, because the top end is in Switzerland and I'd been told that if I'd so much as turned one of Daisy's wheels there I'd have had to pay their annual road tax, £70 sterling.

I wasn't prepared to do that: They've got enough money already.

So I drove Daisy round the bottom bit hoping the top bit, like Como's, would have been less pretty. But I doubt it: At Luino, halfway up the eastern shore, it looked lovely as it sparkled silver in the evening sun beneath its grey mountains. Then, as we drove south, it began to become less appealing.

We stopped for the night near the bottom of the west bank, at Camping Lago Azzurro. The site was large and unattractive and the officious woman at reception insisted on commandeering my passport, the first time this had happened to me.

The lake water beside the camp was smelly and dirty: I wondered if the site should be renamed Lago Bruno. It was near a place called Arona, but I reckoned that name was one letter out. And there were squadrons of bloodthirsty mosquitoes.

The motor caravanner's most important piece of equipment, after lavatory paper and the ignition key, is the fly swat. Before going to bed, you close the doors, put up the flyscreens and turn on the lights. Then it's war. It's you or them. It doesn't matter how long it takes: Everything that moves must be eliminated.

Flies are quite easy. They're noisy and cumbersome, and can usually be accounted for quite quickly. You almost feel sorry for them, although you mustn't allow yourself to: Their buzzing, in that confined space, can prevent all your attempts to sleep. (And sleeping can be hard enough on a hot sweaty night).

Mozzies are a more insidious enemy: More devious in the art of warfare, and more dangerous. They don't come out and fight fair, but hide or play dead until you've gone to sleep.

And even when you get them in your sights they're harder to swat, as they niftily waft themselves out of the way.

That night, I cut and thrust and parried for half an hour (and got far too hot) but even then I feared I wouldn't be able to claim victory.

I was right: The next day I had a dozen new bites. My left foot was swollen with them. My right arm was stiff with a cluster of them round the elbow. There was another in the middle of my forehead.

And as I shaved, I discovered there was one hidden under my stubble when I sliced the top off it and blood poured down my left cheek.

They'd got me despite all my conscientious late-night swatting and despite the fact that I'd spent most of the night lying awake, too sweaty to sleep.

I considered leaving Maggiore immediately, but in the end I was glad I decided instead to drive further up the shore.

Arona had an attractive wisteria-clad waterfront. Stresa and Baveno were beautiful with geraniums and piles of hydrangeas, in every pastel of pink and blue, and monster magnolia trees, as big as oaks, their huge blooms waxing creamy white.

And, through the watercolour heat haze, dark islands loomed alluringly, happily smothered in their hilly jumbles of houses.

THEN I cheated: It cost me £14,200, in two instalments, but I took the toll autostrada back towards France. There were still plenty of exciting tunnels. And, as on all motorways, there was a hold-up.

We were delayed for about 20 minutes, between Milan and Turin, by roadworks which had dinky little cones, much smaller than ours. (Cornettos, I suppose they call them).

It was sweaty, and there were loads of lorries. But none of them belonging to Eddie Stobart. His isn't a global domination, then. Yet.

We drove past kilometre after kilogram of sweetcorn, peaches and vines. And there were little lay-bys with lavatories, which looked like bus stops, as well as proper service areas. I stopped at one of the services for a cappuccino.

Booze was on sale there, but I wasn't tempted: Writing and driving was enough of a challenge without drinking and writing and driving.

I caused chaos at the second toll stop (and yes, it was my fault this time). I got in the lane where you needed a special card, not cash, and of course I didn't have one, so I had to make several irate Itis behind me reverse out again.

After I'd paid my toll, my Italian money had almost run out: I was down to my last two grand. But fortunately Daisy's fuel gauge wasn't in the red (quite).

We left the autostrada just before the Fréjus Tunnel, and got back on to real roads again. Then we ran into more sign trouble: On the continent, they don't like to admit that other countries exist, so we followed signs which indicated a diminishing number of tiny villages on the Italian side of the border, but none of the sizeable towns on the French side.

Eventually, a lone signpost begrudgingly pointed to FRANCIA. Reassuring, all right. But not exactly long on detail.

8

Briançon - La Chapelle-en-Vercors - Vassieux-en-Vercors - Bauduen - Saint-Cyprien - Collioure - Port-Vendres - Banyuls - Portbou - Lloret de Mar - Barcelona - Gavá - Valencia - Villajoyosa - Benidorm - Alicante - Castillo de Baños - Granada - Seville

I'VE got to admit it: Daisy found the French Alps a bit of a struggle. In fact, I've seen them climbed quicker in the Tour de France.

But she gave me plenty of time to admire the view, and the higher we got the more beautiful it became.

There were streaks and stripes of snow forming milk-cow patterns on the dark peaks. With sun on them. And spiky trees and mountain villages and, fortunately, a filling station which was open even though it was early afternoon.

Through Briançon, which claimed to be Europe's highest town and one of its sunniest, past avalanches of Alpine flowers rolling pink, yellow, blue, mauve and white down the boulder-strewn grass. And plunging waterfalls tens of metres high, hurling down enough water to create rivers, not streams.

We twice waited more than five minutes at traffic lights for tunnel-repair roadworks more than a kilometre long. At night the road would have been closed completely from 10 till six, meaning a diversion of 80k.

(Up there, you couldn't blame them for wanting to get it done in the summer though).

We passed two of the most famous villages in sport, Les Deux-Alpes and L'Alpe-d'Huez, where champions live life on the edge of their skis.

Then down to Grenoble and up again, this time to France's most haunting region, the primaevally beautiful Vercors, forbidding with grim menace and combed with cliffs and canyons and chasms.

Through rock arches and tunnels, amazed not to meet Fred and Wilma Flintstone rolling the other way, to La Chapelle-en-Vercors and the airy mosquito-free Camping les Bruyères right in the centre of the village.

There was nobody at reception so I parked Daisy, made myself tea in her christening pot and tried (but failed) to resist scratching blood from my itching wounds.

The village was an attractive no-nonsense place of unassuming pride, clean and well kept, with a handful of shops, a couple of bars and restaurants, and an absence of gaudy signs and neon lights.

Its proudest landmark was a 100-year-old drinking fountain with water flowing from the mouths of two mean-looking bears, commemorating the fact that this (understandably) was the area of the Alps where the last bear was seen.

I didn't know it when I arrived, but I discovered the village had been completely destroyed by the Nazis, six weeks before I was born, because of its support for the French Resistance.

After the war it had all been rebuilt. Even the treasured drinking fountain had had to be pieced together again.

Not surprisingly, there weren't any Germans on the campsite. So in the morning I wasn't woken early by any umlautish behaviour.

There still wasn't anyone at reception when we left, but I managed (with difficulty) to persuade a decorator who was working on the place to accept 28 francs which, according to a price list pinned on a noticeboard, appeared to be what we owed.

Feeling slightly uneasy about Daisy's ancestry, and expecting at any moment to see a sign saying VOLKSWAGENS VERBOTEN, I drove past clanking cow-belled dairy herds to the austere Resistance Memorial, built high on a mountainside above Vassieux-en-Vercors.

Here, I learned how the Nazis had massacred 600 Resistance fighters and 200 local people, young and old, male and female. Many had been forced to watch their homes being burned before they were tortured to death.

An inscription told me not to forget.

From there down to Die (a painfully appropriate place name to an Englishman) on a road gripped in place by a hundred hairpins.

We passed lots of those roadsigns showing huge boulders falling from a great height. They're like the ones that show low-flying aircraft: I'm never quite sure what you're meant to do about them.

From the Vercors to the Verdon, due south along fertile valleys between steep dark woods and over more hairy climbs between more rocky horrors.

One thing we were learning to respect was the continental level crossing. Some of these could be taken at speed, others couldn't. But there was no way of knowing which was which, except that the ones we did slow down for usually lived up to their name, and the ones we didn't usually turned out to be real crockery clatterers and milk shakers.

On by tiny roads (where it was a surprise even to meet a tractor) and across furrowed deep-scented seas of blue-green lavender to the magnificent Lac de Sainte Croix.

GREAT Barkeepers of the World (An Occasional Series): No 3: Bernard Keyser, of the Café du Midi in the beautiful backwater of a lakeside cul-de-sac called Bauduen.

Originally from Alsace (they get around, these barkeepers) Bernard runs the café with his sidekick Bilou beside the boules terrace overlooking the lake.

The two of them always wear shorts, and sometimes wear shoes.

Amid sweet cooking smells, the tables and chairs share the main rumpled road with the traffic (not heavy).

The phone has an old-fashioned ring not heard since Maigret was a lad, and is constantly in use. The place is equally popular with locals and visitors.

A cryptic shout of "Oliday" from the kitchen announces when another meal is ready to be served.

For two nights I sat at one of those tables with my childhood chum Pete Marsh, and we chatted contentedly as we drank beer, pastis and wine, and ate entrecôte steaks, medium rare.

The evening sun turned the water below us a gleaming yellow-pink and sharply silhouetted the mountains beyond, before disappearing behind them.

Pete was there for the summer, staying at the municipal campsite where Daisy and I joined him, to sail his yacht Rip-Rap on the lake.

Between our visits to the Café du Midi, he took me and the delightful camp gardienne, pretty golden-skinned Régine, for a sail. There was more sun than wind, but we enjoyed a memorable afternoon in a beautiful setting.

While I was there, Pete was trying to persuade the authorities to let him take paying tourists aboard Rip-Rap for day trips. But the combination of his certificate of sailing competence and the European Union's laws of fair trading were proving no match for local French politics.

As I left Bauduen, I became aware of a clicking noise coming from Daisy's front offside tyre (or the nearside one, over there). I stopped to investigate, expecting to find a stone lodged in the tread, and discovered instead the head of a large screw which had embedded itself there.

I pondered for a while what to do about it, but the tyre pressure looked OK so I decided on a policy of If It Ain't Broke Don't Fix It. It could have been acting as a plug, and if I'd taken it out the tyre could have gone flat instantly.

It's still there and doesn't seem to be doing any harm, but the clicking isn't as noticeable now. I'd love to know how long it is, though.

Next, with a little help from the autoroutes, to the Mediterranean corner of France where it meets Spain. I booked into Camping Al Fourty at

Saint-Cyprien, previously a quiet fishing port but now overgrown and overrun with tourists (for once, nearly all French). And their yachts. And their dogs, all ridiculously small or ridiculously large. Never in-between.

At night, we campers aren't just up against the insect Enemy Within, there's the Enemy Without as well. The noise-makers: Scooters, obviously, plus other road traffic. Trains. Planes. Radios and TVs tuned to different tastes. Frogs croaking. Grasshoppers playing with themselves (or whatever it is they do). Drunks. Dogs. Birds. Babies. Germans. Sneezers (I heard one camper sneeze every seven seconds for 40 minutes). Smokers coughing. Couples and whole families fighting.

And it's not as if campers stick to the same hours. Some like to make their noise late at night, some early in the morning.

Then there are the bells. Every self-respecting small village has at least one chiming clock, often two, sometimes three. And they don't all keep the same time: It only needs one to be five minutes fast and another to be five minutes slow, and you can end up getting a chime every five minutes throughout the night.

Of course, noises aren't a problem in themselves: They're fine if you're used to them.

At home, I can sleep soundly through jumbo jets screaming into Heathrow every 33 seconds (or however often it is). But if an unexpected chaffinch comes up with an unexpected chirrup on the furthest twig of the furthest tree at the furthest end of the garden, I'll immediately leap from sleep in a state of alarm clock shock.

And the trouble with touring is that nearly every noise is new or unexpected.

Most continentals like to smoke (and cough) but the Dutch are the world champions. From my campsite research, I can exclusively reveal that all Dutch adults and most Dutch children smoke to excess.

(They don't mind what, so long as it will go into a roll or a bowl and can be set fire to).

There was a Dutchman at Bracciano who never took his pipe out of his mouth. He went to the toilet block in the mornings wearing just his shorts and his pipe.

When he got there, I suppose he must have taken his shorts down. But I'll bet he never took his pipe out.

Next morning we drove to pretty Collioure, where French accents merge into Spanish via Catalan: A gently delightful spot, its little port watched over by a distinctive round church tower.

I sat over coffee and croissants as the staff of the harbourside cafés set out their tables and chairs for the busy day ahead. Meanwhile, painted-faced commandos paddled their small boats out from beneath the town's ancient fort, looking menacingly as if they meant modern business.

On to Port-Vendres, a serious harbour this time, with a work bit as well as a play bit but the more interesting for it. And another hard-to-resist row of quayside bars and restaurants.

FRANCE gradually unwound itself beneath the vine-veined hills of Banyuls, finally running out at Cap Cerbère.

Spain started slowly, giving the impression at first that it might be closed: Although we entered Portbou well before siesta time, nearly everywhere was shut and shuttered.

But at least my language worries were over once again, because if my Italian is stagnant then my Spanish is positively arid.

Dos cervezas por favor dimly recalled from the time my old pal Drummond Hislop and I imported a Deux-Chevaux from Brussels to London via Blackpudlian Lloret de Mar about the time England won the World Cup. And that's more or less it.

We'd slept in the car (all you did if you needed a bed was to unhook the backs of the deckchair front seats and attach them to the rear ones) and we went to Lloret not so much because it was on the way but because we thought it might be a good place to drink beer and chat up girls.

I seem to remember we had lots of success with the one, and none at all with the other.

So it was to Lloret, with Daisy as my chaperone, that I headed now. (Well, Tossa didn't sound right somehow).

The coast was beautiful, more rockily rugged than the French side of the border.

It was hard to assess Spanish driving skills at first because nearly every car I saw was French, German or English.

I liked the fact that the roadsigns which showed cameras didn't mean you were in danger of being nicked for speeding, but you were approaching a place where you could stop and take a photo of the view.

Lloret was better looking than I'd remembered it: The palmed seafront was almost elegant, and the little streets in the town almost pretty.

True, there were bars with Happy Hours and English names (THE QUEEN VIC) and takeaways and amusement arcades and discos and tattooists and body piercers and printed T-shirt shops (TO BEER OR NOT TO BEER THAT IS THE QUESTION - SHAKESBEER) and big burned bellies from Brum.

But you can get those anywhere these days. I've seen a lot worse in places that were supposed to know better.

The beach was beautiful, and so were some of the topless bathers. I went to a beach bar, ordered just una cerveza and decided I rather liked the old place.

I concluded it probably hadn't got any prettier over the years: It was just that other places had got a lot uglier. But in a world getting less attractive every day, that represented a considerable achievement.

I needed some Spanish money, so I went to a bank in the wall. A worrying moment, this, when you've just arrived in a new country and your maths are as bad as mine: You're not sure if you're about to upset Britain's Balance of Payments by 100 quid or 10,000. (Don't take my word for it, but I think £2 was worth about 500 pesetas).

We drove beside 50 kilometres of bathing beaches, sandy and full-bodied, then I did something I'd been wanting to do for ages: Put on my Freddie Mercury and Montserrat Caballé tape and played Barcelona. In Barcelona. At high volume.

Driving through Big Bad Barcelona was barmy, but not barking. It was testing, yes, but only in the way that driving through any large city is testing when you haven't got a map, or the first clue what you're doing. It wasn't a brain-bending trip like Naples: A van driver actually let me in when I got in the wrong lane. I was beginning to wonder if the Spanish might be nearly normal.

They're a contrary lot, of course. You only had to look at their language to see that. Just to be different from the rest of us, they put an o on the end of everything: Banco, centro, fantástico, mucho, plástico, teléfono etc.

Of course, this means that where we already have an o they've got to be different again: While the rest of us say Hello or Allo, they (perversely) say Hola.

Obviously I never saw a helpful sign in Barcelona, but I found a way out eventually and ended up 15k to the south at Gavá, and Camping la Tortuga Ligera. It wasn't the site I'd been looking for, which was called Albatros. But that sounded a bit fate-tempting anyway, so I settled for an Agile Tortoise instead.

My first day back in Spain made me think of Fawlty Towers and Mañuel. After all, he came from Barcelona (although he hadn't been conceived when I first visited his country).

But more than that, I thought of all the bad guys in all the bad Western movies. Especially whenever we stopped at a sign saying: CEDA EL PASO.

IN the morning I caught the bus to town, and it had been sabotaged: Some despicable spic had spread a layer of sticky gunge on most of the seats.

A lot of people on the bus knew each other, and they thought it was hilarious that their pals' bums had got smeared with the stuff. Until they discovered theirs had as well.

I wanted to see some of the work of Barcelona's most famous architect, Antoni Gaudí, so I set off in search of him.

I went first to the Casa Batlló, a six-floored office building disguised as a grotto. Without a hint of a straight line anywhere. And no right to be above water.

Its walls grew more colourful as they neared the top, with bubbles of tiles and ripples of mosaics in blue, green, yellow and brown, just as marine life becomes more colourful nearer the surface of the sea.

It was impossible to understand why shoals of fishes weren't pouting at me from its wavy first-floor windows.

Almost as impressive were the nearby street lamps: Big and brown with top-hatted bulbs hanging from wrought-iron leaves and flowers and crowns and bats (long-eared, not cricket). Each had a shapely double-sided mosaic bench at its base.

Next was La Pedrera: A corner building this time (not that that was a problem for Gaudí). It had the same rocky-grotto look but was less colourful, with tangly brown wrought-iron seaweed as railings for its bendy balconies.

On to his most famous building, the Sagrada Família cathedral, still being built more than a century after it was started: A Born Again Crustacean pointing its pincers to God. Barnacled brown with statues and carvings at its bottom. Colourfully sponged with yellow, orange, white and red mosaics at its top.

I paid 800p to get in, but all I could see was scaffolding. Then I looked at the small print on my ticket. It said: THE FEE IS A CONTRIBU-TION FOR THE CONSTRUCTION. (So I wasn't meant to be able to see anything, then).

I paid another 200p to take a lift 65 metres up one of the pincers, then clawed my way up another 35 metres of narrow, winding steps to its tip.

The view of Barcelona was spectacular, but the experience didn't suit me: I discovered I was able to suffer from both vertigo and claustropho-bia at the same time.

As I clambered down, bells blasted eleven in my left ear. I could see they weren't real bells, just loudspeakers. But no church, complete or incomplete, can be without its noisy chimes on the continent.

(Fortunately they still don't seem to chime beyond 12 despite the intro-duction of the 24-hour clock).

Back on solid ground, I made a sweaty midday climb to Gaudí's Parc Güell, with its fairyland entrance between gingerbread houses, its

Cinderella-Castle steps and its fantastic fountains dripping with mosaic monsters.

I think the word gaudi is similar to the Latin word meaning: I rejoiced. (Whether it is or not, I did).

Downhill, through the joyous city that knows the meaning of fiesta but not siesta, to the "real" cathedral. Its façade was intricately carved and statued and beautiful.

But compared with Gaudí's masterpiece, it seemed lifeless. Just as declining Venice and fallen Rome seemed lifeless compared with vibrant virile Barcelona.

Next, to discover Christopher Columbus, misguidedly pointing not towards America but towards Italy as he stood high above the Old Port which has been revitalised with a hi-tech silver-glass complex of shops, restaurants and bars. I quickly downed dos much-needed cooling cervezas.

So to La Rambla, said to be the greatest street in the world, slicing through the city with its portrait artists, pavement artists, face artists, body artists, hair artists, mime artists, escape artists, con artists and piss artists.

Its street-sellers, eat-sellers, meat-sellers, frite-sellers, beat-sellers, beet-sellers, treat-sellers, discreet-sellers, cheat-sellers, seat-sellers, marguerite-sellers and parakeet-sellers.

And its visiting thousands: Eating, drinking, smoking, talking, watching. Or just rambling.

The point about Barcelona is that it surprises you. It doesn't stay still, and it doesn't let you stay still either. You'll go round the corner and the next building you see won't be straight-faced like its neighbours, it'll be a wittily-wobbly Gaudí gobsmacker.

Or you'll find a restaurant with a huge lobster on the roof. Or cable cars which come up from nowhere to sway sky high above the port, between lighthouses which are covered in giant footballers.

I had a Catalan Salad at a tapas bar just off La Rambla. A bit of everything: Ham, cheese, salami, asparagus, red pepper, tomato, onion, olive and plenty of proper lettuce (not Tonsil Tickler).

I also had a bottle of vino tinto and a basket of bread. And the bread was a problem: To me, it was stale. But when you're abroad, how do you know it isn't meant to be?

As you crunch your way through it, are the staff laughing at you behind your back? Or would they be deeply hurt if you complained? And would you be showing your ignorance?

In France, they serve you guinea fowl and quail and starlings and sparrows and all sorts of other little feathered creatures that might have flown over the cooker a couple of times but clearly never actually settled on it.

Yet if you say a dicky-bird about them being underdone, the staff get most upset and can't understand what you're complaining about.

So I said nothing about the bread. Mind you, The Chauffeur says I never complain back in Britain either: I just put up with whatever I'm given. But even if you're not going to complain, it's nice to know whether or not you've actually got something to complain about.

At most campsites 50 per cent of the taps are red and 50 per cent are blue, no matter what the temperature of the water that comes out of them.

In truth, 90 per cent of them ought really to be blue. But I got an unexpected bonus when I went to wash the next morning, and discovered the water from the blue tap was nice and hot.

The water from the red one was cold, mind you.

When I'd checked in at the Agile Tortoise they'd asked me to hand over my passport, and as I left they handed it back. Or they thought they did.

I wasn't aware that there were any other Brits on the site, so when they gave me a British passport it seemed reasonable to assume it was mine.

But fortunately I checked it. And saw this ugly face framed with thick, dark hair staring out at me. (I may be ugly but my hair, such as it is, is a little thinner and lighter these days).

So I gave it back, got the correct one, paid my 4,280p bill, and drove off. But it could have been awkward: Supposing the other bloke had already been given mine, and had driven off with it.

I'd have had to spend the rest of my travels pretending to be him. And wearing a dark wig.

Naturally when we left all the signs said BARCELONA, no matter which way they pointed, but we managed to find our way across winding white cliffs to Sitges. After that the land flattened out, although the sea and the mountains were never far away.

Daisy and I took the N340 from the Costa Brava to the Costa Blanca. And it wasn't pretty: There were dirty factories and big out-of-town sales centres supplying caravans and boats and swimming pools. And warehouses and filling stations and motels and restaurants and campsites and massive messy advertising hoardings and (unlike in Italy) huge hypermarkets.

I stopped between Tarragona and Valencia for a coffee and a doughnut (they like doughnuts in Spain, even though they can't spell them) and I felt a long way from home. But I was reassured by the familiar sight of the Centre Court at Wimbledon (just round the corner from where we live) on the telly in the corner of the bar.

One good thing about driving on the continent is that when you're used to dealing in miles, kilometres can seem quite friendly. You'll see a sign saying VALENCIA 240, but given a reasonable run you can soon lap them up.

Most of the roads have kilometre markers, and if things are going your way they'll roll away nicely. (Five miles are about eight kilometres).

We drove through Valencia and it was a clean elegant city with nice modern buildings spaciously laid out among well-leafed trees.

Some of the older bits were more cramped, but pleasant-looking enough. It seemed like a place on the way up. But I've never seen so many queues at traffic lights.

Perhaps the locals should start ignoring them and speed up the traffic flow, like they do in Naples.

We found our way out all right, despite the fact that halfway through they suddenly changed our signs from ALICANTE to ALACANT.

After Valencia, Spain began to look more like bandido country. The houses became lower and flatter, built for mean hombres thrusting out unshaven chins stickily matted with cigarillo spittle.

We ended the day's drive at Camping Sertorium, 6k south of Benidorm. It was big and bossy, with lots of tannoy messages I didn't understand. But I don't think any of them were for me: I wasn't expecting any phone calls.

I was hot after the day's drive and the site was right by the beach, so I put on my jellies and dived into the big cooling white breakers.

Unfortunately, though, the waves were too strong for my right jelly and tore it from my foot. When I came out, refreshed, I spent ten minutes searching for it, but it had vanished.

I returned to Daisy, changed and had a drink. But an hour later I decided to go and have another search for my missing jelly.

I'd noticed there was a strong current running towards the northern end of the beach. And that's where I found it, about 50 metres from where I'd lost it. Upside down and covered in seaweed, but undamaged.

(I felt really pleased: I'm fond of those jellies. They remind me of Brighton, one of my favourite places).

Another thing about that site: There were dozens of cats on it, mainly because a couple of them had recently had kittens.

Of course, that's fine by me. I love cats. And so, it seems, do the continental campers. In fact they like to take all kinds of pets with them on holiday, even birds in cages.

It was time for another Wash Day, so I acquired a couple of tokens from reception and headed for the camp's washing machine. In the ladies' washroom.

I felt a bit shy at first when I went in, but then a lot of camps have uni-sex toilet facilities anyway. Also, I wasn't likely to see much I couldn't see on the beach.

But I did have the element of surprise (as was clear from the looks on the faces of a couple of larger ladies who were giving their chests a good swill as I entered).

I managed to wash a couple of loads OK and got out of there in one piece.

Then I got clever: I rigged up my washing line between the top of Daisy's ladder and a nearby tree and, to draw it nice and tight, drove Daisy a couple of metres forward.

There was no question of my washing not drying this time: The day couldn't have been sunnier, and there was even a bit of a sea breeze to help. It was dry before I'd completed the second of my half a dozen swims that day.

And I was careful each time to keep a firm foothold in my jellies.

GREAT Barkeepers (Continued): No 4: Tito Rodriguez, of the Mojito Beach Bar, nowhere in particular but on a little spit of pebbly shore between the waves just north of Villajoyosa, Costa Blanca.

Tito, who looks like Fawlty Mañuel but with a few more qué on the clock, runs the bar (named after a vicious drink, not a vicious insect) with his vain assistant Toni, who went off to do a bit of bodybuilding and hair-styling halfway through his shift.

Tito keeps faith with his well-travelled barkeeping kind by originating from the diagonally opposite corner of Spain, near La Coruña.

His bar is popular mainly with locals, who roll up in their cars at most hours of the day and night. As in Italy, I was struck by how little English they were able to speak. I'm not complaining, just observing.

But I was surprised: After all, much of the music they hear and many of the adverts they see are in English.

(I wonder if I know something the advertising agencies and the pro-gramme planners don't).

The Mojito was a great place to be, although I didn't have much clue what the locals were on about even before I got stuck into the cervezas.

(I can't tell you how many I had because I can only count up to tres).

What I do know is that, as at Bauduen, when the evening sun turned pink the craggy mountains defied the laws of drinking and came sharply into focus.

Next morning, I drove Daisy into Benidorm and had a Full English Breakfast on the seafront: 425p for bacon, egg, sausage, beans, toast, orange juice and a pot of dishwater tea.

(I wondered how many millions of cups of tea would be ordered by Brits in Benidorm before one was served to their liking).

Then I watched the package parasols multiply as my compatriots basted their bodies for another baking day on the beach.

I was only in Benidorm for a couple of hours but I don't think there was a Premiership football shirt I didn't see.

With its skyscrapers and its grock shops, you could hardly call the place beautiful. But the sea and the mountains certainly were.

I realised why most Brits don't bother taking their cars, though: The parking was fine, but the one-way system was a nightmare.

On The Chauffeur's orders I'd checked Daisy's oil that morning, and again it was on minimum. Daisy had now done nearly 6,000 miles.

This running in was taking its time, but something had to be done so I stopped at a BP filling station. And quickly became confused

I'd clearly understood before we set off that all engines, petrol and diesel, used the same oil. Here, it seemed, there was a different oil for each.

I wanted to do the best I could for Daisy, but as my grasp of the mechanics of Spanish and my grasp of the mechanics of motors battled it out in the relegation zone I found myself agonising over what oil I should buy her.

The cashier invited the growing queue of customers behind me to debate my case with him, and the feeling of the meeting was that I should go for the stuff marked VISCO DIESEL.

I bought a litre, but just to be on the safe side I gave Daisy only a little of it to start with so I could see how she took to it. She purred along happily enough. So we stopped, and I gave her the rest.

(Four Out Of Five Cats Prefer Viscos).

In Alicante, we followed our usual policy of driving straight in (which is easy) and then trying to drive out again (which isn't).

Most cities not only have CITY CENTRE signs (in their own language) but, to help you still further, they also have neat little bullseye target signs for you to aim at.

I found Alicante airily attractive with broad palmed streets, quays full of yachts, and beaches full of bathers.

We discovered a way out eventually, and passed ponds of flamencoing flamingoes, which weren't pink, a lake which was, because of pollution, a new mock-castle housing development, which was about the ugliest I've ever seen, derelict windmills (tilted at, I suppose) and signs to La Manga golf course, where I definitely wouldn't have needed my umbrella.

Near Almería I saw six clouds. They were only little white things but

I thought I should mention them because they were the first I'd seen for a week.

The land looked thirsty: Scrubby with rock and cactus, pointy Paramount hills and dried-up river beds. Very little growing for profit. And very little traffic.

Then it became lumpier, with cement sand dunes. And less scrubby. There were derelict houses. Too many. For long stretches the roads were beautifully surfaced, but you wondered why they bothered.

Further south, on the flat bits, there was lots of commercial growing. But always under protective plastic, giving the ironic impression from a distance that vast areas of this driest of dry land were flooded.

We stopped for the night at Camping Castillo de Baños, beneath the Sierra Nevada.

I parked Daisy on a pitch just 20 metres from the sea and went straight in for a cool swim off the stony beach, pleased to be a two-jelly man again.

I KNEW I'd like Granada. I had happy memories of it before I even got there: Of Ena and Elsie and Co.

Then there was the Shrewsbury version, where I went to see The Beatles with my mate Drummond when we broke out of the high-security compound known as Shrewsbury School.

They had second billing on the Helen Shapiro Show, before they'd had their first Top Ten hit with Please Please Me.

The Alhambra was well signed, and parking was easy. (They didn't seem to have any heightist hang-ups in Spain).

I paid the usherette my 750p and went to see the palace, the Casa Real, which was fabulous: Not so much grand, more delightfully kitsch, the lower sections of its walls colourful with patterns of tiles in blue, brown, green and orange, which wouldn't have looked out of place in any period of English suburbia.

Its arches, ceilings and upper walls were less colourful, but intricately carved with fish and leaves and flowers and fruit. And shields and stalactite castles and Moorish scripts.

Its courtyards, each with a different water feature, hinted at a grander scale but never became big enough to be impersonal like most of the stately buildings that have been put up since.

I reckoned I'd never seen a more fascinating building. Even in Brighton.

The palace gardens, though not old, were wonderful too. Especially in the way they merged with the buildings so you hardly felt the join as you moved out of one and into the other.

They had pebble-patterned paths and neatly topiaried low hedges ambushed by rose and oleander. And ivy-shaded arches and arbours and tall conifers and peaceful water, sometimes gently springing and flowing, sometimes a still green sanctuary for lilies and goldfish. But, again, never forsaking intimacy in favour of showy splendour.

I'd rarely seen more beautiful gardens, either. Except perhaps at Hidcote, in Gloucestershire, where they call the different sections rooms: Just the word to describe the bits of Granada garden bordering the Casa Real.

The Alcazaba fortress was remarkable for the amount of it that's still left and for giving you the best half an hour's Granada viewing you could wish for, including (despite the fierce July heat) snow on the top of the accurately named Sierra Nevada.

But the fortress didn't hit you between the eyes like the palace. It did-n't surprise: It was what you expected an old fortress to look like.

We followed the bullseye targets to the centre of town, where parking was about as easy as it is in towns everywhere. We eventually found somewhere that seemed to be legal, and I left Daisy for an hour while I took a stroll and drank coffee at a tree-shaded café in the main street.

The town was busy and lively and attractive enough, though not par-ticularly beautiful or remarkable. But who cares when you've got one of the most magnificent buildings in the world? Not to mention all those Corrie characters.

WE headed west, through 200k of olives struggling to survive on little more than sand, stone and cement, to park beside a nomadic gathering of Aussies and Kiwis at Camping Sevilla, right at the end of the Seville Airport runway.

For most campers, airports mean good news and bad news: Good news if you want to find it. (It's the one place every city always has clear signs to). Bad news if you want a bit of peace.

I had the best of both worlds: I found it easily. And the planes made me feel sufficiently at home to give me a good night's kip.

In the morning I left Daisy behind and caught the bus into Seville, where I went first to the Plaza de España, a grand three-storey semi-cir-cular sweep of civic pride, built 70 years earlier, with columns and arch-es and towers and domes and ornately balustraded bridges and a foun-tain rainbowing in the sun.

At the base of its façade there was a wonderful sequence of ornately and colourfully tiled scenes and maps of Spain's provinces, in alphabetical order from Alava and Albacete to Zamora and Zaragoza. I counted 49 provinces, but there were a lot more scenes than that because Seville itself made several reappearances.

Buxom gipsy women kept trying to persuade me to buy flowers from them. But they were very pushy, and despite being a romany myself I had to remind them more than once to keep a Seville tongue in their heads.

Next, to the María Luisa Park, shady with trees and water and gaudy (but not Gaudí) frog-statued fountains.

Then past the somewhat unsettling sight of an armed cop with a pony-tail, to the Alcázar palace where I got the better of the automatic entry ticket machine to marvel at Moor carvings and tiles and courtyards like the Alhambra's.

I didn't fork out for one of the mobile phone-type tape machines, which most people had to their ears, for fear it might try to clutter my mind with facts and dates, and stop me appreciating what I saw.

(It's like in art galleries: If you spend too much time studying the names of the artists and the titles of the paintings, you forget to look at the art).

Again, the wall tiles were timeless. And above them the carvings were intricately worked but here, unlike the Alhambra, sometimes inlaid with colour: Gold, red, brown and blue.

Everything was on a bigger scale than the Alhambra, but not unmanageably so.

It went on and on, with upstairs bits and basement bits. And wonderful walled gardens, again less intimate than the Alhambra's.

And fountains and trees and low trimmed hedges. And fewer flowers, but miles of tiles on walls and seats and garden buildings to give more pattern and colour.

Then, to the cathedral. It was a magnificent construction, carved and statued to infinity. But Gaudí had spoiled me for cathedrals, as Arles had spoiled me for markets.

On to the cat's cradle of pedestrianised streets, squares, courtyards and alleyways of the Barrio Santa Cruz area: A jumble of little houses and shops and bars and restaurants including the magnífico Bodega Santa Cruz, with its slabby floor, shabby plaster and scarcely-varnished wood. Busy with character and life and lack of ceremony.

I ordered a cerveza and grilled sardines, because that's what the locals next to me were having. And, like my neighbours, I had the price of what I'd ordered marked on the wooden bar counter in front of where I stood by one of the noisily, cheerfully efficient white-shirted barmen, with a piece of chalk produced from behind his ear.

Never, in that frying pan of a city, was a beer so welcome. How could

I have whinged, less than a month ago, about the cold and the rain?

In common with the other bars in the city there was a notice, in Spanish and English, saying:

THIS ESTABLISHMENT HAS A COMPLAINT BOOK AT THE DISPOSAL OF THE CLIENTS WHO WISH TO REGISTER A COMPLAINT

I'd be amazed if it had ever had any entries.

Next, to the river, broad and green and full, although it was impossible to imagine where all the water could have come from, and the Plaza de Toros, where there was to be bullfighting that evening.

I didn't go to the ticket window marked either SOL or SOMBRA, though. I know it's not as bad in the flesh as on the telly (where they show all the goriest bits again in slow motion) but I didn't have the stomach for it.

And my sister's a vegetarian, for heaven's sake.

Across the river to the less touristy Triana district, and an unexpected, frothily-poured pint of Kilkenny at the darkly-welcoming Madigan's Irish Pub.

Then, past an electronic sign which said the temperature was 44 degrees at 16.02, to return to the shade of the María Luisa Park.

And there I was all but knocked down by a workman's truck.

It was just like being back home in Kew Gardens: You wouldn't believe the amount of traffic they have at Kew these days. When it cost 1p to get in, they didn't even allow bicycles.

Last time I went, admission cost £5, and that gave you the chance of being hit by any number of cars, vans, trucks and tractors from the moment you entered the gate.

Most of the benches there have plaques with long-winded dedications saying how much So-And-So (1880-1990) Loved These Gardens.

I like to take The Chauffeur to sit on one in the Rhododendron Dell which just says DAVE'S BENCH. (Even if it's already in use and all the others are empty).

But I've told her that if my days are ended by a vehicle in those gardens I'll want a plaque, with a full description of what happened inscribed on it. That'll show them.

(One good thing about Kew, though: It's always been safe to take kids there for a good clean kick among the fallen autumn leaves because it's that idyllic rarity among urban green space, a dog-free zone).

Anyway, the important thing is that the park-keepers of Europe have spared me long enough to tell you that Seville is baking (not barking) and wonderful.

And that Bodega Santa Cruz... Well, the sooner some of you workers take a lunch break there the better. (I know: I was that worker).

Next morning, Daisy and I checked out of the Sevilla (2,482p for two nights) and set off for the Algarve.

9

Faro - Cape Saint Vincent - Sagres - Sines - Areia - Lisbon - Nazaré -
Vila Nova de Gaia - Oporto - La Coruña - Avilés - Gijón - Llanes -
Zarautz - San Sebastián - Saint-Estèphe - Pauillac - Ars - La Rochelle -
Saint-Marc-sur-Mer - Rennes - Mont-Saint-Michel - Saint-Malo

DRIVING to Portugal was a bit like driving to Wales: We headed west
and crossed a big bridge, then grey cloud covered the sun. It didn't actually rain, but it certainly thought about it.

The country looked much the same as Spain, though: Red, rocky and
scrubby. With cactus and olive and orange trees.

We parked (with difficulty) near the harbour at Faro and I managed
(with equal difficulty) to withdraw a suitable sum of money on my bank
card. (I reckoned one pound was about 300 escudos).

Then I walked past McDonalds and the amusement arcade and the
Original Levi's Store (surprised to find it wasn't in America) and through
cockney accents to the Chelsea restaurant. (Well, at least it wasn't the
Arsenal).

I had shrimp salad, a Coke and a coffee for 1,960 Es. The menu was
in English as well as Portuguese, and the waitress understood me perfectly.

As for her own language, it looks like Spanish when you see it but it
certainly doesn't sound like Spanish when you hear it. To my ear, it
sounds more as if it comes from far eastern Europe rather than far western Europe.

I added up all the Portuguese words I knew:
PORTO + VINHO VERDE = 3
Not a bad starting point. But at least this sum of my knowledge meant
that Portugal (like most other countries) was somewhere I needn't have
any language worries.

I soon learned that the Portuguese, like their neighbours, had to change
the spelling of words here and there just to be different again.

They often changed l to r, for example. So, reading from l to r, the
Spanish playa (for beach) became praia, and plato (for plate) became
prato.

But I was also to learn that, unlike the Italians and the Spanish, a lot of the locals were capable of unleashing the most daring stabs at my language. Presumably because their Atlantic nation is more outward-looking.

It was sunny but windy in Faro, and a sign said the temperature was 28 degrees at 12.56. I didn't see a beach.

That afternoon we drove past massive advertisement hoardings screaming, in English:

VILLAS AND APARTMENTS FOR SALE WITH GOLF RIGHTS
NEW BLACK HOLE SLIDE AND SPLASH WATER PARK
KRAZY WORLD MEGAFUN FOR CHILDREN AND ADULTS
ZOOMARINE NEW SEALS SHOW
EXPLORE THE WORLD OF AMAZONIA LIVE SHOWS (But with a picture of a big fierce alligator, not a big fierce woman).

We kept going west until we could go no further, crossing headland heathland to join English and German coach parties at Europe's Land's End, windswept Cape Saint Vincent, where a dozen stallholders sold food, drink, souvenirs and warm woolly jumpers.

As is the way with Land's Ends, there wasn't a lot to see: It was more a place to go to than to look at. There was a powerful-looking lighthouse, squat, sturdy and red atop low white-washed buildings. And cliffs. And miles of blue-green Atlantic, not rough despite the stiff breeze. And that was about it.

But it was dramatic, as endings often are. And it was impossible not to think of all the soldiers, sailors and travellers who'd have felt joy or sorrow, hope or despair as they'd pitched past that landmark and that light to enter or leave the Med.

Later, I parked Daisy high above a sandy cove and climbed down a cliff path for my first Atlantic swim of the year. The water was cold, but it was beautiful.

And the best thing, after a month of the Med, was that there was a tide. Kids had built castles and written their names in the sand. I sat on a rock in the early evening sun and watched the water creep up the beach until all the traces were covered.

We stayed at the parque de campismo at Sagres, and I summoned up two-thirds of my Portuguese to order vinho verde to drink on the camp bar's terrace as quiet darkness swallowed the hardy little clifftop town beneath me.

The wine wasn't all that green, but it was the perfect refresher: Both sweet and sharp to each mouthful.

Our night there cost 1,300 Es. Then we drove north along rough roads (I think that's what my notes said: They're the untidiest words you can write, those, when you're driving) and beneath grey West Welsh skies.

We stopped at Sines where I drank a tall glass of tepid too-milky coffee among the fishermen and the fishing boats and the quayside haggling over silver seas of mackerel-sized sardines.

After that, the weather and the roads both improved (slightly) and we drove through wooded hills and past straw-shaded roadside stalls piled with oranges and lemons and melons and watermelons.

We did the last stretch to Lisbon by autoestrada. I hadn't intended to, but I followed a signpost saying LISBOA and we found ourselves facing a row of tollbooths with no escape route.

I wanted the campismo nearest the city, but had great difficulty finding it. When I finally saw it I let out a loud cheer, but it was full. In fact, it was overflowing: There was a queue of cars and caravans and motor caravans stretching out into the street.

We had no chance of getting in that day, so we headed west to the coast and Campismo Orbitur, near Guincho, and got in. Just: It was packed to the pine branches, and it was a challenge to find a space big enough for Daisy.

I drove round the camp twice before managing to squeeze her in between a couple of tree trunks. The ground wasn't very flat, but it would do.

I was glad we weren't towing a caravan like the two French families who came in after us and raced each other round the site to try to find a corner they could manoeuvre into.

Later, amazingly, it got even fuller. And privacy went out of the window as campers set up their vans and tents, tables and chairs, food and washing just half a fart apart.

I knew campsites could be full in high season. That's why we'd set off in May. But I hadn't expected it this soon. I decided I'd have to leave Daisy to stand her ground for the next two nights.

I walked into the prosperous-looking village of Areia, and watched the incongruous sight of an out-of-time old goatherd and his inattentive dog accompanying their tinkling charges slowly along the main street between smart new commuter homes.

Then I went to a little restaurant and had grilled sardines and salad accompanied by half a bottle of vinho verde, two large glasses of porto and Rod Stewart whinily wishing that he knew what he knew now when he was younger.

Quite right: If only he'd known to stay with The Faces. (Now there was a band).

The bill (no reduction for Rod): 2,650 Es.

During the night there was an Atlantic gale. I heard much flapping of canvas and plastic, and feared for some of my neighbours' homes. Daisy just rocked gently on her strong German haunches, but in the morning she was nearly buried beneath pine needles.

I took the 7.35am bus, Stagecoach like our local trains at home (except it was only five minutes late), along the coast road past white-horsed seas and through heavy sand-drifts to the local station, Cascais, to catch the 8.05 coastal commuter special to the capital.

My fellow commuters were like commuters everywhere: Mostly quite young and quite smartly dressed, yawning more than smiling.

The girl next to me, in a floral skirt, was reading Orgulho e Preconceito by Jane Austen (the only bits I recognised were Sr Collins and Sr Bennet, but she appeared to be enjoying it).

The man in neat shirt and tie opposite me was less fortunate: He had to look through Microsoft Windows.

THE first things you notice in Lisbon are the trams. Small, racy, bell-ringing and usually yellow, they get everywhere. At speed.

I had near-misses with a couple of them (unlike Gaudí who died after being hit by one in Barcelona) as I climbed from my seaside station to the Alfama district with its small slanting streets and squares of cobbles.

I visited the cathedral and found it introspective and plain, not extro-vert or ornate like others I'd seen. Judging by the battlements on its roof I'd say it may have suffered from a split personality over the years, try-ing to make up its mind whether it stood for Love or War.

Up to Lisbon's most famous landmark, the Castelo de São Jorge, which had no trouble deciding what it stood for: A sentry for centuries over the capital, its walls and towers well fortified and its cannons trained menac-ingly on the broad silver-grey Tagus Estuary.

There was no charge to walk round the castle, but I paid 300 Es to visit the Camera Obscura on top. I love those things: There's one at Greenwich. You stand in a darkened room and watch as the 360 degrees of your surroundings, the city, the river, the ferries, the cars, unravel in front of you on a giant horizontal precursor of the satellite dish.

Unlike at Greenwich, I got a commentary, in English, from one of the two lively young girls in charge. What's more, I got it all to myself because I was their first customer of the day.

Down to the Baixa area, its design more elegant and ordered than much of the city because it had to be rebuilt after being destroyed by an enormous earthquake 250 years earlier. This time I was hoping I would-n't get a world-shaking exclusive.

I walked round Rossio Square, midday hot with pedestrians and traders and shoe-shiners and traffic, uncertain whether I'd be safer keeping clear of the sun or the buildings.

The locals seemed to regard the sun as the more immediate threat, so I followed their lead and carelessly risked being crushed by tons of falling masonry.

I had lunch, served by black-tied, waistcoated and aproned waiters at the art-nouveau Café Nicola, chunkily mirrored, glassed, lit and furnished in silver: Refreshing gazpacho Andaluz soup, endive salad with Roquefort sauce, fizzy water and crusty rolls (not stale). The bill: 1,720 Es.

To the waterfront and the spacious passenger ferry terminal, proud with marble columns and coloured tiles depicting the shields of Portugal's provinces: Less hectic than it would have been before they first bridged the Tagus in the 60s but still busy enough with sailings fanning away across the water every few minutes, as befitted this most seafaring of nations.

It was time to catch a tram, so I waited for a No 15 which would take me back down the estuary to the Jerónimos Monastery.

But when it came it was a real disappointment: It wasn't one of the clanking characterful things I'd seen nipping round town, it was hi-tech and highly-articulated. A smooth-running air-conditioned modern monster.

The monastery was old, though. And magnificent: Ornately carved inside and out with saints and seahorses and elephants, its columns and arches growing from floor to ceiling like palm trees. Much more impressive than the cathedral.

By now, I'd noticed there were also proper trams running on my route, so on the way back I waited for one.

I let a swish cool giant slide by, then got what I wanted: Hot and uncomfortable aboard a jolting old wood-cabined rattler reminiscent of a perfectly preserved Edwardian seafront shelter, air-conditioned only by the wind from its wide-open windows, and furiously ringing its bell at every corner to tell the world to keep out of its way.

Next, another climb: This time to the Biarro Alto district of antique shops and secondhand stores and bohemian bars and cafés, where groups of men seriously and noisily played cards and dominoes on tin tables beneath shady trees.

And I had a welcome dois cervejas before commuting by train and bus back home to Daisy.

IN the morning, I eased Daisy out from between her pine trees, paid 3,190 Es for her release and aimed her north up the coast.

Our first stop was Nazaré, a pretty little fishing village until the scent of tourist cash began to taint its salty nostrils and it set about netting the grocks instead.

Its hideously expanded centre was sardine-packed with visiting cars and coaches, souvenir shops and cafés beneath high-rise holiday blocks. With too-plump landladies on the street corners greedily touting for trade, waving signs at every passing purse and bumbag saying: QUARTOS CHAMBRES ROOMS ZIMMERS APARTAMENTOS.

Meanwhile, half a dozen wrecks from a once proud-prowed, beach-based fishing fleet crumbled to sand alongside the eager shoals of sunbathers.

We drove on, passing several houses with prettily-patterned tile fronts to another Campismo Orbitur, this time near Vila Nova de Gaia, just south of Oporto and the River Douro.

Here, there was plenty of room. In fact they seemed rather relieved to see us, and that night I was one of only three customers when I ate in the camp restaurant.

Next morning, I caught a No 57 bus to Oporto. I didn't have a time for it: All I knew was that there was supposed to be one every 25 minutes. After waiting what seemed rather longer (although this one wasn't Stagecoach) I joined two other passengers on board.

It was a real bone-shaker: It bounced along at high speed, revving and hooting as it criss-crossed the narrow cobbled streets of Vila Nova, showing little respect for other road users but stopping with great frequency and even greater suddenness to sweep more passengers up or hurl them down.

Soon all the seats were full, and it was standing (well, jitterbugging) room only as a crush of forty locals, mainly large ladies of shopping age, clung determinedly to their self-respect.

Eventually Oporto came into view, heaped high above the Douro in the morning mist.

We crossed the steel grey Dom Luis double-decker bridge by the lower level and wound our way through wider but still cobbled streets, past more tile-fronted buildings, to journey's end beside a red telephone kiosk (just like the ones we used to have) near the Praça da Liberdade.

I was right by the main railway station, so I went to have a look at it. And it was brilliant, its huge ticket hall wonderfully tiled with stirring battle scenes and other epic events from Portugal's past.

Oporto wasn't rich. Even near the centre many of the buildings were shabbily begging for urgent repair, and many of the shops were old period pieces: Dark and bare inside, their names quaintly gilded on black glass outside.

But it was real, with no pretences or pretensions. And it was gorgeous.

I walked down to the river and the Church of Saint Francis, and it was a real Lo and Behold job: A joyful tumult of gold leaf and flower and cherub and angel and saint and whirligig and curlicue as far as the eye could see.

Below, huge catacombs contained the numbered tombs of former members of the congregation, laid down beneath statues of stone skulls like cases of port in a cellar.

But not improving with age.

Next, the grand Palácio da Bolsa, the former stock exchange building completed less than a century before. Its huge main hall was bedecked with the crests of friendly trading nations. Its highlight: The dazzling Arab Room, cribbed from the Alhambra and almost as intricate, but more colourful in gold, green and red.

Back to the imposing Plaça da Liberdade, triumphant testimony to a democratic freedom gratefully retrieved less than 25 years earlier, to sip an ice-cool strawberry milk shake at a shady table on one of its elegant mosaic-patterned pavements.

(All right, I admit it: It was a McDonalds).

Then a climb to the cathedral, solidly serious on the outside like Lisbon's. But I can't tell you what it was like inside because when I got there it was closed for lunch, and the time had come for me to get a taste of what Oporto is really about.

I descended by steep steps and alleys, between food stalls and clothes stalls, beneath balconies and washing, to the Douro's little quayside market (a proper one, not a grock trap) then walked back to Vila Nova across the Dom Luis bridge.

My first Port of Call was Taylor's, where they welcomed me with a cool glass of white port in the big reception hall of their opulent lodge as peacocks paraded in the rose garden.

Then I was shown round the cellars with their huge vats and smaller (but not small) barrels, before being given a glass of 1991 Late Bottled Vintage which I drank on the terrace with its magnificent view of the city and the river. It was all free.

My second Call of Port was Graham's, just as opulent looking, with another spacious reception hall displaying bottles and old leather-bound ledgers and other exhibits.

No free drink before the tour this time, but afterwards I got three glasses: One white, one 1992 Late Bottled Vintage and one ten-year-old tawny. With nice little biscuits. And, again, all free.

My third Thought of Crawl was Ferreira: Less posh perhaps (their reception area was more like a warehouse) but after the tour I was given a glass of white and a four-year-old tawny. And loads of biscuits.

My fourth Fall of Cork was Kopke, where there wasn't a reception area and they didn't bother with a tour (perhaps thinking that in my case it wouldn't really be worth it).

They just sat me down in the gallery overlooking their vats and barrels and gave me two glasses of white and three glasses of red, a ruby, a ten-year-old tawny and a 1992 Late Bottled Vintage. And each glass seemed to be better than the last.

In fact, I enjoyed them so much I wondered in a fleeting moment of conscience whether I should fall into their trap and actually buy a bottle.

Fortunately, though, I was still quite capable of working out that that was out of the question: It could prejudice my integrity as a writer.

So I slurred my excuses and left. I'd had a dozen glasses of port and half a barrel of biscuits. And they hadn't cost me an E.

But the best thing was that the No 57 stopped right outside the door.

I SLEPT well, thanks more to the port than to all the late-night air-raid sirens and early-morning explosions that disturbed the peace of the campismo.

But if such belligerent sounds meant Portugal had been deprived of democracy again overnight, there was no indication of it when we crossed the Douro and drove north, as the land grew greener with sweet-corn and vine among wooded hills, to La Coruña, in Spain's north-west corner.

La Coruña was surprisingly modern considering its long seafaring his-tory (including the departure of The Armada).

I drank coffee beside the docks, which still contained a couple of fight-ing ships. But the main fleet was for the benefit of fishmongers, not war-mongers.

Then we drove along Spain's spectacular north coast, rugged with rocks and sand, stopping for the night high above the waves at Camping los Cantiles, near Luarca. A beautiful site, with a beautiful view. And beautifully kept, with blue hydrangeas and pink geraniums. But a cool reception.

The place seemed to be run by a mother and son. I don't know if they'd just had a row and thought I would be a good person to take it out on, or if they each separately took an instant dislike to me. But when I got there I was made to feel my arrival was a bit of an inconvenience.

That night, I was lulled to sleep by the lapping of the waves. In the morning, I woke to a cloudy grey Atlantic seascape with rocky cliffs and headlands just like Cornwall.

And to prove the point, just as we were leaving, it started to rain.

I still had 10,500 escudos in my pocket, so I decided to change them into pesetas at nearby Avilés. I parked Daisy (eventually) and found a bank calling itself: CAMBIO EXCHANGE CHANGE WECHSEL.

Then I ran into computer trouble of a high order.

A fat cashier with a moustache spent nearly ten minutes calling up and keying in all kinds of information including my full name and nationality (slowed down by many a consultation of a hefty handbook) and swept 1,210p in my direction.

Even with my dodgy maths I knew that wasn't right, and shoved them back. He then angrily adopted a Take-It-Or-Take-It attitude, and relations between us, already cool, sank below zero.

It's good news for the world that I've never attempted the job of managing other people's money, but even I spotted what he'd done before he did: He'd keyed in 1,500 Es instead of 10,500. I indicated this to him, and he reluctantly agreed to start again.

He spent another five minutes discordantly fat-fingering and thumbing his keyboard, and threw me 8,468p. I've no idea if that was the correct amount, but it represented a sizeable victory.

So I signed the form he hurled at me, and took my money.

East along that Cornish coast, in that Cornish weather. I stopped for diesel, and decided I'd better check Daisy's oil again. It was below the minimum, even though it was only 1,500 miles since I'd last dosed her.

My poor Daisy seemed to be running out, not running in. I administered her another litre, this time down in one.

Gijón was a big, ugly place which couldn't decide if it was there for industry or tourism. But it had a fine sandy beach full of under-dressed holidaymakers doing what holidaymakers do everywhere: Kidding themselves they're having a great time, no matter what the weather.

The sea was grey and menacing, with breakers big enough to keep half a dozen surfers on their toes.

Giddy from winding roads, between misted mountains and unblemished beaches, to Llanes, with more sand and surf and a little harbour (and a name which looks as if it might feel more at home in Wales than in Cornwall) where I straightened myself out with a coffee and a roll.

We stopped for the night above Zarautz and its broad sweep of beach and knobbly lighthouse promontory, where the Pyrenees came down to meet the Bay of Biscay.

Here, as happy campers huddled together in their vans and tents, it stopped raining and started pouring.

Next morning, I drove to San Sebastián early enough to be able to park Daisy without difficulty, and I watched it come to life. In sunshine.

It was a real Basque beauty, its bay a threequarter circle of natural harbour, inviting sand and an elegant esplanade wonderfully adorned with wrought iron.

A large sign, complete with artist's impression, showed me they were building a new Kursaal entertainment complex, which surprised me because the only Kursaal I knew was the one in Southend.

You know: Where The Kursaal Flyers came from, and heroically rhymed the words laundry and quandary in their song, Little Does She Know (That I Know That She Knows That I Know She's Two-Timing Me).

The Old Town was superb, with its narrow paved streets and its tall geranium-balconied buildings. I had coffee in stylish Constitution Square while, above me, the Virgin Mary kept her hilltop watch over the city.

LEND an ear, Vincent. I've seen your favourite models line-dancing across France, turning first this way then that with the sun, just as their French name, tournesol, so perfectly describes.

Here, they brazenly turn their blooming yellow faces towards us to show off their shining glory. There, they coyly turn their green heads away from us for fear we might deflower their modesty.

Daisy and I drove north through a million sunflowers to Bordeaux and, as the vines became more plentiful and the châteaux more prosperous, the Médoc.

The state of repair of the Médoc châteaux was astonishing: Most grand old buildings need of a bit of cash spending on them nowadays, but not these.

The little green beauties they owed their existence to were still coming up with the maintenance money.

Many of the rows of vines had roses (red, of course) growing at the ends of them. Apparently, this used to be a traditional early warning system for disease: The roses would be affected first, then action could be taken to protect the vines.

It was time for us to pick our way through another wine list: Margaux. Saint-Julien. Latour. Pauillac. Mouton-Rothschild.

At Saint-Estèphe, where I stopped for coffee beside the dirty brown waters of the Gironde, I was alarmed to learn that the forbidding grey concrete complex of towers and domes on the opposite bank was a nuclear power station.

(I hope it never Chernobyls over the vignobles: Those early-warning roses would really have their work cut out).

128

We returned to Pauillac and booked in at the Camping Municipal. Then I made an appointment to visit nearby Château Pichon-Longueville.

Hi-tech and high finance, it turned out to be owned by the giant Axa insurance group.

I was shown round the science-laboratory underground chambers where the wine is made, but not round the château itself, which isn't inhabited any more but is used just for business entertaining.

It all seemed a long way removed from the land. You almost got the impression that if it hadn't been for the fact that it's the end product, the wine would have been a bit of an inconvenience.

In fact, the stainless steel vats looked rather like a smaller subterranean version of that nuclear power station. Oh well, business is business.

We left Pauillac in the morning, and drove to the tip of the Médoc where I paid 215 francs for a bumpy half-hour ferry crossing of the mouth of the Gironde.

Next, to La Rochelle where I forked out another 110 francs to take the toll bridge to the flat featureless Île de Ré pointing pointlessly out into the Atlantic.

It was jammed with grocks on foot, on bikes and motorbikes, in cars and vans and coaches. And such natural beauty as it possessed was scarred by the services they seek: Souvenir stalls, snack bars and camp-sites.

Popular though it was, I couldn't see its attraction. Near the far end was a village called Ars. I'm afraid that word summed up my feelings for the place.

I had a crêpe beneath the lighthouse, and left.

La Rochelle was far more interesting and attractive, especially round the fortified Old Port. With yachts (proper ones, with sails). And cafés and restaurants (proper ones, on wide pavements beneath awnings in front of attractive old buildings). And stalls (proper ones, forming a street market selling arts and crafts).

And the station was a belter. In the same division as Huddersfield (yes, the first) with magnificently ornate façade proudly displaying SNCF sign and tricolores. And tall round clocktower designed to reflect the fortifications of the Old Port.

Up the crowded coast, past the packed Sables-d'Olonne, to the climax of the trip: Saint-Marc-sur-Mer, in Brittany, where 45 years earlier the great Jacques Tati excelled at tennis, table tennis and pyrotechnics, and immortalised summer at the seaside in the most charming film ever made, Monsieur Hulot's Holiday.

I dropped Daisy off at Camping de l'Eve and, without once stopping my humming of the film's theme tune, strode into town to see if they remembered its star.

And they did: A street sign on the front of the post office announced that the main square was called Place Jacques Tati.

Not only that, but there was a statue of Monsieur Hulot on the little wooden ship's deck of a promenade overlooking the beach, in typical pose: Leaning forward, hands on back of hips, trousers at half mast, jacket open and hat rim awry.

The pipe in his mouth had been broken off, but to compensate for this someone had stuck a toothbrush behind his ear. And somehow it seemed entirely appropriate.

Best of all, the outside of the Hôtel de la Plage (one of the other stars of the film) was almost unchanged.

I went in for a meal, and as surprisingly large ships passed surprisingly close to the beach on their way in and out of next door Saint-Nazaire I sat at a window table and watched this year's supporting cast:

A teenage lad wearing only swimming trunks, but carrying an umbrella. A boy in a jumper two sizes too long for him, kicking a football against the rocks. Two cartwheeling girls. A little brother showing off to a littler sister how many press-ups he could do.

At 9.30, with no hint of sun in the evening sky, the teenage lad (still wearing only swimming trunks but now minus umbrella) reappeared, strode purposefully down the beach and dived unhesitatingly into the unwelcoming waves.

By 10, as light grey evening turned to dark grey night, the lone football boy had acquired five pals and a full-scale match was in progress: Long jumpers versus short jumpers.

Kids climbed on the rocks, couples ambled arm in arm, dogs were walked, and the beach was the busiest it had been at any time since I'd arrived.

To this day, if Jacques the Genius had been wanting to bring Monsieur Hulot and his Holiday to life, he couldn't have found a more suitable background to set them against.

During the night it became wet and windy. And cold. I knew I was nearly home. It was time to get the cricket sweater out again.

Between green fields and beneath grey clouds to Rennes, a pleasing blend of old and new and large and small, with lopsided little half-timbered bars and cafés and bigger, more dignified civic buildings as befits the Breton capital.

A group of young morris dancers performed self-consciously to an accordion in front of the Mairie, trying to remember to smile through their concentration. They looked just as daft as British ones but sounded less ridiculous, without bells on.

Pausing only for Daisy gratefully to lap up yet another litre of oil, we headed for France's north coast.

One thing about Mont-Saint-Michel: You can't miss it. Although it was raining hard, a roadsign said we were 22k away when I first saw its famous profile piercing the grey-washed skies.

And what a popular attraction it was, with a sea of mudflats on one side and a sea of parked vehicles on the other.

I joined the thousands of dripping refugees (driven from the beaches by the rain) as they impeded each other's progress in trying to climb the cobbled path to the top, between the ice cream stalls and the souvenir shops.

It cost me 30 francs to park Daisy, 40 francs to enter the abbey and two francs for a pee. I hope they put all the money to good use: They must take more in a week than Wembley Stadium could take in a year.

It wasn't ornate with wonderful works of art. But it was an incredible creation, if only for its size. There weren't just buildings up there, there were gardens too. Maybe they deserved all that money of mine just for having had the daring to do it.

It was time to check into our last campsite on this trip, Camping du Nicet, just outside Saint-Malo.

SO what are we campers like? Well, we're: Practical, organised, efficient. (That's why the Germans are so good at it). Clean, tidy, caring, sharing, uncomplaining, easily satisfied and content with our lot.

We're happy to make our own entertainment: Husbands and wives will sit for hours playing cards, chess, draughts, dominoes, dice, backgammon, Scrabble etc. (They find it easier than having to talk to each other).

And you wouldn't believe what we take with us: Tables and chairs and boats and bicycles and barbecues and washing machines and pets and children and every conceivable convenience and encumbrance.

Of course, like everybody else, we have our own pecking order. We motor caravanners, for example, are vastly superior to the conventional caravanners: Those misguided people who (laboriously) hitch and unhitch their mobile home so they can (just as laboriously) tow it along behind them.

They're a strange breed: Not the type to clean the car once a week. More the type to clean it once a day.

At Bracciano, I watched a middle-aged Brit conscientiously clean his for 45 minutes. Then his wife came out of their caravan, and they polished it together for another 30. At Pésaro, I saw a geriatric German with a large broom strenuously sweeping sand off a path a good 20 metres away from his van.

But even the caravanners are infinitely more exalted than the statics: Those sad folk who choose to spend their holidays in a mobile home that isn't even mobile.

They've condemned themselves to putting up with all the head-banging inconvenience of living in a confined space, but with none of the free-range benefits of being able to get about. Staying in the same place and looking at the same sights all the time.

You've seen them in England: It's not as if most of them even choose particularly attractive places. They're often stuck by a busy road or a rubbish tip or a sewage works, and there's no escape.

For them, camping isn't a means of exploring the world. It's an end in itself. Like playing house: Many of them have created their own little gardens, so they can't even get away from the work-a-day chores of weeding and watering.

Although it pains me to say it, there is one group above us motor caravanners in the pecking order, though: The tenters. Those who travel by car or motorbike or pedal bike or on foot (or by canoe in the case of some of our fellow campers at La Charité on the Loire) free from the worries of height barriers and other bureaucratic restrictions.

But I didn't envy them having to put up or take down their homes when it was too wet, or sweatily battle to hammer their pegs into rock-hard ground when it was too dry.

Our last night cost us 162 francs. This camping business was becoming expensive: It was time to go home. I did some housework, giving Daisy a wipe and a sweep, then we drove into Saint-Malo.

The Chauffeur had told me to get some wine, so I stopped at a supermarket and bought a case of Sancerre to export home, because it's a nice, crisp, dry… Oh all right, because we'd liked the place it came from.

Then I parked Daisy beneath the walls of the Old Town. Saint-Malo was a forlorn sight that morning as the rain swept in from the sea.

But it was built for it: Stone-solid against anything an unfriendly northern climate could throw at it. Attractive enough, but with no time for the fripperies or refinements of the south.

I sat at a pavement café (glad of its protective awning) and had petit déjeuner of orange juice, croissant, and coffee. And as the wet cobbles sloshed beneath the wheels of a new day I said Au Revoir to the continent.

The Chauffeur had booked Daisy and me a £148 passage to Portsmouth aboard the Brittany Ferry Bretagne.

When we got to the port their computer was expecting us so, along with a full cargo of 600 vehicles and their occupants (mainly Brits), we had a smooth boarding. And a smooth crossing.

Back home, I gave The Chauffeur a cuddle. And I looked up oleaginous. It meant: Oily. Maybe not the perfect word to describe oleander, but ideal to describe my travels with Daisy.

YEAR TWO

Daisy Among The Cráic Addicts

THE chief beauty of this book lies not so much in its literary style, or in the extent and usefulness of the information it conveys, as in its simple truthfulness.
JEROME K JEROME, *Three Men In A Boat*

10

Pembroke Dock - Rosslare - Wexford - Gorey - Avoca - Kilkenny -
Waterford - Clonea - Ardmore - Youghal - Ballymaloe - Kinsale -
Skibbereen - Castletownshend - Baltimore - Creagh - Ballydehob -
Mizen Head - Barleycove - Crookhaven - Sheep's Head - Macroom -
Blarney - Mallow - Cork - Glengarriff

CARAVANNING: The new Rock 'n' Roll. That's what I'd heard on the radio. Great: It meant Daisy, The Chauffeur and I were trendy (although it was hard to believe as we queued for the ferry with all the other Old Age Travellers and their motor caravans at Pembroke Dock in West Wales).

The oilcoholic Daisy had been given a clean bill of health during the winter: If I'd studied the small print in one of her many handbooks, I was told, I'd have realised it would be quite normal for her to lap up several litres of oil in her first few thousand miles. (She'd been grateful for another dose shortly before we set off).

It was early May, and we were on our travels again: This time to Ireland.

We joined about 500 other passengers aboard the Irish Ferry Isle of Innisfree and slipped out of misty Milford Haven (making a better job of avoiding the rocks than many before us) to a Gael Warning from the skipper: "Now it's windy out there, so it'll be a bit bumpy now."

He said something like that anyway, although the combination of his Irish accent and his Irish loudspeaker made it hard to be sure (to be sure).

Certainly, the group of grey-faced French schoolkids sitting in a circle and gazing gloomily into paper bags (FOR YOUR CONVENIENCE) would have been in no condition to argue. Especially the one who'd just missed his target.

As we crossed the Irish Sea the winds were behind us, so we reached rainy Rosslare 10 minutes early. At first sight, there appeared to be as much water lying on the land as off it, but a cheerfully optimistic sign said: WELCOME TO THE SUNNY SOUTH EAST. Another told us, thoughtfully: STOP FOR RED LIGHTS

The Chauffeur switched on Daisy's headlights (although it was still afternoon) and we headed up the coast. The first things we noticed, apart from the weather, were:

1. The houses were smaller.
2. The churches were bigger.
3. The post boxes were green.

We joined a gaggle of bedraggled campers, English, Irish, German and Dutch, at the Ferrybank campsite on windswept Wexford seafront. Cost: 10 punts a night (about 8.50 sterling) for the three of us. Facilities: Basic, but including a cosy little TV room where a notice on the wall said: NO SMOKING AT ALL (at all).

Our Irish camping guidebook had told us that the town centre was just a five-minute walk from the site, over a bridge. But if it wasn't the longest five-minute walk in the world, it was certainly the most exposed: Mallory and Irvine may or may not have conquered Everest. They'd never have made it across that bridge, though. Not in just their tweed suits and hob-nail boots.

Wexford, once we got there, was wonderful: Many of the shops in the narrow main street sold modern goods (computers, mobile phones etc), but all the buildings were small and old-fashioned. It was as if the likes of WH O'Smith and FW O'Woolworth had never existed.

There were loads of bookies, barbers and butchers. And masses of bars, cafés and restaurants, all incredibly busy. One establishment, Macken's, announced itself as a BAR OFF-LICENCE AND UNDER-TAKER (all equally revered in Ireland).

We went into welcoming Tim's Tavern, with its MENU FROM THE LAND and MENU FROM THE TRAWLER, and from the moment my first pint of Guinness was creamily poured, in two settling stages, I knew I was going to feel at home.

(As any Irishman will tell you, the perfect pint of Guinness should take six and a half minutes to serve).

Most of our fellow customers were wearing Manchester United shirts: The Irish seemed to have managed to separate themselves from our government, but not from our football.

A notice on the wall referred to CLOSING HOURS, not Opening Hours as it would have done in England. (A more crucial consideration, I suppose).

Talk, even in drink, seemed to be quieter, more discreet, than in the pubs back home. Conversation in Ireland is too important, too cherished an art, to be to raucously bandied about in public.

Next, to the friendly Sky and the Ground (beneath the Heaven's Above restaurant) where important old lettering above the bar proclaimed: TEAS COFFEES COCOAS HERBS SPICES STOUTS PORTERS

WHISKEYS BRANDIES TOBACCOS SNUFFS WINE MERCHANTS.

And here the cráic, as well as the Guinness, was excellent: Four guitarists and a drummer of varying ages and hair lengths came and sat at the table reserved for musicians and, to the obvious pleasure of a growing audience, unassumingly started a gentle music session (unplugged, but not diddly-diddly) which included a lilting interpretation of Jimi Hendrix's All Along The Watchtower.

In the morning, more rain battered Daisy's roof but this time in the form of heavy showers between spells of cheerful sunshine which lit up the old town quay as well as a pair of passing trawlers.

I kept my washing activities to a minimum in the spartan toilet block: Showering didn't seem to take on such a high priority in chilly Ireland as in sweaty Spain. And anyway, I didn't fancy forking out for the tokens.

North through gorse-hedged fields, confused by signposts which pointed in many more directions than the roads, to encounter:

1. A couple of hitch-hiking pensioners (but we were too surprised to think of stopping to give them a lift).

2. A Dalmatian dog (which did its best to run under Daisy's front wheels).

3. Half a dozen magnificently slow drivers (not all of them on board tractors).

To busy little Gorey, where dozens of disconcertingly young mums paraded with buggies full of babies as older folk filled the town's benches to take advantage of the few moments' sunshine and admire the chaos on road and pavement.

The Chauffeur parked Daisy outside Whytes the Newsagents where a notice in the window said PAPAL BLESSINGS ARRANGED (but there was no sign of the Holy Father) and we went for morning coffee at The Country Kitchen, frantically busy of course and proud of a menu FOR VEGETARIANS OR FOR A CHANGE.

On the way out I was nobbled by a young lad who told me he was selling scratchcards in aid of handicapped kids. I gave him two punts, but failed to win a car.

As I walked away, he happily called after me: "Now congratulations, you've just been ripped off by a charity now."

North again, taking in our first stretch of Irish dual carriageway, to Arklow where we stopped for diesel. I got out and was about to start filling Daisy when a man came and stood beside me and started talking about the weather.

In Ireland, of course, this isn't at all unusual. But I'm not stupid: I soon twigged. He was a pump attendant. (I remember them well).

Narrowly avoiding a couple more stray dogs, we drove to the pretty village of Avoca. (To you: Ballykissangel).

We parked near a sign saying ROAD UNSAFE FOR HORSE CARAVANS (nothing about Cat Caravans) and walked past Ballykissangel Mini Market to Fitzgerald's Crafts Shop.

Here, there was a real panic on: A red-haired girl had left her Visa card behind, and the staff were desperate to find her and return it.

(Unfortunately the description of her didn't narrow things down much: A red-haired girl? In Ireland?)

So to Fitzgerald's Pub, Ireland's most famous TV bar, to raise a pint of Guinness in memory of the gorgeous Assumpta beneath signs saying: MISSING WIFE AND DOG - REWARD FOR DOG and THEY'VE FOUND SOMETHING THAT DOES THE WORK OF FIVE MEN - ONE WOMAN.

By sunlit valleys of dripping trees and bluebelled river banks to misty Wicklow Mountains and boulder-strewn Wicklow Gap, where a fast-flowing mountain stream was too full of itself to know which route to take.

We stopped at the summit viewing point but unfortunately, that day, the view had been cancelled.

We passed signs saying DANGEROUS BRIDGE AHEAD. (But not why or in what way: Would it give way beneath us?)

Through the village of Hollywood and across the Liffey to Naas, in the heart of horse and gorse country, where every car was blowing its horn in celebration of a wedding which had taken over the town.

Then more confusing signs, this time telling us: DO NOT PASS. (We wondered whether they meant we should stop immediately, but decided they were just telling us we weren't allowed to overtake).

Across the evergreen plains to the ancient and modern city of Kilkenny where, as usual, most of the local dogs came out to greet us.

The Irish didn't seem to have got the idea of dogs at all: They tended to leave them to fend for themselves, rarely keeping them under control or taking them for walks.

(When you saw them taking their horses for a walk, though, they were always on a lead).

To the Tree Grove campsite and a warm friendly greeting from boss man Dan on a wet unwelcoming evening. Farmer Dan had clearly decided that rotating grocks had one big advantage over rotating crops: He could chat to them.

And so he did (at length) telling us all about the delights of the area and his wife's pregnancy.

When he'd finally finished, we handed over eight punts for a one-night stay, left Daisy and walked past the imposing castle into Kilkenny where we visited Cleere's Theatre Bar, full of old photos and posters of fondly-recalled productions.

There was English football on the telly, Spurs v Chelsea, so naturally the locals were taking a keen interest.

I did wonder what they made of the recruitment ads for the British Army at half-time, but didn't like to ask. (Subject: How to treat a bomb victim).

The place was packed (obviously) and next came the live music: A did-dly-diddly session this time, played at the reserved table by Mick Walsh and pals, squeezing, strumming and tapping away beneath an intimate oil portrait on the wall of a pint of Guinness.

Again the performance was shyly understated without a hint of show-manship or presumption, just a trace of Guinness froth on the top lip of each of the musicians, which couldn't be wiped away once each new number had begun. And again it was good cráic: People got up and started dancing, although there clearly wasn't room for it.

We paid five punts for a tape of Mick's music, like the good grockles we were, and he never stopped thanking us.

Then it was back through the rain-glistening streets past the butcher, the baker and the bookmaker to the dry cosiness of Daisy.

Sunshine and rain again in the morning. (Oh, all right then: Rain and sunshine). But the toilet facilities were adequate, if basic, and the hot showers were free.

Past a thousand ugly bungalows, built to suburban tastes but miles from any suburb, to Waterford where we left Daisy near the People's Park (more continental-sounding than English) and walked into town along the river front.

To the City Square shopping mall, our closest Irish encounter yet with the outside world, to be transported forward in time by the sight of 21st century Specsavers, Next and Burger King.

We explored the pedestrianised city centre streets, busy with young people, bars, cafés, restaurants and Shaws department store, proudly boasting in large letters above its main entrance: ALMOST NATION-WIDE.

Like most places in Ireland, Waterford seemed to be plagued with mas-sive roadworks which severely restricted the traffic flow.

But of course I should have realised: After hurling, fishing, racing and football, digging holes in the road is an Irishman's favourite sport.

So to see what Waterford is famous for: The Crystal Glass Factory. A serious attraction this, complete with café, tourist information centre, bureau de change and grand piano accompanist beneath purple chandelier in the middle of the huge gift shop.

And, horrifyingly, The Chauffeur managed to drop a giant glass candlestick (price: 109 punts) on to a glass shelf.

A tremendous crack reverberated around the room, a hundred people stared at us and a blue-uniformed girl assistant was on the scene in less than five seconds.

But fortunately no damage was done. (Other than to our nerves).

We paid 3.50 each to do the factory tour and watch the three main stages of the glass-making process: Blowing, cutting and engraving.

The blowers looked the jolliest: Ruddy-faced full-bellied men puffing away like an oompah band in teams of three or four, and paid piecework for every item that passed inspection. (If any member of the team failed to complete his appointed task satisfactorily then none of his team would be paid).

It was hot work, and most of them looked as if they might have been known to down a pint or two of Guinness afterwards. They reminded me of rugby forwards whose job was to feed the nimble threequarter line of cutters and engravers.

The cutters had a gentler, cooler job, with machines to do all the hard work. The engravers were the most skilled, paid by the hour and sometimes spending weeks honing the same piece.

All the skilled work was done by men. Women were involved only with quality control and with packaging. The reason given for this by our (girl) guide was that the company couldn't afford to give women the lengthy training required in case they then decided to leave and have children.

The Chauffeur wasn't too impressed with this argument, and we took it as another sign that in some respects Ireland still has a little way to go when it comes to keeping up with developments in other parts of the world.

SOUTH to wealthy suburb-by-the-sea Tramore where I bought milk at a small supermarket and the cheery checkout girl greeted me as if I was an old friend.

The radio was on, and the voices coming from it sounded just the same as on ours: Terry Wogan, Henry Kelly, Alan Green etc. Once again, I felt quite at home.

Along the rocky coast, past much-needed ports in a storm and over foam-spattered roads, to find (eventually) Clonea and Casey's Caravan Park.

We took a number of wrong turnings first, owing to the fact that the

Irish didn't yet appear to have discovered the No Through Road sign.

(Our camping guidebook somehow seemed to be worded in a way that made it easier for us to work out with hindsight how we should have found camps than how to find them in the first place).

When we finally got to Casey's it appeared to be closed: The toilet block was locked, and there was nobody about.

But on our second circuit of the camp we spied a rustic fellow leaning on a shovel, and asked if he knew whether it would be possible for us to stay the night.

"Now of course you can," he said. "And I'll bring you your toilet block keys in five minutes now."

He went on to apologise for the fact that the weather had broken, implying that up till now they'd had nothing but sunshine in these parts.

He didn't fool us, though: This corner of the isle looked just as emerald as the rest.

Resisting the risk of drinking too much tea beforehand, we awaited the promised delivery of the toilet keys.

(One good thing about Ireland: The water doesn't make the tea as scummy as it does in London. Well, it probably hasn't passed through as many people's bodies).

Our man was as good as his word (well, almost). Just 20 minutes later he was back to give us our His 'n' Hers keys.

And he turned out to be none other than our proprietor, Mr Casey himself, another rotator of grocks and a devoted Man United fan who was keen to spend the next half an hour chatting about his team and bemoaning the jealousy of the ABUs (those whose idea of football loyalty meant supporting Anybody But United).

Mr Casey's place was far plusher than our first two camps, the toilet block boasting patterned tiles, ornate wooden entrance doors and classically-columned portico that any suburban bungalow owner could have been proud of (in town or country).

It was a large site, but we had the whole place to ourselves apart from a Kiwi couple who were spending a year touring Europe in a bigger relative of Daisy's.

Clonea beach was magnificent, although when we were there the weather wouldn't have tempted you to lounge about on it.

We took a brisk evening walk along it, then headed for the welcome shelter of the Strand Hotel bar.

WEST on a bright breezy morning, to the accompaniment of Mick Walsh and his diddly men, past contented dairy herds munching the world's greenest grass to the pretty village of Ardmore, almost deserted ahead of the new summer season but with another impressive stretch of beach where a sign instructed us:

LEAVE ONLY YOUR FOOTPRINTS ON THE SAND

To the walled port of Youghal, pronounced Yawl (or Y'all if you're from the southern states of America).

It was most famous for having been clapboarded up to become a New England fishing village for the film of Moby Dick, starring Gregory (Ahab) Peck and his crew.

Those exciting days were still commemorated by the existence of Moby Dick's Bar beside the harbour.

Next stop: Shanagarry and the scrumptious Ballymaloe Cookery School Gardens, creation of TV cook Darina Allen, with fruit, veg and herbs well guarded by trees, hedges and wicker scarecrows (male and female).

Its highlight: The octagonal gothic folly of its Shell House, with walls and ceiling fantastically smothered in seashells of all shapes and sizes from around the world.

Obviously, lunch in the brightly-painted Garden Café, fresh shrimps with homemade mayo and salad followed by green gooseberry compôte with vanilla ice cream at 7.40 a head, was delicious.

Inland to Midleton, narrowly avoiding half a dozen more stray dogs, and Cork City. We decided to postpone the pleasures of Cork for another day, and headed instead for Kinsale and the coast.

But before we left we had time to notice that Cork was twinned with Coventry, Rennes, San Francisco and Cologne (which must make Coventry a twin of San Francisco).

We also noticed that Irish railways still had proper old-fashioned signals, not just lights, like we used to have.

In Kinsale The Chauffeur parked Daisy beside the yacht-filled harbour, outside Dino's Traditional Take-Away, and we walked into the sunny town centre with its bright red benches, where the bars, restaurants and shops were each painted a different colour: Red, blue, yellow and green, including the Blue Haven Hotel (yellow) with its old clock giving the high-tide times as well as the time of day.

It was like a colouring-book version of Salcombe in Devon. (All right, so it was a bit twee, a bit over the top, designed to bring in us grockles by land and sea, but you had to give them credit for making the effort).

Prices of properties in the window of estate agents Victoria Murphy and Daughter (also yellow) weren't cheap. You didn't get much for less than 150,000 punts, but the descriptions were encouraging:

ONCE AGAIN THE AREA IS RURAL AND YET HAS NEIGH-

144

BOURS
THE ACCESS ROAD AT PRESENT IS BUMPY BUT THIS WILL
BE IMPROVED SHORTLY
THIS PROPERTY IS SITUATED MORE OR LESS IN THE TOWN

Both the scenery and the place names became more Irish as we headed west through Ballinspittle and Clonakilty.

We ended the day at The Hideaway campsite, Skibbereen, where we got another friendly welcome, this time from the Lady of the Camp.

Next morning we drove beneath threatening skies, between white bluebells, to the little creekside quay at Castletownshend where we watched a crafty heron angularly angling for fish in the shallows, virtually invisible against the slate-grey shore.

The steep main street (oh all right, only street) was so narrow that The Chauffeur had to drive Daisy on to the pavement to avoid the two trees which sprouted from the middle of it.

The village was home to Edith Somerville, and here she and her cousin Violet from Ross, County Galway, wrote the Irish RM stories as Somerville and Ross.

Next: The little harbour town of Baltimore, to walk the perilous cliff to its comical conical beacon, a welcoming white landmark for yachtsmen and fishermen, and to admire the miraculous views over land and sea.

We asked at the post office if there was anywhere we could have coffee, and the postmaster said he'd be happy to serve it to us in his tearoom.

But, he warned: "There'll be no cakes now, because it won't be open till June."

(It reminded me of Nigel Jenkins, one of my Strawberry Hill golfing pals, who went on a fishing holiday in Ireland. One morning the weather was so dreadful that he and his mates decided to forget about fishing and go to the pub instead. They walked in and ordered drinks but the landlord said he was sorry, he couldn't serve them because he wasn't open yet. If they went and sat down, though, he'd bring them drinks to have while they were waiting).

To lovely Creagh Gardens, their green peace punctuated with rhododendron, camellia, azalea and magnolia, where a notice informed us in words far too British to be British:
LADIES AND GENTLEMAN WILL NOT AND OTHERS MUST
NOT PICK THE FLOWERS OR SHRUBS

The highlight here: The romantic walled garden, a cheerful coming-together of stick and stone and slate and gravel and glass and hedge and fruit and veg and herb and lupin and foxglove and hen and goose and buttercup and daisy and the ugliest, most cantankerous turkey you ever met.

A couple of gardeners were busy preening and planting for the new season: A fine sight for those of us who are keen gardeners, but only in our minds.

It made me think of the pleasure we get from all the cookery programmes on the telly: We spend hours watching others going to endless trouble as they intricately prepare exciting home-made meals, then we go out and buy boring ready-made ones from Sainsburys.

With spectacular views, past Roaringwater Bay to Ballydehob and its bookshop-café called Clara, where two locals were agreeing what a lovely day it was. (Well, it was only drizzling).

As is the rule in Ireland, we placed our order at the counter, then they brought it to us. A sensible arrangement: There's nothing more tension-inducing than sitting at a café table waiting to be served when you haven't even got as far as placing your order.

(Unlike in England, though, they wouldn't think of asking you for any money until you left).

Through trendy-looking Schull, proud of its planetarium, past ocean-blue views of distant Fastnet Rock as dull afternoon turned to bright evening. So by pink seas of thrift to Ireland's Land's End, Mizen Head.

An understated Land's End, this, with no souvenir stalls or burger bars or ice cream vans, but you did have to pay to walk across the bridge to the lighthouse and the Mizen Vision Centre (sponsored by Murphy's Stout) which told us tales of lights and lifeboats and heroism and disaster.

To nearby Barleycove Holiday Park and another friendly reception, this time from a boss man spattered with fresh-season paint who refused to take more than five punts from us because the camp's facilities weren't fully open.

We walked beside untrodden beaches between hedges of pink fuchsia and fields of yellow iris to Crookhaven, a cluster of pubs, shops and homes clinging together for company beside a tiny quay.

We ate and drank at the Crookhaven Inn but were the only customers, gaining the impression that the village wouldn't be there at all if it wasn't for the tourists who would flock in to fill it later in the season.

The camp was in the quietest location so far: There aren't many places in the British Isles where, for long periods of time, you can't hear any human or mechanical sounds, but this was one.

In the morning we sat over breakfast and watched a fox and two rabbits snootily ignoring each other on a hillside less than 50 yards from Daisy's open side door.

Sunnily by rugged roads, beside calm reflective waters and nesting swans, to Ahakista with its memorial to the 329 who died aboard the Air

India jumbo jet which dived into the sea 14 years earlier off this most peaceful of coasts.

Next: Cut-off Sheep's Head. The Chauffeur took Daisy as far as she could go, then we walked the last boggy mile to the lighthouse which was manned for the day by a couple of maintenance men happily drinking tea in their shirtsleeves.

The air was still, and we marvelled at the smoothness of Bantry Bay. (If there was one thing I'd confidently expected it was that Atlantic breakers, crashing across from the other Baltimore, would have been beating the hell out of it).

And it was nice not to have to worry about snakes: I all but sat on a basking adder one similarly sunny day when The Chauffeur and I were walking the Pembrokeshire Coast Path.

By tiny winding roads, as green as grey, beside the bay to Bantry (where a civilised proportion of the businesses were closed for lunch) to buy campers' provisions at the Super Valu supermarket.

Across country, with many a hold-up for cattle, to the old market town of Macroom where my eye was caught by a bookmaker's sign: MARGO ANN MURPHY.

Forget William Hill and Joe Coral, the name was too attractive to resist. And so was Margo: She was blonde, she was beautiful, and she was generous. (Well even I can pick a winner occasionally).

So to an informatively chatty welcome at Blarney Caravan and Camping Park. And in the morning we set off to do what you go to Blarney to do: We paid 3.50 each to get into Blarney Castle, climb to the top and queue (with coachloads of Americans) to kiss the Blarney Stone.

But I failed. You had to lie down, crane your neck back over the battlements and kiss the stone above you while a bossy local held on to your legs.

The Chauffeur managed it all right but, try as I might, I couldn't get my lips to make contact with it: My nose (one of my finest features) kept getting in the way.

Oh well, it should have improved my ability to sniff out a grockle-rooking gimmick even if it didn't increase my gift of the gab.

We declined to pay for an official I-Kissed-The-Blarney-Stone certificate (one punt) or photograph (six punts, 11 punts or 21 punts including postage).

IT was time for Cork Races, not as you might expect at Cork but more than 20 miles away at Mallow: A lively little town where The Chauffeur had to stop Daisy to allow a huge congregation to spill out of the church on one side of the road into the pub on the other, and the Tina Turner tribute band I CAN TINA was billed to appear at the Central Hotel.

To Kepplers Restaurant in the main street, where we had On The Pig's Back (bacon and cheese baguette with a plateful of salad: 2.95 each).

Then we drove to the racecourse, where the large crowd seemed to be made up mainly of priests and children. Both groups enjoyed betting (half the punters queueing for the Tote were kids) but the priests seemed to have the edge when it came to drinking and smoking.

Making full use of my extensive knowledge of Irish racing, I decided the system I should follow was that of backing horses trained by anyone called O'Brien. And I'm pleased to say that this gave me a couple of modestly-priced winners.

Back for a second night in Blarney, where we ate at Mackey's Restaurant (Tourist Menu: 10 punts each including Hot Corned Beef in Parsley Sauce).

Then in the morning we returned to Cork on the N20, joining it correctly so we didn't have to obey the roadsign which said: WRONG WAY TURN BACK.

The Chauffeur drove us through the shabby outskirts to the centre of Ireland's second city, situated Paris-style on an island joined to the rest of the world by more than a dozen bridges, and managed to park Daisy in busy Grand Parade beside The Goat Broke Loose restaurant.

Coffee and croissants at Calypso's Coffee House helped to heighten the continental atmosphere (as did the fact that our waiter was French and spoke almost no English, so it was easier for us to conduct our negotiations with him in his language).

I went to the lavatory for a pee but unfortunately it wasn't one of the great flushers, as had been observed by one of my predecessors who'd scrawled above the bowl:
SO WHO DID THE BIG BEIGE FLOATER? FECKING VEGETARIANS

Light drizzle fell as we explored Cork's intimate little streets of restaurants, bars and bookies. Then for lunch at characterful Le Château Bars in curving Saint Patrick's Street, all old wood and tiles, where we got a cheery welcome from a barman who insisted on bringing my patiently-poured pint of Murphy's to our table when it was finally ready (even though he was busy giving Irish Coffee making lessons to a group of Frenchmen).

We set off back across country towards Bantry Bay, and were intrigued to see a sign saying MICHAEL COLLINS MONUMENT. We followed it, and came upon the eerie spot where the Sinn Fein leader was ambushed and shot dead by Republican colleagues who reckoned he'd betrayed his country to the English.

Past stunning coastal views to Glengarriff, on the neck of the Beara Peninsula, and the sort of friendly welcome we'd come to expect, this time at Dowling's Caravan and Camping Park.

But here there was one snag: Midges. The basins in the men's toilet block were crawling with them, and I couldn't bring myself to have a wash.

The cráic was good, though, as Mr Dowling himself and his mate Jim, a refugee from Grimsby, entertained a crowd of us on flute and squeeze-pipe in the camp bar over smooth pints of Murphy's ("Born in Cork, Raised All Over").

11

Ring of Beara - Ring of Kerry - Killarney - Gap of Dunloe - Macgillycuddy's Reeks - Cahersiveen - Dingle - Dunmore Head - Dunquin - Brandon Creek - Gallarus - Great Blasket Island - Castlegregory - Foynes - Limerick - Corofin - The Burren - Thoor Ballylee - Cliffs of Moher - Lahinch - Doolin - Ennis - Galway - Carraroe

WE woke early on the sort of sunny morning Irish folk normally experience only in their songs or their sleep, and set off to drive round the Ring of Beara.

First stop: Hungry Hill, and a boggy yomp to Ireland's highest waterfall. It was a lovely spot, but it was hard to avoid the suspicion that some of the footpath markers might have been positioned as much to lead us grockles into the boggier bits as to keep us away from them.

(Or maybe, as The Chauffeur suggested, it was simply that the softer bits provided the easier places to stick the posts in).

Then between matt grey mountain and gloss green sea to the fishing port of Castletownbere and the sociable Old Bakery Café where a huge group of locals of all ages were happily gathered together round one of the big wooden tables.

Past squat homes in every shade of green, yellow and pink to beautiful Beara's spectacular climax, its western tip, where an unexpected Alpine cable car swayed high above the swirling sound to Dursey Island whose little rock companions The Bull, The Cow and The Calf were the only obstacles between us and America.

A signpost, equally unexpected, pointed in the other direction to Moscow (3,310 km).

Next, Beara's bigger, more famous next door neighbour, the Ring of Kerry, and its distant misty islands shimmered into view.

The Chauffeur parked Daisy and we walked between thrift-pink banks to scrunch the grainy sand of deserted Ballydonegan Beach between our bare toes.

Then we drove on beneath Viennetta-layered rocks, beside bright yellow iris and bright pink foxglove (but pale compared with the gaudily-painted villages of Allihies and Eyeries) and past sudden schools and cemeteries and even more sudden Gaelic Football grounds and a little white calf alone and lost on a big brown beach.

(And I'll tell you something about the tourists we saw who were riding bikes: They looked so smug and so superior to us motorists, as if they'd never used an engine in their lives. But I bet they all had cars elsewhere, and had only hired bikes for the day).

We stopped to make tea and toast in Daisy just two dry-stone walls, three cows and a gorse bush away from the rocky shore. Rarely can food have been eaten in a lovelier setting.

Through the beauty of Kerry's magnificent sheep-filled, tree-gladed Lake District to a friendly, if flustered, welcome from the inexperienced girl receptionist at the well-appointed Flesk campsite just outside Killarney.

We walked into town, and if ever there was a tourist trap this was it: Visitors were the only reason for its existence. It was full of Americans, English, French and Germans.

There wasn't a proper shopping centre, just a long street of bars, restaurants, gift shops and guesthouses waiting to gobble up the grocks.

We ate at the Crock o' Gold, and soon saw why its grateful owners had called it that: First we were given a businesslike reception. Next we were conveyor-belted through our meal. Then we were efficiently relieved of our money.

In the morning we drove past lovely Lough Leane to the Gap of Dunloe in the foothills of Ireland's highest mountains, Macgillycuddy's Reeks, doing our best to ignore the lines of insistent jarveys with their horse-drawn jaunting cars, who started soliciting us for our custom before we'd even got out of Daisy.

We had coffee at Kate Kearney's Cottage and hiked the four-mile road to the top of the Gap, an attractive winding route by humpy bridges punctuating gorse and boulder, black lake and white stream.

The road was meant to be closed to motor traffic, although we encountered plenty. But the biggest danger to us walkers was the jaunty jarveys in their cars full of fleeced fares, travelling at great speed and making little attempt to avoid us.

Back to Daisy, then over the misty Reeks to spiral down spectacular Ballaghbeama Gap and pick up the Ring of Kerry at Sneem where a statue in the main square proudly remembered its local hero, Steve (Crusher) Casey, former World Heavyweight Champion Wrestler.

Round the Ring past a hundred rocky outcrops and islands, across green slopes dotted with sheep and cottages, to the Scariff Inn to accept the invitation displayed with pride on the sign outside:

ENJOY IRELAND'S BEST KNOWN VIEW (FOG PERMITTING)

To Waterville, with statue of another local hero standing right in the middle of the seafront: Charlie Chaplin. No, he didn't come from these parts but spent happy holidays here in his later life with his young family.

Next: Ballinskelligs and another Ring, the Skellig, with theatrical views of the spiky Skellig Rocks dramatically spotlit at sea by shafts of early evening sun.

Past parquet-patterned peat fields to Cahersiveen and the friendly Mannix Point campsite, complete with campers' sitting room full of books, photos, piano, guitar and (quite unnecessary) turf fire, run by the wonderfully welcoming (and named) Mortimer Moriarty.

Here, The Chauffeur and I ended a beautiful day drinking red wine and watching the red sun sink behind Valencia Island.

Next morning, under more blue skies, we drove against the high tide of oncoming tourist coaches to Killorglin, where the locals hold a three-day drinking festival in mid-August to celebrate the start of the harvest.

(In any other country, we reckoned, they'd wait till all was safely gathered in. But fair enough: Best to celebrate first, in case anything goes wrong later).

And so to the bit we'd been most looking forward to: Europe's most westerly point, the Dingle Peninsula.

WE strode the sandy strand at Inch. (They still called beaches strands in Ireland). And we strolled the garish streets of Dingle Town, its bars and restaurants deliciously served up in every colour under the still-shining sun.

We stocked up with food at the Super Valu store, where the friendly checkout girl happily went off to weigh the vegetables we were supposed to have already weighed ourselves (and nobody behind us in the queue gave us a hard time or tried to make us feel guilty for holding them up).

Through a profusion of fuchsia to park near Dunmore Head and ignore an unhelpful sign saying NO ENTRANCE PRIVATE PROPERTY to walk to the rocky tip.

(That was a serious problem we'd encountered in Ireland: They seemed to be far too possessive about their coast. There weren't any public cliff walks).

We stood and gazed across the rock-cluttered sound at the bleakly beautiful Blasket Islands, and then we saw it: A huge sea creature.

We watched with mounting excitement for half an hour as it swam backwards and forwards beneath us, and wondered what it could be.

It was at least 20 feet long and had a large fin on its back and a smaller one on its tail, which swished powerfully a good four feet from side to side.

We drove on to the weather-beaten village of Dunquin, where Ryan's Daughter was filmed, to a teashop where they were happy to serve us even though it was six o'clock. (Not something you could expect to happen after about 4.30 in England).

We asked them about our sea sighting, and the feeling of the meeting was that we'd seen a basking shark (which seemed fair enough in that sunny weather).

Along the coast to the tiny quay at Brandon Creek, from where the explorer Tim Severin sailed the Atlantic in a leather boat to demonstrate that Saint Brendan could have been the first person to do it, 15 centuries earlier.

(Saint Brendan is supposed to be buried in Galway, but nobody's explained how he got back there. Perhaps he also became the first person to fly the Atlantic).

Next: The remarkable Gallarus Oratory, a dry-stone church standing perfectly preserved like an upside-down boat despite being more than a millennium old.

Even more remarkable was the fact that the curator was still there to welcome us in and show us the introductory video, although it was now eight o'clock. (In England he'd have been off at five).

We checked in at the Teach an Aragail campsite a couple of fields away and, with the place to ourselves apart from a two German tenters, we sat over supper and watched another red-sea sunset end another glorious day.

For the first time on this trip the camp facilities were unisex, but as on all the other sites they were adequately equipped and included a communal campers' sitting room as a refuge from inhospitable Irish weather.

Irish, not English, was the first language around here but the locals were just as friendly as everyone else in their country, and refused to let us go by without giving us a wave or a one-fingered salute. (No, not that sort of one-fingered salute).

We parked Daisy beside the deserted little beach at Ferriter's Cove and set off to walk through wild orchids along the cliff towards an inviting headland.

But once again barbed wire barred our progress.

The Irish are proud of the fact that their country has no large estates in the hands of private landlords (unlike Scotland) but smaller landowners seemed to be doing their best to deprive the rest of us of the pleasure of this most beautiful of coasts.

To the Blasket Heritage Centre which looked from a distance like an oil storage depôt but, inside, movingly told us the heroic story of the brave but ultimately futile battle which the Great Blasket Islanders fought with the wild Atlantic to keep their community and their way of life alive.

We felt we owed it to those hardy islanders to see for ourselves where they'd lived and worked, so we took the little ferry with its fiddling skipper (music, not money) to make the three-mile crossing.

Even on a calm mid-May afternoon it was an adventure, but in the old days the islanders didn't have engines: Strong men with oars had to undertake the journey, often in far less friendly conditions, at times of birth, marriage, sickness or death.

We walked among the dry-stone ruins of people's lives and visited the tiny craft shop run by a woman from Cwmbran in South Wales, the nearest thing the island now has to a full-time inhabitant.

She told us she lived there for eight months of the year, and in times of heavy weather went as many as three months without seeing another person.

There was also a trendy little café run by a poshkin English mother and her teenage son. She was having trouble with her mobile phone. He couldn't get his pocket calculator to work.

(I wondered how much sympathy the pair of them would have got from the old islanders for their technological plight).

Gales were forecast for the next few days so they caught the ferry back to the mainland with us along with a couple of builders who had been working on the island, leaving the woman from Cwmbran to her lonely life among the ghosts of a departed world.

We watched a procession of trawlers and small boats running for the safety of Dingle Harbour, ahead of the forecast danger, as we drove back along the curling coast road that clings to the cliffs by Slea Head.

Up Ireland's highest pass, the Connor, which cuts the Dingle Peninsula in two, to admire Ireland's best views: North across Galway Bay to Connemara, south across Dingle Bay to the Ring of Kerry.

To Castlegregory, confused as usual by the Irish signposts: Some had been converted to kilometres, but many were still in miles.

To add to the confusion, all the Irish speed limit signs were in miles (assuming 30 meant 30 mph not 30 kph, which would be less than 20 mph).

The spelling of the place names, too, was a lottery. (Was it Connor or Conor?) But I suppose that just served to indicate what a low opinion the Irish have of English (which is fair enough).

We checked in at the Anchor Caravan Park, a bossy camp where the harsh régime included hard lavatory paper (surely taking nostalgia a little too far) and an excess of notices telling us how to behave. Perhaps that's why the place appeared to be particularly popular with Germans.

It was in a nice situation, though, beside a lovely sandy strand.

The weather forecasters got it right for once: Wind and rain gave Daisy a noisy battering during the night, although The Chauffeur and I slept snugly inside.

(A very inexact science, meteorology: A bit like medicine. I suppose it's because both are still in their infancy. I once heard a forecast which said there was a 50 per cent chance of rain: I still wonder what action I was supposed to take. Actually forecasters like to play safer these days, spending as much time telling you what has happened as what will happen. And as a rule they don't even get that right).

We took the road to Tralee, complete with painted markings saying first SLOW then SLOWER. A set of traffic lights was notable for its rarity value.

One thing that surprised us was the variation in fuel prices. Diesel for Daisy was much cheaper than petrol, but the price fluctuated hugely from garage to garage: Sometimes less than 50 pence a litre, sometimes more than 60.

I've always been intrigued by flying boats, so our next stop was the little Shannon port of Foynes with its fascinating Flying Boat Museum and its proud boast that it was once The Centre of the Aviation World.

From here, in the 1940s, the first regular non-stop commercial passenger flights operated between Europe and America. Film stars, tycoons and wartime leaders (travelling incognito through neutral Ireland) passed this way before conventional land-based aircraft rolled in to eclipse their eccentric pioneering predecessors.

We climbed to the top of a hill beside the museum (which is in the old terminal building) and looked out across the broad sweep of the grey Shannon, imagining the spray and the roar and the excitement of the belly-flop comings and goings of those proud ancestors of today's self-satisfied jumbo jets.

But we're indebted to Foynes for something far more important than its contribution to the history of aviation: It was here that late one wartime night chef Joe Sheridan was serving coffee to some cold damp American passengers and decided to give them something a little stronger.

"Hey, buddy, is this Brazilian coffee?" asked one of the Americans.

"No," Joe replied. That's Irish coffee."

THERE was a dear cat called Daisy
Who became decrepit and lazy

But her death brought new life
To me and the wife
And now we've gone caravan crazy

(All right, I'm sure you can do better. But when in Limerick).

It wasn't the most beautiful town in Ireland, but its streets were lively with shoppers and mums and babies and buskers and groups of school-girls trying to outdo each other with the length of their skirts. (Yes, the length. Not the shortness).

To Arthurs Quay shopping mall where the lavatories cost 10p but the girl taking the money said we could come in for free provided we told her we'd been in before.

And now a question: What's the most used word in Ireland? That's right: It's not "Begorrah" or "Bejaysus" or "sure" or "loike," it's "now."

This was confirmed to me in Limerick as we paid for supplies at a supermarket checkout:

"Now how are you?

"Now 10.75.

"Now your receipt.

"Now enjoy your day."

Sometimes it's simply used on its own, as a full sentence, in its own right: "Now." Just like that. Meaning: "Now what a lovely day" or "Now can I help you?" or "Now here we are then."

Next stop: Corofin Village Caravan and Camping Park, just off Corofin's unspoiled main street with its little gathering of pubs and restaurants.

To McNamara's Bar (glad this time of the real fire) for a perfectly poured pint of Guinness, then for posh nosh at the Gairdín Restaurant.

I had:

Duckling and guinea fowl sausage with apple, Calvados and onion confit.

Carrot and coriander soup.

Roast rack of lamb with parsley mash, confit cabbage and glazed shallots.

Parfait of pineapple and almond with coconut and figs.

She had:

Lobster terrine with chervil sauce.

Toasted nut salad with walnut cream.

Fillet of beef with basil, ratatouille and juniper.

Lemon tart with blackcurrant and yoghurt.

With wine and coffee: 57.50 for the two of us. (Less than £50 sterling).

Next morning we drove past more of the shrines and monuments which the Irish love so much, to visit the world's most incredible rock-ery, the giant lunar landscape called The Burren where Arctic, Alpine and Mediterranean flowers colourfully commune together in the cracks between the grey slabs of limestone.

We walked and ran and jumped on its alien surface, amazed not to experience weightlessness and alarmed to encounter fellow explorers who'd forgotten to put their spacesuits on.

Irish stew (in the name of the law, as Spike Milligan used to say) at The Burren Centre tearoom in Kilfenora, then to Poulnabrone Dolmen, a 4,000-year-old balancing act of a grave in the form of a slanting stone table.

(Call me a cynic, but I bet it's fallen down and been been put up again a few times since it was first erected).

IF the Americans like Italy, then they love Ireland. (There's even more of it in their blood).

But for once it wasn't Americans we tangled with at our next grock stop. Or English. Or French. Or Germans. It was, of all people, Irish. A whole coachload of them.

We were at Thoor Ballylee to visit the hopelessly romantic, hopelessly impractical, hopelessly damp old tower which the fifty-something WB Yeats got restored as a home for his young wife and their children.

The idea was that we would tour the tower in a group as a taped com-mentary kept pace with us, floor by floor, telling us about the place and its former owner.

Unfortunately, though, the Irish being more renowned for talking than listening, the entire commentary was drowned out by the excited chatter of our fellow visitors: About the view, the weather and Mrs Murphy Nextdoor's son-in-law's indifferent treatment of Mrs Murphy Nextdoor's daughter (etc).

The result was that we learned very little about the work of WB or about his uncomfortable home. But if the doggerel he left on one of the outside walls of the place was anything to go by we weren't missing much:

I the poet William Yeats
With old millboards and sea-green slates
And smithy work from the Gort forge
Restored this tower for my wife George
And may these characters remain
When all is ruin once again

(I don't know about you, but I reckon it makes my Daisy catterel look like pretty high-class work).

The best thing about the tour, though, was the close-up view we got of a peacefully-nesting kestrel in a glassed-off side turret, apparently unaware of the hundreds of visitors who came to stare at her every day from all of three feet away.

It was nearly time for The Chauffeur to leave me again and return to work. We'd been told she could get a flight home from Galway Airport, so we drove there to try to get her a ticket.

Impressive signs indicated it for miles, but when we got there it wasn't much more than a shed in a field. What's more, it was closed.

Back by Clare country lanes through saluting locals and early-evening milk herds, as mad farm dogs rushed out to try to bite Daisy on the axle, to camp again at Corofin.

First call: Bofey Quinn's Bar where a young Frenchman was trying to teach another how to order an "arf of Arp" and a singing, dancing Irish hen party were merrily tossing about a giant blow-up willie.

Next: Daly's Bar, where a young sober three-piece band (flute, squeeze-box and keyboard) was playing for the pleasure of the older less sober regulars.

Soon, the drinkers began to take the floor: First for a couple of gentle waltzes, then for full-blooded traditional Irish set-dancing.

For dance after dance, happiness and concentration filled their faces in equal measure as they zig-zagged about the bar on diddly-tiddly feet in time to the hypnotic repetitive rhythms while the studious young musicians stuck determinedly to their task.

We were witnessing the sort of impromptu yet disciplined pleasures of a Saturday night in the pub that hadn't been seen in England since the days Thomas Hardy wrote about (and even he was seeking to preserve the idyll of a way of life which was already changing his beloved Wessex for ever).

More and more locals flooded in through the door. At 10.30 the place was busy. At 11.30 it was packed. Then at 12.15 everybody stood up for the National Anthem (just like they used to do at the cinema when I was in short trousers) and they all went home.

In the morning we drove through fields covered with more rock than grass to the fearsome Cliffs of Moher. The moher and faher of all battlements.

For two miles we precariously threaded our wind-lashed way along the top, keeping as close to the edge as we dared and wondering all the time if each step might be our last.

We looked out over the barren Aran Islands, grateful our lives didn't depend on having to battle our way to them by small boat.

Above the roar of the seething sea, wheeling squealing gulls yelled like kids in a playground as they mocked us land-lubber interlopers.

Selfishly, The Chauffeur would keep stopping to peer over the edge (just to show she's got a better head for heights than me).

Every time she did so, I became weak with fear, partly at the thought that I'd miss her and partly at the prospect at having to explain in court that I hadn't shoved her over for the insurance money. If she went, I thought, I'd have to go too (on both counts).

Next to Lahinch, where white seas pummelled the rough edges of the famous golf links as sweater-fattened players battled to reach the frantically flapping flags.

A sign outside O'Looney's Bar advertised: SURF SEAFOOD AND STOUT. (Continental translation: Sun, sea and sex).

One snag about the Irish countryside: It's covered in black polythene.

Farmers use it to wrap their rolls of hay in, but when they cut it open to feed their cattle the wind gets hold of it before they do and it ends up like so much funeral drape clinging from every fence and hedge.

We saw loads of it, along with notices by the roadside telling its owners to keep it under proper control.

Along the coast, where the white lines and the cat's eyes disagreed about the position of the centre of the road, to Doolin where we checked in at O'Connors Riverside Camping and Caravan Park (because it was the closest site to the three village pubs).

We'd heard that Doolin was the home of traditional bar music, so we set off to find some. The first pub was O'Connors and it was packed, at eight o'clock. There wasn't a spare seat anywhere, although the music wasn't due to start until 9.30.

When it did, it was excellently performed by half a dozen enthusiastic players on flute, fiddle and drum. But it wasn't the same as the night before. It wasn't the real thing, for the locals: It was a put-up job, for the tourists.

The second pub was McDermotts, and here it was the same story: Four excellent musicians performed to a bar crammed with foot-tapping visitors. But there was hardly a local in sight.

The third pub was McGanns, where the music of another four players was as diddly-diddly and as plunkety-plunkety as ever, and just as well received by just as many customers. But...

This was theme-pub Ireland: Why else was it that when I tilted back my head to drain my glass of Irish coffee (the sweetest bit's always at the bottom) there was an old bicycle, rustic and rusting, hanging from the rafters?

We'd now arranged for The Chauffeur to fly home from Shannon

Airport, but before she left the following afternoon she gave me a parting gift: She helped me work out how to use the camp washing machines so I'd have some clean clothes for the next stage of my trip.

We drove to the pretty market town of Ennis (where the customary dogs and festival bunting were out to greet us) and stopped at the Ennis Gourmet Store to sit at one of the three tiny tables, amid shelves of fine food and fine wine, and eat bowls of chicken salad which was as good as you'd find anywhere.

On to Shannon to see The Chauffeur off on her AB Airlines flight to Gatwick (74 punts). I tried to persuade her to give up work and stay in Ireland, but no luck. So Daisy and I set off inland without her, to see Lough Derg.

MISSING The Chauffeur's company I tuned Daisy's radio to Clare FM, just in time to catch the Lost and Found slot. Lost: One handbag containing ferry ticket. One dog. One cat. Found: One cow. After that, the Deaths Notices (including removal and funeral arrangements).

It reminded me of my local newspaper days when I had to write everything including the Stars (under the name of Horace Cope).

Lough Derg was beautiful. Very beautiful. It looked like Windermere. But compared with the sea it was dull: Passive, not active. Neither the land nor the water excited me as the coast had done.

I pointed Daisy west towards Galway, and so we wouldn't feel too lonely on our first night without The Chauffeur we returned to my favourite County Clare village, Corofin.

I was warmly welcomed back at Bofey Quinn's by Trish the lovely landlady, and waffled away happily with her and a couple of the locals about Manchester United, The Troubles (as decades of Irish murder and mayhem are euphemistically called) and the meaning of life. As well as death.

In the morning I chatted with three hairy-legged French cyclists who had stayed at the camp overnight.

They were a cheerfully optimistic lot and their bikes were loaded front and back with vast quantities of gear, in bags and sacks and panniers which sprouted in all directions.

The only things they'd left behind were strings of onions and garlic.

They didn't mind how hard it rained, they said, but they didn't care for strong winds: The cyclist's worst enemy.

After much thought, I decided to grow a beard: Having to shave every morning in an uninviting toilet block was one piece of pedantry I could do without.

Besides, it would be a surprise fancy-tickling treat for The Chauffeur when I got home.

Through the land of lough and rock and tower and cattle crossing to Galway City where I parked Daisy (for free) beneath the unattractive cathedral, its weather-worn copper dome dripping green gunge, candle-like, down its grey walls.

Beside the River Corrib, where fishermen stood waist-deep in the rushing waters, to coffee, topped with cream, at Maggie's Café.

(If they offer you cream in Ireland they don't mean a little drop of dribbly stuff, they mean a large lump of floppy stuff).

Through the famous Spanish Arch, which looked old despite a board on it saying RAINEY (ESTD 1913) HISTORIC BUILDING SPECIALISTS, to the docks, well past their prime, where more than a hundred swans easily outnumbered the trawlers and yachts.

The city had a lively young population, a fair number of whom were playing a ferocious game of football in front of a good attendance of plump pigeons on a sunlit patch of grass in the middle of the main square.

The little streets of the city centre were busy with brightly painted shops, bars and restaurants.

(I don't know if anybody's ever worked out how many bars there are in Ireland, but I'll have a go: Wexford is said to have 93 bars and has about 16,000 inhabitants. The total population of Ireland, North and South, is five million. Wexford is a typical town. Therefore Ireland has 29,070 bars. One for every 172 inhabitants. QED).

I entered one of them, Tigh Neachtain's, darkly cubicled, with wooden floors, panels and screens, and dimly lit by stained glass windows.

The only relief from the gloom came from the rows of bright bottles behind the bar and the colourful posters on the walls recalling the many festivals that had taken place in Galway during the pub's 150-year history.

Pints of dark stout, deeply surveyed atop dark tables from dark benches by a handful of lugubrious lunchtime locals, did little to lighten the mood.

One old drinker made a determined effort to start a conversation with another, raising a number of topics of national and international interest without eliciting any response.

He finally drained his glass and took his leave with the words: "It's been a pleasure speaking to you now." (Without a hint of irony).

Of all the theme pubs in all the world...

So to Connemara, to make sure it was as beautiful as I'd expected, in deteriorating weather that the Irish call misty and we call pissing down.

Across the wastes of bog and rock to Connemara's bottom left hand corner, Golam Head, where the grey ocean finally put a merciful end to this most beautiful but inhospitable of landscapes (although not before the last hint of dead-end road had had wild orchids growing in the middle of it).

We headed for the Carraroe Caravan and Camping Park, a place of little shelter on an exposed Atlantic hillside. It was pretty basic. Primitive even. But then what can you expect for four punts a night?

I walked through the mist into Carraroe Village to visit one of its three pubs where I quickly noticed three things:

1. All the customers were male.
2. They all drank pints of Guinness.
3. They all spoke in Irish.

Feeling like the uncomprehending foreigner I was, I pretended to be more interested in studying the old photos on the walls than in chatting with my fellow customers, drank up and returned to Daisy for an early night.

12

Connemara Isles - Clifden - Castlebar - Cong - Louisburgh - Achill Island - Keel - Blacksod Point - Ballina - Tobercurry - Strandhill - Drumcliff - Mullaghmore - Donegal - Killybegs - Bunglass - Rosbeg - Burtonport - Crolly - Glenveagh

IT was time to play my first round of golf on Irish soil (well, some of the time) at the ruggedly beautiful Connemara Isles Golf Club.

The first problem was finding it: My Irish golfing guidebook had said visitors were welcome, but I'd passed it a couple of times in each direction before I finally recognised the secret sign:
GAILF CHUMANN OILEAIN CHONAMARA

I drove along a bumpy track and entered the thatched clubhouse, expecting a cool reception from a typical golf club secretary (grumpy, middle-aged and male).

Instead, I was warmly greeted by a delightful dark-haired shy-smiling colleen. Her name was Rita, and she was the sort of girl any man in his right mind would want to propose to.

Could I play a round? Now of course I could and it would cost me 10 punts for the day, no matter how many holes I played now.

And would the bar be open at lunchtime? Now of course it would, and at any other time I wanted it to be now.

So I handed over my money, bade Rita a fond farewell and set off to find Poll 1 (314 slat). There were only two snags:
1. The Irish mist had developed a capacity to move at more than 40 mph.
2. The course, besides being the most beautiful, was also the most difficult I'd ever played.

I don't want to sound like a name-dropper, but I've tackled some pretty tricky courses in my time: Turnberry for instance. There, the most notorious hole is the 413-yard ninth, Bruce's Castle, where you have to hit your tee shot over the sea.

Connemara Isles may only have been a nine-hole course but it was far harder: On the fifth for example (380 slat) you had to cross the sea not once but twice.

One good thing: I had the course to myself, apart from the oyster catchers, the herons, the pied wagtails and the cuckoo. That cuckoo: Every time I addressed the ball it taunted me with its mocking call.

I didn't even know what it was doing in those weather-beaten parts. I'd always thought cuckoos were more the type to seek out the easy life in the Home Counties. (Although maybe it was thinking the same about me).

At least the greens were, well, green, even if they did have something in common with every other course I've ever played: Just as I approached one, the greenkeeper would appear from nowhere and prevent me from playing by starting to mow it.

But then in Connemara maybe it's important that they cut them immediately before you arrive because the grass grows so quickly. (A bit like curling, where the players frantically sweep the ice as the stone approaches).

As for the rough... Well, the term could have been invented here. But it was as beautiful as the rest of the course: I've known men sufficiently confident of their sexuality to play golf with pink balls. Here, that would have been hopeless: They'd never have been able to find them for all the wild orchids.

(Things you wish you'd done: 1. Brought a bag of old golf balls. I had hundreds of them at home, but had over-confidently brought just a dozen new ones. 2. Brought a pair of waterproof shoes. I had some heavyweight winter ones at home, but had naïvely brought my lightweight summer ones.)

I've been known to play to a handicap of 18 but after my morning round I was 52 over par, even allowing for the most lenient interpretation of the Lost Ball and Out of Bounds rules.

I'd lost eight balls, and my feet were soaked from looking for balls in the knee-high rough.

At least the lovely Rita was there for me at lunchtime to serve me reviving Irish coffee and sandwiches and sell me 10 more nearly-new golf balls (80p or one euro a shot) from a basket behind the bar carefully positioned to catch the eye of a gullible visiting English hacker.

In the afternoon, neither the course nor the weather was any easier. I told the greenkeeper how much trouble I was having, and the gist of his reply (politely put and softly spoken) was that I should stop whingeing and try playing when there was a real wind.

There were no bunkers, but who needs bunkers when you've got beaches? And where there wasn't sea there was bog and ditch and gorse (Genetically Modified I'd say, judging by the strength of it).

I don't often play golf on my own, but it does have one big advantage.

You can make as much noise as you want: Sing when you're winning and shout obscenities at yourself when you screw up.

At least, I thought, if I got a hole in one it wouldn't cost me much to buy every player in the bar (ie me) a drink. Some hope.

Playing in those conditions certainly teaches you to Ca Canny, as the 15th poll (sorry, hole) at Turnberry is called.

It also teaches you to keep your head down. (Well there's not much else you can do in all that weather).

One of the most painful experiences, I found, was being able to see your ball sitting gloatingly out to sea on a sandbank but being unable to reach it.

My Strawberry Hill golfing pal Brian Donaldson wouldn't have been able to bear it: He hates losing golf balls, and would have been off to get himself a snorkel and flippers.

(Brian is a magistrate, and swears the following story is the truth, the whole truth and nothing but the truth: He was sitting on the bench with a chairman who was hard of hearing and had just sentenced a defendant to jail. Chairman, to defendant: "Have you anything to say?" Defendant, under his breath: "Bugger all." Chairman, to lady clerk: "What did he say?" Lady clerk: "Bugger all, Sir." Chairman: "Are you sure he said bugger all? I could have sworn I saw his lips move").

As I hacked my way towards the seventh green for the fourth time, a little old van pulled up beside me and the none-too-smartly-dressed driver leaned out of the window and asked: "Now are you making plenty of pars now?"

When I explained that I'd had more lost balls than pars, he reached behind his seat, among the breeze blocks and the barbed wire, and pulled out a handful of balls.

"Now here you are now," he said. "I'm the club captain now and we can't have you losing your balls on our course. You'd better have some of my old ones now."

By the time I'd played 36 holes, I was 98 strokes over and 14 balls under. I wasn't just misty-eyed, I was misty all over. And my lost balls had cost me more than my day ticket.

But a lovely hot shower was included in the price, and I got a parting souvenir to take away with me: When I stowed away my soggy golf gear, I noticed all my clubheads were covered in shamrock leaves.

BACK to Carraroe camp, which was run by a lively lass called Tina who lived in a caravan and wore a natty line in rugby shirts.

She was friendly and helpful and exceedingly energetic, running at great speed across the site from customer to customer as required, usually accompanied by two big black dogs which had trouble keeping up with her.

Into Carraroe village again to check that the Guinness was in good nick and to listen to the locals chatting away in Irish.

And when they spoke English for my benefit it was so Irish it sounded Scottish.

They didn't seem to have any swearwords of their own, because it was ours that kept cropping up whenever their conversation became particularly earnest.

(That's another thing you notice about the Irish: They swear far more than we do. Men, women and children are forever feckin' and fockin' whatever language they're speaking).

I got chatting with a pleasant young Irish lad "from the east." He'd come to Carraroe for his work and put a brave face on things, saying how lucky he was to be living in such a beautiful area and what a wonderful opportunity it was for him to observe its traditional culture.

But I felt sorry for him because he didn't speak Irish and so was excluded from most of the pub talk and local activity: An outsider in his own country.

When I got back to Daisy I made the mistake of turning on the light before shutting the door.

The result was that we were instantly invaded by a million midges and I had to spend 20 minutes frantically swashbuckling at them, smashing the flyswat into several pieces in the process.

Swapping The Chauffeur for the golf clubs had its advantages and its disadvantages: They were just as hard to handle, but a lot less cuddly. The golf had made me tired enough to sleep well, though.

In the morning I visited the remarkable Coral Strand. No, not an Aussie soap star but Carraroe's main claim to fame: Its amazing beach which looks like sand but is in fact billions of bits of limestone.

I crunched across it and ran it through my fingers, admiring the beauty of its tiny tangly fragments.

I didn't realise at the time how much of it was sticking to my shoes: Daisy was full of the experience for days afterwards.

We set off to drive north, and almost collided with a Guinness lorry. (What a way to go that would have been).

By bog and boulder and cloud-caked mountain along the jagged coast, with little grass, few sheep and fewer cows (but the usual crop of sore-thumb modern bungalows) towards Clifden.

There's no doubt about it: They really do take a pride in their roadworks in Ireland.

166

As we approached some near Kilkieran we passed no fewer than 17 big orange and black warning signs proudly stating (in both English and Irish):

MAJOR ROAD WORKS AHEAD
SLOW
PREPARE TO STOP
DIVERSION 300 METRES
WARNING YIELD AHEAD
SLOW
DETOUR AHEAD
WARNING YIELD AHEAD
SLOWER
DANGER NARROW BRIDGE AHEAD MAX SPEED 15 MPH
CAUTION CONSTRUCTION TRAFFIC CROSSING AHEAD
CAUTION DEMOLITION OF BRIDGE IN PROGRESS
SLOWER
REDUCE SPEED NOW
DETOUR
YIELD TO TRAFFIC ON BRIDGE
SINGLE LINE TRAFFIC

And we weren't even on a busy road.

Clifden, the main town of Connemara, is where British heroes John Alcock and Arthur Whitten-Brown, having completed their historic first non-stop flight across the Atlantic from Newfoundland, naïvely assumed that any piece of Irish land was innocent until proved guilty, and crash-landed in a bog.

Poor old Alcock wasn't able to enjoy his fame for long, being killed in a flying accident (with harder landing) less than a year later.

Eighty years after their achievement I visited the hillside sculpture of a plane wing which salutes their memory high on a seaside hilltop.

(Incidentally, one of the most politically incorrect jokes I've ever heard was about Alcock and Brown and Linford Christie, but I've no intention of going into that here).

Lunch in Clifden, which was a colourful grockle-welcoming town even in the cats-and-dogs mist, with plenty of pubs, restaurants and gift shops (besides bookies, barbers, butchers and roadworks).

So, safely seatbelted, to tackle the turbulent air miles of the heady Sky Road, with its gull's-eye views over creeky coast and rocky island, to Letterfrack, hiding among the rhododendron bushes where two wilds, the Atlantic Ocean and the Connemara National Park, collide.

Beside lough and waterfall, where the only farming is of fish and peat, beneath gunpowder skies, to Castlebar and the caravan park at swanky

Lough Lannagh Holiday Village: 12 punts for the night for just Daisy and me, three times as much as the previous night but with free use of their fitness centre.

(They must have been joking: After playing 36 holes of golf I wasn't nearly fit enough for a fitness centre).

Into the town, lively with drinkers of all ages, to discuss with locals over a couple of pints of Guinness, among other important topics, the entomologically etymological conundrum of whether swallows are called swallows because they swallow midges.

(You don't order a pint of Guinness in Ireland, by the way: You just order Guinness. They naturally assume you want a pint. And it's true, it is good for you: A couple of pints at lunchtime and a few more in the evening, and there's no need to eat. You've had all the nourishment you want).

I WOKE on a bright breezy morning to the sound of church bells playing Ave Maria.

Of course it's impossible to forget when you're in Ireland that you're in a Catholic country: Apart from anything else, there are statues of Jesus, Mary and Joseph (in various permutations) all over the place, usually so gaudily painted as to be in dubious artistic taste.

We drove into town to get diesel (I'd seen a garage where it was less than 50p a litre) and I asked the pump attendant to check Daisy's oil. He did so, and told me with some confidence that she could do with a litre.

But I was a little alarmed when he then asked me where he should put it. Fortunately I was experienced enough by now to be able to show him.

The main street was full of kids dressed as cowboys and cowgirls giving the impression that we might have lost our way and somehow ended up in Calgary, but I was told they were there to take part in a line-dancing championship.

Between miles of fuchsia hedges, their little pink lanterns flashing in the wind, we drove beside lovely Lough Mask, surely big enough to be able to apply for official EU status as a sea.

It was still rare to pass a local without getting a wave. Elsewhere, people wave at boat passengers and train drivers. Here, every motorist was made to feel important. Most oncoming drivers waved too, as if it were a "God be with you" blessing.

To another vintage film village: Cong. No, nothing to do with giant apes but the location for The Quiet Man, starring John Wayne and Maureen O'Hara, which was made here almost half a century earlier.

(In Ireland, to every pub a theme, to every village a film).

I ate rhubarb pie at The Quiet Man Coffee Shop, served with a huge helping of cream and a huger helpful of nows, and confessed to the lad behind the counter that I'd never seen the film.

He was only too happy to fill me in, treating me to a lively and entertaining re-enactment of the plot, complete with actions, and proudly informing me that the fight scene lasted eight and a half minutes and was the longest to have been filmed up to that time.

I also discovered he'd cooked the rhubarb pie. (Such versatility).

Beside Lough Corrib, spawning frog-green islands and boat parties of anglers, to be flagged down by a burly young motorist standing beside a small red car.

I cautiously opened Daisy's passenger window just a crack, making sure the door was locked, and asked him what he wanted. He informed me:

1. He was from Donegal now.
2. His car was hired now.
3. His wife (of whom there was no sign) was unwell now.
4. He had no money now.
5. He had no petrol now.
6. He'd be grateful for 20 punts now. (Now).

Too unnerved to do anything else, I complied with his request. Then I tried not to show indecent haste as I waved away his suggestion that I give him my address so he could return me my money, and continued on my sunny scenic way.

Through mountainous Joyce Country (no relation to any Dubliner) to well-coached tourist stop Leenaun between the Devilsmother mountain and the deep grey sea.

Up the Atlantic coast once more, encountering a cyclist who insisted on riding on the right and a tractor driven by a boy who couldn't possibly have been over 14, to Louisburgh, which sounded and looked like a Wild West frontier town with its wind-blown main street of bars and its Trading Post crafts and antiques store.

A passing priest stopped to admire Daisy. He greeted me cheerfully and said he didn't want to worry me but... Four priest pals of his had once been travelling in a similar vehicle across the Californian desert when it had overturned, killing the lot of them.

To Old Head, where a sign said PLEASE PARK ON ONE SIDE OF THE ROAD ONLY and the little quay fought a brave broadside battle against the Atlantic breakers of Clew Bay.

Then to the moving National Famine Memorial, a powerful sculpture of a three-masted barque rigged with human skeletons pointing pitifully towards the new hope of the New World.

Across the causeway to Ireland's windiest corner, Achill Island in the bottom left-hand corner of County Mayo, desperately beautiful but hopelessly exposed.

Keel Sandybanks Caravan and Camping Park had the best view of any Irish site we'd been on: Over a massive sweep of strand to the buttressed cliffs of Cathedral Rocks, ascending gloriously to Minaum Mountain.

From inside Daisy, the setting couldn't have been more picturesque. But to step outside was to understand why the Blasket Islanders had given up their struggle to keep their Atlantic community alive.

The cráic was good over the road at the Minaum View Bar though: There, I walked right into the middle of the Achill Island Celtic Supporters Club's end of season celebration.

The big bar was packed with members, all in their green and white football shirts, and a live band was playing Celtic songs.

Some members drank and sang. Some drank and danced. Some just drank.

A hen party had also managed to elbow its way in there, and its members too were drinking and dancing and singing.

As at Corofin, the girls had the (clearly traditional) Irish blow-up willie, and again this was being merrily tossed about the bar.

I was amazed that so many people should want to live on this windswept bit of land, but not that they should have chosen drinking as one of their main activities. (There were two other busy bars in Keel village).

Behind the bar, along with the Celtic photos and pennants, was a huge gallery of pictures of Republican heroes and martyrs and a large library of books about the Nationalist cause (not to mention a drinks can labelled Semtex).

Incongruously, there were also several pictures and busts of Laurel and Hardy (not noted, as far as I know, for the strength of their Irish Republican beliefs).

This was the first overt display of Nationalist passion I'd encountered, but the natives were friendly enough and I didn't feel intimidated. Much.

All the same, I was glad I'd chosen to wear my green jumper that night.

It was sunny but windy again in the morning as we drove back along fantastically rhododendroned Atlantic Drive above more stunning strands.

Then north to the Belmullet Peninsula and cruelly named Blasksod Point, deserted in the cold wind but far more attractive than it sounded, with its little fishing quay and a sturdy lighthouse.

It was now June, but smoke still billowed from the chimneys of many of the bungalows (including the modern ones).

We spent the night at the Belleek Caravan and Camping Park just out-side Ballina. I walked into town, and quickly learned one thing: Not everyone in Ireland likes traditional Irish music.

I was in a pub where a programme of diddly-diddly stuff was being shown on the telly. Suddenly, the man sitting next to me at the bar threw back the remains of his Guinness and stormed out, yelling: "Now I can't stand it any more now. All they do is play the same tune all the time now."

Personally I can face the music (although I can see his point). It's the slushy ballads I'm not so sure about, as they sentimentally whine about such clichéed old Irish characters as Emma Gration and Donny Gall.

(And have you ever noticed how the tune of When Irish Eyes Are Smiling always ends up as Glasgow Belongs To Me? Go on, try it: See what I mean?)

In the morning the sun remained but the wind had vanished as we headed for County Sligo past more beatific salutes from drivers and bystanders.

(More than once, I caught myself handing out Papal blessings in return).

Another thing about driving in Ireland: The sign for a crossroads isn't a heathen x like ours, but a religious +, bigger vertically than horizontal-ly, presumably in prayer for a safe passage.

IT was time to show another Irish golf course who was boss: I chose Tobercurry, a nine-hole parkland course set beneath the lovely Ox Mountains (partly because I liked the name and partly because it looked a lot easier than the last one).

Beside the car park was a big officious notice saying green fees must be paid before you played, and warning:
COURSE RANGER ON DUTY

I asked a young lad playing on a nearby green what I should do about paying, and he did his best to dissuade me from doing anything at all: "Now they're very liberal about green fees, very liberal now," he told me.

But being an honest English chap (not to mention being more than a little scared of the threat of the ranger) I went into the clubhouse to see if there was anyone I could give my money to.

The place was deserted, but I put 10 punts in an honesty box beside the secretary's office and hoped that would be enough to cover me for the day.

I was about to set off for the first tee when an old jalopy drove into the car park, so I asked its driver if he fancied a round and he said he did.

He was called Des Casey, and if he wasn't a member he didn't bother to pay a green fee.

He carried a small golf bag containing half a dozen battered old clubs including one wood (which he never used) and he wore a smart golf cap, its sartorial effect somewhat devalued by bearing the slogan:
THE JCB MAN ON TOUR WITH THE BIG BAMBOO

"Now I've only played 10 times in me life now," he assured me, and as we went round he kept asking me lots of innocent questions about which club to use and how to hit the ball.

But he wasn't as green as he was Irish looking, because he matched me stroke for stroke the whole way round.

By the time we'd finished, I was glad we hadn't been playing for money: He'd have made Paul Newman look a novice among hustlers.

But in these sunnier, easier, inland conditions I was much happier with my efforts this time. I didn't lose any balls, and finished the round a mere 26 over par: A major triumph after my traumatic experiences at Connemara Isles, which could have set my golf back five years.

They say cricket is an Indian game which just happened to be accidentally discovered by the English. Well, the same could be said of golf, the Irish and the Scottish: Golf is ideally suited to the relaxed Irish attitude to life.

I also liked the way the sexes seemed to mix more easily on the golf course in Ireland than in England: In nearly every Irish clubhouse I saw notices announcing mixed competitions.

Back home, male and female golf club members tend to keep apart as they attempt to observe an uneasy truce which can break out into open warfare if ever a member of one side is reckless enough to invade the course at the wrong time.

Des left at lunchtime, and in the afternoon I had the course virtually to myself. But I did something I hadn't done before: I played golf with a priest wearing a dog collar.

Father Gallagher was his name, and he was playing with his friend Doctor Flannery. I caught up with them at the 15th tee, and they invited me to join them.

The father told me:
1. He'd been a missionary in Korea.
2. He'd been 6ft 4ins tall.
3. He was in his 80s.
4. I should never make the mistake of thinking my ball was on the green before I'd hit it.

He and the doctor were as friendly and welcoming as everybody else in Ireland. The doctor, who was also in his 80s but didn't half give the ball a clout, offered to play me again the following day if I wanted. But I said I had to move on.

As you drive round Ireland you often see people (mainly men) walking the country roads miles from anywhere. I know you do in England, too, but not normally wearing suits and ties.

(Once again I was reminded of Hardy's Wessex).

I saw a couple of such men as we drove to Strandhill on the Sligo coast, where we passed a sign saying: THIS LAND IS POISONED FOR PROTECTION OF SHEEP.

(I still haven't worked that one out).

WE checked in for two nights at the Strandhill Caravan and Camping Park, among the sand dunes, and I was lulled to sleep by the sound of the Atlantic rollers.

Next day I played another round of golf, this time with a Northern Irishman, Benny McDermott (captain of Clones Golf Club, no less) at Strandhill, an altogether posher course where a single round cost me 20 punts.

The place was well named (by Strand out of Hill) in a lovely setting between the glorious beach and beautiful Knocknarea mountain, said to be the burial place of the warrior queen Maeve, Ireland's answer to Boadicea.

The 13th hole, The Valley, was a belter, with a narrow fairway snaking downhill to a tiny green hemmed in between huge dunes.

Benny and I enjoyed each other's company and had a good game, but the course couldn't match Connemara Isles for either difficulty or beauty.

The following morning Daisy and I drove east along the coast to Rosses Point, a tidy little village popular with yachters, their channel marked by the colourful Metal Man, nearly 200 years old, standing tall in mid-river.

Then to Drumcliff and WB Yeats's simple grave, bearing the epitaph he wrote himself:

Cast a cold eye
On life, on death.
Horseman, pass by.

(Well, at least his poetry had improved a little with age).

They certainly took their hero pretty seriously around here: We even passed a sign to YEATS UNITED FOOTBALL CLUB.

Next: Mullaghmore, an idyllic fishing village with another fine beach, its peaceful beauty tarnished for ever by the brutal killing of Lord Mountbatten whose boat was blown up in the bay by the IRA soon after he'd chosen to make his home there.

So to County Donegal and Donegal Town: I walked into the centre past Saint Patrick's Church, shaped more like a Disneyland Castle, with its notice saying ABSOLUTELY NO PARKING.

(And wondered if there'd be Absolution for sinning motorists who disobeyed it).

The town was a letdown: I'd been looking forward to seeing this part of Ireland, but here was a humdrum sort of place, quite small, with a handful of bars, cafés and souvenir shops lining the main square (or Diamond).

It wasn't even the capital of County Donegal (which is Letterkenny) but it was the country bits I'd come to see, so we set off in search of them.

First, I got a friendly garage attendant to fill Daisy with diesel: 68 litres at 52.9p a litre = 36 punts. Just round the corner they were selling it at 57.9p a litre, so I reckoned I'd saved well over three punts in just a few hundred yards.

Across the Oily River to Ireland's premier fishing port, Killybegs. (I knew when I was nearly there from the stench of fish in the air which came out to meet me).

This was no grockle show, but a serious business of life and (sometimes) death. Big notices were there to tell us so, and warn us to watch out for forklift trucks and other quayside hazards.

There were more than a dozen monster trawlers in port, each one a match for any ocean in the world. Most were being busily hosed, painted and patched in readiness to do battle again with the Atlantic waves.

A number of empty berths awaited the prayed-for return of brave husbands, fathers and sons far from home, out there earning a living the hard way.

Beside Donegal Bay, calm but grey on an early summer afternoon, past more modern bungalows clearly lacking for the vernacular, to Bunglass and (through a farmer's gate) the highest cliffs in Europe.

Light rain had begun to fall, so I took my golf umbrella with me. It was all so different from the Cliffs of Moher, where to have done so would have meant certain destruction for the umbrella and almost certain destruction for anyone hanging on to it.

I thought of The Chauffeur and how sorry I was that she wasn't here to admire the awesome view, but how glad I was that she wasn't able to put the fear of death in me by showing off her head for heights again.

I'd heard of springy turf, and I suddenly realised what it meant as I bounced across the grass at the top of those cliffs. I wondered how many enthusiastic hikers had accidentally trampolined themselves over the edge.

On a heathery slope near where I'd parked Daisy the message TÍR ÉIRE was written in stones to warn would-be wartime invaders that this was a neutral country.

(How many of them would have understood it, though?)

By traffic-free roads through peat and bog to Glencolumbkille, having to stop for a rebellious sheep which sat in the middle of a narrow bit of road refusing to budge even when I hooted and shouted at it.

In the end I got out, pretended I was a dog and worried it out of the way.

Over rocky Glendesh Pass to the Donegal tweed town of Ardara, to be reminded along the way of the worst thing about being a motor caravanner: The others.

With the exception of tractors, motor caravans (apart from Daisy, of course) are the slowest vehicles on the road, and that afternoon I became one of a dozen drivers to be held up by one (French).

Nothing would make monsieur move over as the queue behind him gradually grew longer. I didn't just feel embarrassed, I felt guilty by association.

On to the miles-from-anywhere coast village of Rosbeg and the even-more-miles-from-anywhere campsite at Tramore Beach to sleep again in Daisy among towering sand dunes, with views of strand, sea and mountain to rival those on Achill Island.

Through more Irish-speaking country with roadsigns urgently yelling AIRE! and DAINSEAR! but with no subtitles for English readers (although the BED & BREAKFAST signs were English enough) to Dungloe, the nearest thing to a town round here, its main street proudly laid waste by roadworks of gargantuan proportions.

Along that stranded coast of Donegal to Burtonport with its fisherman's co-operative society and harbourside memorial to the eleven local lads who lost their lives in two separate shipwrecks in the 1970s.

It must have been a mighty blow indeed for the community when the second disaster struck less than two years after the first.

Next, to Crolly village and Leo's, family pub of folk-rock group Clannad, whose pictures and discs of gold, silver and platinum covered the walls.

A young Dutch couple were there to pay their respects, and the visitors' book showed it wasn't just fans from all over Europe who'd passed this way: Addresses included America, Australia, South Africa, Japan and any other place you can think of.

I had some lunch and bought a tape of A Night in Leo's Tavern to remember my visit by. (Well, it would make a change from Mick Walsh, my travelling companion since Kilkenny).

One thing, though: The tape they were playing in the bar wasn't Leo's or Clannad's, it was All-Ireland's biggest favourite (and mine): Van the Man Morrison.

So on my tuneful, duneful way to follow a signpost saying IRA: We drove down a narrow lane past a football ground that was heavily fortified behind a wall and barbed wire, but it all ended peacefully enough beside a picnic table overlooking a small quay and a fine strand.

(I managed to work out later that the sign had been carefully doctored from its original TRÁ, meaning beach).

Signposts were something of a gamble in Donegal, I discovered: Sometimes in Irish, sometimes in English, sometimes in broken English, sometimes just broken.

Next: Bloody Foreland. (Once again nothing to do with the IRA, but named to describe the way its red rocks glinted in the evening sun).

Across the wall-of-death slopes of misty-murky Muckish Mountain to the Glenveagh National Park, heart of the Donegal Highlands.

I paid two punts to deposit Daisy at the Visitor Centre car park, and set off to walk the two miles up the valley, between lough and mountain, to much towered and turreted Glenveagh Castle.

It was a bit like the Gap of Dunloe, except that the threat of those racy jaunting cars seemed tame compared with the threat of the racing minibuses laid on here for those who didn't fancy the walk.

The castle tour guide did her best to clutter my head with dates, but suffice to say the place was a bit of a fraud, being less than 130 years old.

It was up to its antlers in opulence though, and there was nothing wrong with its highland views. (I had to keep reminding myself I was in Ireland, not Scotland).

Owner No 1 had earned well deserved loathing throughout the land for evicting nearly 250 tenants from the estate.

Owner No 2 had vanished mysteriously from Inishbofin Island (probably as a result of his womanising) and had never been seen again, dead or alive.

Owner No 3 had been a decent chap who had generously given the place to the nation.

Grace Kelly and Greta Garbo were among the guests who had been pampered here.

The gardens were wonderful: A series of rooms in different styles separated by ramparts of rhododendron.

Best of all was the walled garden, a joyous mixture of fruit and veg and flowers and topiary and statuary, a line of massed lupins marching colourfully across its centre.

13

Sligo - Letterkenny - Portsalon - Cardonagh - Malin Head - Moville - Derry - Castlerock - Portstewart - Portrush - Bushmills - Giant's Causeway - Ballycastle - Carrick-a-rede - Fair Head - Glens of Antrim - Portaferry - Belfast - Newcastle - Kilkeel - Warrenpoint

I FANCIED another day at the races, so I drove back to Sligo Town and booked in for two nights at the Gateway Caravan and Camping Park.

There was said to be an arts festival on. I had a suspicion that the arts referred to might consist mainly of drinking and diddly-diddlying so I left Daisy and walked into town, past the statue of Wherever-you-are Bet-I-was-there-first Yeats, to check it out.

Beneath bunting to McGarrigles Bar, where a sign said TRAD SESSION TONIGHT.

Clearly Trad here had nothing to do with jazz, because no sooner had I ordered a pint of Guinness than seven student-aged musicians began scraping, beating and blowing the night away on their pipes, fiddles and drums.

It was good cráic, but was it art?

(If there are 29,070 pubs in Ireland, then there must be more than 87,210 musicians because every pub had at least three. Average age: 20).

Next bar: Shoot the Crows (themier than ever) and another three strummers and fiddlers hard at it in a lovely lively licensed old corridor of a pub overflowing with mirrors and glass and partitions and tiles and benches and the local cráic pack. A business efficiency expert's nightmare, but efficiently doing great business.

Finally to McLaughlin's Bar, which advertised:
1. Guinness (of course).
2. Music (of course).
3. Oysters.
4. Frank L Ludwig reading a selection of his poems.

Frank L (late of Hamburg but now resident of Sligo) certainly looked the part, with his long black hair, small moustache and large pipe.

177

And he was a very contented poet, smiling and laughing happily at his own poems despite the lack of hush from the Man United section of the crowd in the little back bar.

As in other pubs, one corner had a sign saying RESERVED FOR MUSICIANS (like it might say RESERVED FOR NON-SMOKERS in other countries: Non-smoking not being a readily-grasped concept in Ireland, least of all by Frank L).

It wasn't long before the music started, as 50 cráic addicts crammed into a room barely big enough to contain 20.

Soon, Mr McLaughlin himself joined in with his guitar.

(In Ireland the chances are that if a pub is called McLaughlin's or McNamara's or whatever then that's the name of its landlord, unlike in England where the proprietor isn't normally the Marquis of Granby or the Duke of Clarence).

The place was packed with German people, French people, English people, Northern Irish people, even local people, as the more pressing arts of drinking and singing took over from the poetry, and Mr McLaughlin and his pals led us along with the Wild Rover and all the other old favourites.

(Originality is never the object of the exercise during an Irish music session, although one guitarist did break ranks at one point to give Elvis a good belting).

When I got back to camp at about 1am, I found the gates locked. I managed to climb over them, but had a bit of a bumpy landing on the concrete below. Such is the lot of the arts lover.

(Next morning, I was told I needn't have climbed over: All I had to do was to open the side gate).

Race Day: Sunny and windy, so for once the races might not be abandoned. (Apparently they nearly always are at Sligo: It's something to do with the course being built on a bog).

I spent the morning at the camp, writing postcards, and none of my fellow campers went out while I was there: Kids chatted and played games, adults chatted and played house, but nobody went anywhere.

The site was smart and clean, but it wasn't pretty. It didn't have beautiful views over lovely countryside: It was in the suburbs right beside the junction of two busy roads.

I wondered once again why camping folk bother to travel for miles so they can do just the same things as they do at home.

I set off to walk to the races, and stopped off in town for a burger at a fast-food restaurant. I wasn't a bit surprised to discover that the idea of fast food didn't come easily to the Irish: They're far too friendly and helpful for that.

I gave my order to a girl at the counter, and she insisted I shouldn't take it to a table myself: I should go and sit down and she would bring it to me.

And so she did but not until some ten minutes later, by which time I'd become a lot hungrier and she'd had a good natter with most of her colleagues and several other customers.

I arrived early at the pretty little course, with its view over town and mountain, to watch the horses arrive (some in posher boxes than others) and the bookies prepare their pitches and wrap themselves in their leathers and leggings to protect themselves against the Home-Fires-Burning weather.

One thing about the Irish: They're much freer with their racing tips than the English, who tend to keep their opinions to themselves.

I suppose it's because they're keener on talking (and what more important to talk about than racing tips?)

The man guarding the stable gate was happy to mark my card for me (although I later discovered he wasn't an official gate-guarder at all, just a compulsive amateur one: I noticed him again several times during the afternoon, standing purposefully and importantly beside doors and gates all over the course. It was his hobby).

Gradually, the farmers, priests, children and other punters started to arrive. The big barn of a bar began to fill up as a man with a drill put some finishing touches to it, and boys went about smothering every bit of level space in beermats.

(They love beermats in Ireland, and will never serve you a drink without one).

Unfortunately, though, the wind came in through the barn door and blew most of the mats on to the floor before enough customers had arrived to weigh them down with their drinks.

The official proceedings began with a video on the bar tellies instructing people how to place a bet (as if it didn't come naturally enough to an Irish person).

A couple of heavy showers swept in shortly before the first race, but for once they weren't enough to stop the meeting going ahead.

Although the crowd couldn't have been more than about 3,000, I counted 53 bookies and 26 Tote tellers (one for every 38 men, women, children and priests). All were doing good business.

Apart from the bar, only one small stand offered any protection from the weather and there wasn't a lot of room in it. It was a lovely viewing track, though: You couldn't hope to see your money go down the drain more clearly.

Racegoers had different ideas on how to dress, especially the women.

Some were in summer frocks and some in winter woollies. (No prizes for guessing which ones were on a winner).

The bar, like the stand, was completely packed, and as at Mallow it was almost impossible to get to the Tote windows for the dozens of kids in the queue.

A face-painter and a traditional Irish story-teller were there to entertain them if the pleasures of punting should start to pall.

I decided to stick to my system of backing horses trained by anyone called O'Brien and also to follow JS Bolger, because his was the biggest horsebox and it had made quite an entry after all the little ones towed by farm trucks and Land-Rovers.

Unfortunately the O'Briens had an off day, but the Bolger plan worked a treat and gave me a generous-priced winner.

It was time to resume my search for the arts so I headed for the Adelaide Bar, unable to resist the lure of:
THE GINGHAM DIVA CHLOE POEMS IN UNIVERSAL RENT-BOY

"Kicks drag right in the Millennium," said the Sligo Arts Festival programme. "Chloe Poems is a witty gay transvestite socialist poet."

It was too artistic to miss, but unfortunately when I got there a notice on the door said: THIS PERFORMANCE CANCELLED DUE TO CIRCUMSTANCES BEYOND OUR CONTROL.

Oh well, back to the art of Guinness drinking.

IN the morning we returned to County Donegal, through sunshine and showers so fierce that sometimes Daisy aquaplaned across flooded roads beneath blue skies.

Breakfast at The Beanery in Letterkenny, and then more signpost trouble: Every sign in Donegal was either to somewhere you'd just come from or to somewhere you didn't want to go to.

Still, it was all beautiful so I suppose it didn't really matter which way you went.

Behind a dustbin lorry saying MAKE DONEGAL GLITTER DON'T DROP LITTER (wondering if WB had got here before us again) to rocky Fanad Head where the whitewashed lighthouse battled to keep its head above the whitewashing sea.

Then to the Knockalla campsite, across the sandy bay from the village of Portsalon.

I left Daisy and walked beneath the dunes and mountains, beside the golf course, to the little village quay along the second best beach in the world.

(Well, the local guidebook said it was the world's second best beach although it didn't say who'd worked it out or how, or what the best one was. But I couldn't see any reason to argue).

I passed through the timewarp of the old brown door of a little establishment with no name (but generally known as Rita's after its nonagenarian proprietress) and it couldn't decide if it was the village pub or the village shop.

At one end of the room were jars and tins and packets and postcards and Bisto and Brillo and Cookeen and Jammie Dodgers. At the other: Beer pumps and tobaccos and bottles of booze, Jamesons and Haig and Sandeman and Martini.

From the ceiling hung brooms and beachballs and galvanised-iron buckets. All the fittings, including a couple of old benches, were of wood, as was the well fag-ended floor.

Nobody appeared, within living memory, to have been too bothered about the state of the décor.

And at the high counter: The boozers, a dozen of them, all men, seated on high stools (one of which doubled as a step-ladder for reaching the items on the higher shelves) and looking like the original audition for Whisky Galore.

It was still early evening, but they'd already had a heavy day and the conversation was well past its prime:

"I've enjoyed our chat now, apart from the bullshit."

"I can't remember the way home now, you'll have to show me."

You couldn't fault them for stamina, though. The talk may have been slurring to a standstill, but the drinking wasn't.

From time to time little schoolgirls would come in to buy sweets and fizzy drinks and get an early introduction to words they weren't supposed to know. But none of them seemed at all impressed, interested or concerned.

A local dad came in for a pint accompanied by his daughter (aged about 10) but nobody seemed to find the mixture of old and young, drunk and sober, degenerate and innocent in the least bit awkward or embarrassing.

And all the time, through the window to the right of the groceries and the left of the liquor: The finest view in the world. (Oh all right, the second finest).

I tell you one thing about Donegal: It never got dark. Not because of moonlight, and certainly not because of street light, but because the sunlight never disappeared.

As I walked home to Daisy, along that out-of-this-world beach, at 10.40pm, there was a golfer happily hacking his night-time way home to the still-visible 18th flag.

The next day I played the course myself. Twice. And it was wonderful, a lovely, relaxed, informal jumble of shared and crossing fairways among the dunes, with a clientèle to match: I was the only man there who didn't have either his wife or his dog with him to keep him company.

The following morning we drove past a sign saying NO BURIAL OF ANIMALS ON BEACH and back through Letterkenny to join the Inis Eoghain 100, the spectacular 100-mile drive round the Inishowen Peninsula.

First stop: Buncrana, where Eamon Friel The Mobile Barber was doing good business in his van parked in the main street.

Over slithery Mamore Gap, with its phrenologist's view of bumpy Dunaff Head below, to Cardonagh for lunch at The Coffee Shop beneath the great grey battleship of the Church of the Sacred Heart.

Religion (as you might expect) was the subject under discussion among my fellow customers, and in particular the Good Lord's last-minute decision to switch the birthplace of the Baby Jesus from Cardonagh to Bethlehem because of the locals' inability to come up with the required three Wise Men and a Virgin.

North to Five Finger Strand, too wild for swimmers but surely at least the third best beach in the world, and radio superstar Malin Head, Ireland's most northerly point (although not in Northern Ireland) and taker of a hundred Test Match wickets.

(It's a condition of Radio 4's cricket coverage that at least one must fall during every Shipping Forecast).

I parked Daisy at its summit (fair, rising slowly) beside the old Lloyd's signal tower which used to report every passing ship, and scrambled down to the rocky shore to feel the sea spray on my face beneath a group of white stones on the headland turf spelling EIRE and a group of white sheep spelling nothing in particular.

If Malin Head is Ireland's most northerly point then The Curiosity Shop, just an outcrop away, must be Ireland's most northerly antique shop.

I stopped there to buy a couple of its postcards of Ould Donny Gall and envisaged some of the cast-iron cast-outs from local farmhouse kitchens adorning the suburban living rooms of Philadelphia.

East through Stroove to Inishowen Head, its black and white lighthouse gazing across Lough Foyle at the bitter-sweet beauty of tortured Ulster, to the busy fishing port of Greencastle and the pleasant resort of Moville.

I didn't see many campsites on the Inishowen Peninsula, so I was grateful for a friendly welcome at the Moville Holiday Hostel where I was told I could park Daisy and make use of all it had to offer.

They tried to persuade me to come inside to sleep, but Daisy and I had been through a lot together so I decided to stay faithful to her.

The place was clean and well appointed, with excellent toilet facilities, dormitories and common room.

I'd noticed there were lots of hostels in Ireland, and if this one was anything to go by they were clearly good news for cyclists, walkers, backpackers and any travellers who'd come without a Daisy.

Moville, once in the mainstream as a stopping-off point for Transatlantic liners, was now just a quiet backwater despite the attractions of the lively Hair of the Dog bar beside the harbour, prop: Mike (Easy Rider) Dobbins, late of California via London and Amsterdam.

I spent a happy hour chatting with Mike over a couple of pints before returning to Daisy for an early night, past the tractors and other farm vehicles parked outside the bars in the main street waiting to take their owners home when they baled out at closing time.

THROUGH Muff, with an open mind but without flag or barrier or checkpoint or police or guard, into demonised Ulster. The only clue that we were changing countries: A discreet little notice warning us to make sure our motor insurance was valid.

We drove into Derry (or Londonderry, depending on your point of view) and after a moment's hesitation to reacclimatise myself to funny old sterling I left Daisy at a Pay and Display beside the River Foyle and set off to walk the city walls.

To start with, I could have been in Chester. There was plenty of grafitti, of course, as in any British city. But it was as much about football as politics: CHELSEA FC alongside BRITS OUT.

The big difference came when I reached the part of the walls where Chester has the Roodeye, happy gathering place for racegoers. Instead, Derry had the Bogside, tragic scene of the Bloody Sunday killings.

Up here, the old British bastion bristled with modern surveillance towers and cameras as well as ancient cannons. Below, the Bogside fought back with its house-high murals yelling: YOU ARE NOW ENTERING FREE DERRY and NO CONSENT NO PARADE.

A plaque beneath the walls remembered Stephen McConomy, "Murdered By A Plastic Bullet Aged 11 Years On The 16th April 1982. Always Remembered By His Loving Mother, Brothers & Family."

The city centre was a thriving, optimistic place with not one but two shopping malls and all the usual British stores: Littlewoods, Woolworths, M & S etc.

In fact the problem for an adventure-seeking nomad like me was that it felt a bit too much like home. I liked the colourful Craft Village though: It reminded me of Galway.

Past the grim MOD firing range and the grimmer HM prison to sandy Magilligan Point, thinking how typical it was of the British forces of law and order to grab all the nicest bits of land.

Beside magnificent Magilligan Strand to dramatic Downhill, high on a windswept headland and once home to the Bishop of Derry, its ruined palace a castle at one end and a house at the other, its round folly of Mussenden Temple clinging precariously to the cliff, the whole lot perched on top of a railway tunnel.

Past the well-fortified police station into the little resort of Castlerock, with another fine strand and a great golf course among the dunes.

But it was an austere sort of place, more Scottish than Irish, with a Presbyterian Church hostel on the seafront and a sign on a nearby lamp-post saying ALCOHOL FREE AREA and warning of £100 fines for anyone caught drinking in public.

I was beginning to realise that the divide between Ireland's two parts was a little wider than Lough Foyle.

We checked in at the Castlerock Holiday Park and for the first time on this trip I was directed to park Daisy on a specific pitch, although there were plenty of spaces available and no sign of anybody else rushing to occupy them.

In the morning: East to Portstewart for a breeze along the alchohol-free prom. It was the perfect place for a seaside holiday with its mountain views and its row of little gift shops, cafés and amusement arcades. But it was oh so British: We could have been in Colwyn Bay.

A lively sculpture of an old sailing boat with fish-caked hull stood in memory of Jimmy Kennedy, the man who wrote Red Sails in the Sunset and spent his early life here. (Unfortunately it was green not red, though).

Another thing I noticed: Officious traffic wardens on the prowl. (I hadn't seen many of them lately).

Next: Llandudno, aka Portrush, on a brasher scale with bigger amusement arcades and the Water World indoor swimming complex beside the harbour.

I treated myself to the Large Ulster Fry all-day breakfast at the Hidden Cove Café just off the main street, a popular meeting place for the locals, its flower-printed wallpaper and carpet remaindered from the 1970s.

Then I walked beside the sea beneath huge painted wooden hoardings notifying passers-by:

ALL HAVE SINNED & COME SHORT OF THE GLORY OF GOD

THE BLOOD OF JESUS CHRIST HIS SON CLEANSETH US FROM ALL SIN
BELIEVE ON THE LORD JESUS CHRIST & THOU SHALT BE SAVED

I sat on a sunny outcrop and watched three fishermen hauling their nets into their open boat a few yards off shore.

But it seemed they hadn't said their prayers that morning because along with their pathetically small haul of fish they pulled out dozens of old plastic containers, sheets of polythene and other debris.

They'd have been better employed as dredgers.

One thing about this area: They didn't half take a pride in their public lavatories. There were hundreds of them, all beautifully kept and many of them newly built.

(Presumably because the outdoor discharging of drink would be regarded as even more unsightly than its outdoor consumption).

To another cliffhanger: Beautiful Dunluce Castle, its ruins clinging impressively to the rocks 100ft above the deep green sea, its sights set on the Scottish Isle of Islay less than 30 miles away.

Past the Bushmills Church of the Redeemer to the Old Bushmills Distillery (with high proportion of Southern Irish vehicles in the visitors' car park).

The world's oldest licensed distillery, it narrowly survived American Prohibition (which killed off a hundred other Irish distilleries).

I joined a guided tour and learned how to make whiskey: You take malted barley, yeast and water, then you mash it, ferment it, distil it, mature it and bottle it.

Simple, really, although rather hot and noisy in the early stages. All you have to do then is to drink it.

The best whiskeys are matured for up to 25 years in oak barrels. The percentage lost through evaporation is known as The Angels' Share.

Our tour guide was a nice girl called Lynda who had teeth a bit like Janet Street-Porter's. (But at least they had the effect of reminding me that Ulster's might not be the least attractive accent in the world).

A wee free dram of 10-year-old single malt was served to us in the bar at the end of the tour, but out of deference to Daisy I didn't join in the sample tasting of ten other whiskeys.

So to Northern Ireland's most amazing natural phenomenon: The Giant's Causeway. Despite its name it wasn't huge, but what defied belief was that it hadn't been made by a giant's (or a human's) hand.

It stuck out towards Scotland, among perfectly normal sensible cliffs, like a three-dimensional game board of hexagonal checks fit for Heroes of Halma.

I sat in the sun on one of its thousands of stone column seats and watched the moves of its pieces: The hundreds of visitors who were there to marvel at it.

Past more strands of gold (thinking that Nature, at least, hadn't discriminated between North and South in this beautiful country) to make the winding descent to rocky little Ballintoy Harbour which was being watched over by a glorious white folly of a holiday home: By Art Deco Cubist out of Giant's Causeway Columnist.

My next aim was to walk the hair-raising rope bridge to Carrick-a-rede Island, but although we got there before six, it was closed. Now that wouldn't have happened in the South now, to be sure now.

(Incidentally, if the most used word in the South is now, then the most used word in the North is aye. As in Scotland, but without the och).

Then to Silvercliffs Holiday Village near Ballycastle, a cheerful town (despite the customary ban on drinking in public).

I had a couple of pints of Guinness in the welcoming Central Bar (although it wasn't as smoothly or as lovingly poured as in the South).

I was disarmed to see a series of photos on the wall showing a building being blown up, and bloodied victims being carried from its smoking ruins.

I asked about them and was told, matter-of-factly, that they were of the Marine Hotel just round the corner. It had been blown up by the IRA and one person had died.

Next, to pub No 2, the House of McDonnell (three doors down from the Paddystani takeaway) where the atmosphere was enlivened by six diddly-diddliers: Two blowers, two bangers, one twanger and one scraper.

I'd been told closing time wasn't too strictly enforced in these parts, mainly because the besieged police had bigger problems to contend with.

And so it proved: At 11 o'clock, when the bar was supposed to close, it began instead to fill up. The pub clock stood permanently at five to 11 and the cráic was as good as any I'd found in all Ireland.

At 12.20 on my watch (10.55 still on their clock) I thought it was time to be faithful to Daisy once again and applied to be ushered out through the side door, the front door having long since been barred to all comers (and goers).

Next morning the sun shone again. I decided to stay another day and walk back to Carrick-a-rede, so I set out to discover if doing a coast walk was any easier here than in the South.

Nobody at the campsite knew if there was a path, so I walked down to the tourist information office in the town to find out. And, being British, it was closed.

All day Saturday and all day Sunday. In the middle of June.

As far as I could tell, though, there wasn't a path. So I decided to take Daisy along for the ride.

IF you haven't got a head for heights, don't go to Carrick-a-rede. Or if you do, don't look down. I walked the lurching rope bridge 80ft above rocks and sea, and didn't enjoy the experience in the slightest.

With any luck I'll never have to repeat it (so long as I remember to steer clear of the Himalayas).

The bridge is highly strung every year by salmon fishers who use the island during the summer months. They've certainly got a lovely work-place (even if it was more nerve-racking to get to than the 22nd floor of Canary Wharf).

Back to Ballycastle to walk beside the harbour, where you can get a ferry to Campbeltown in Scotland and where a rough stone memorial celebrates the excitement of the historic moment when Guglielmo Marconi marvellously made wireless contact from here with Rathlin Island just six miles away, 100 years before.

(Rathlin, Northern Ireland's only remaining inhabited island, was also the making of Robert the Bruce, who returned from there to defeat the English at Bannockburn after admiring the determination of history's most famous spider, and of Richard Branson who was rescued here after ditching in the sea on one of his many unsuccessful balloon trips).

I had lunch at the Beach House Café, and drove to the accurately named Fair Head. There, I finally got my coast walk: A six-mile round trip back towards Ballycastle, with only one barbed wire fence to cross, and miraculous views of Scotland: The Mull of Kintyre, which was sup-posed to be 13 miles away but looked far closer, Ailsa Craig and the Ayrshire coast.

Once again I was grateful to Saint Patrick for his Zero Tolerance Policy on snakes as I tramped the heathy heathery cliffs on a balmy afternoon that would have had them out of their vipers' nests and basking in the sun by the squirmful back home.

(I remember reading about a mad adder professor at one of the Welsh universities who thought there weren't enough of the unwelcome things in his homeland, so planned to breed them in his laboratory and release them on the Gower Peninsula. I imagine the tourist industry there need-ed him about as much as the Northern Irish one needed The Troubles).

I didn't have those cliffs all to myself. Apart from other walkers, I also encountered rock climbers and mountain bikers. But it couldn't have been more spectacular. My coast walk (I had to admit) had been almost worth the wait.

Next day we set off, on one of Ireland's mistier mornings, through fuchsia hedges which gave the South something to think about, by Torr Head to Cushenden village, created by Clough Williams-Ellis, architect of Portmerion (of Prisoner TV fame) but in this case comfortably Cornish rather than eccentrically Italian.

Daisy was badly in need of diesel so I stopped to fill her up at the next village, Cushendall, and found that here in the North the price had suddenly shot up to more than 70p a litre. In hard cash: Serious sterling, not play-money punts.

One thing I wouldn't want to have been doing for a living: Trying to run a filling station just inside the Northern Irish border.

(Incidentally, I found Northern Irish banknotes most confusing. They came in a huge variety of different makes, each with their own idea of what they should look like: Bank of England, Bank of Ireland, Northern Bank, Ulster Bank, to name just a few. Even the locals must have trouble keeping up with them all. The place must be a forger's paradise: Nobody would ever be able to tell a fake from the real thing).

So, through the pelting mist, to the part of Antrim that sounds like a malt whisky tasting, the Glens: Glenarm, Glencloy, Glenariff, Glenballyemon, Glenaan, Glencorp, Glendun, Glenshesk and Glentaisie.

I decided to sample Glenballyemon and Glenariff. And they were delicious (with water): Clean, smooth and peaty, and as unspoiled as any bit of Ireland I'd seen.

From a glorious taste of the glens to a lovely white port, Carnlough, where we drove under an old railway bridge that looked like a cardboard cut-out but, like the harbour beside it, was built from the limestone it once helped to export.

Next: Afternoon tea at Carnfunnock Country Park, where a brass band played gentle non-military melodies and the scents of the herbs and flowers in the walled garden perfumed the air after the rain.

Kids got happily lost in the Ulster-shaped maze and there was a magnificent collection of sundials, some bizarrely beautiful, some beautifully bizarre. (Just a shame that on the cloudy day I got there they'd all stopped).

Through villages keen to show where their Loyalty lay, with Union Jacks flying from the lamp-posts, kerbstones painted red, white and blue, and NO SURRENDER and GOD SAVE THE QUEEN etched in the middle of the road, to Carrickfergus and Newtonabbey, as the cranes of Belfast Docks came poking into view across the mudflats.

I decided to visit Belfast the next day, so a rare encounter with a motorway took us to Bangor, County Down, a more brazen resort than its

Welsh namesake.

Along the much caravanned but unspectacular sea side of Down's nether appendage, the Ards Peninsula, to its southern tip, Portaferry (not to be confused with Porta-Potti) where we checked in for the night at the little campsite just down the steps and across the road from the welcoming Fiddler's Green pub.

Up the prettier side of the appendage, beside Strangford Lough, past a notice on a gate saying NO SHOOTING (which looked like good advice in this part of the world) to Newtownards and back to Belfast.

Past massive Stormont Palace and the huge Harland & Wolff shipyard, where they built the Titanic, to East Belfast's Freedom Corner, its angry murals shouting: IRISH OUT and HANDS OFF ULSTER.

(But as in the South many of the locals still wore shirts in support of the same team, Man United, and all the many churches still stood in the name of the same God).

I parked Daisy near the Central Library to walk down Royal Avenue, busy with shoppers, and again it all seemed so British (as long as you disregarded the police Land-Rovers disguised as battleships and the armed cops on point duty).

I was reminded of Manchester city centre (which also received its share of The Troubles when a massive bomb blew it apart).

Past the Prince Albert Memorial Clock Tower, grand but not handsome, to Belfast Cathedral, Saint Anne's, austerely erected in the name of a no-nonsense God and containing the unfussy grave of Lord Carson who led the opposition to Irish Home Rule and has been revered or reviled (according to taste) ever since.

There weren't many black faces in Belfast, but then who needs racial divisions when they can be provided just as readily by religion?

I passed the Official Manchester United Superstore, which was doing super business, and the Liverpool Football Club Superstore, which wasn't.

Next: The over-the-top City Hall, with a dome to match Saint Paul's and survivor of as many bombs, its main entrance lurking behind a giant Diamond Jubilee statue of Albert's other half, the Empress Victoria, its interior much marbled, muralled and stained-glassed despite being less than 100 years old.

With Daisy for company again, to West Belfast and the Falls Road where the flags on the lamp-posts were black and the slogans screamed: RUC NOT WANTED HERE and A PROPER POLICE SERVICE NOW.

Then, a few hundred yards and several million disagreements away: The Shankill Road, submerged like an English village fête beneath waves of red, white and blue bunting, every wall daubed with red hands and fists and slogans yelling: ULSTER FREEDOM FIGHTERS and ULSTER VOLUNTEER FORCE FOR GOD AND ULSTER.

So, beneath more Republican flags, we left that divided city by the Ormeau Road to return to County Down and the holiday town of Newcastle, where the Mountains of Mourne sweep down to the sea.

I slept among those mountains at the beautiful (and beautifully kept) campsite in the Tollymore Forest Park. And before I went to bed I followed one of the forest trails for a walk beside fast-flowing streams, as the sky reddened and the sun went down on a lovely Northern Irish evening.

In the morning I drove into Newcastle to buy a copy of the Racing Post (to study the runners at Royal Ascot) and was tactfully asked whether I'd like it in a bag, as if I'd chosen a naughty mag from the top shelf.

I also noticed the old-fashioned courtesy of the locals' conversation. Even when they clearly knew each other well, they didn't use first names. It was: "Lovely morning, Mrs Kennedy." And "Aye, it is that, Mr Graham."

To another major fishing port, much Union-Jacked Kilkeel, where I sat on the sunny quayside and watched the busy scene as trawlers eased their way through the narrow harbour mouth, hulls were being painted in all colours, and mountainous seas of nets were being checked.

Up Carlingford Lough to another attractive resort, Warrenpoint, with its pleasantly old-fashioned seafront, park and bandstand. A delightful place, yet previously known to me (like so many other peaceful corners of pretty Northern Ireland) only for the spilling of blood: The gruesome slaughter of 16 British soldiers on the same day as Lord Mountbatten was killed.

14

Newry - Rush - Trim - Malahide - Donabate - Balcarrick - Dublin -
Portlaoise - Cashel - Clonmel - Caher -Glen of Aherlow - Tipperary -
Birr - Athlone - Knockcroghery - Roscommon - Longford - Ardagh -
Ballykeeran - Mount Temple - Moate - Clonmacnois - Mullingar -
Reynella - Charleville - Athy - Kildare - The Curragh - Shankill -
Sandycove

I OFFLOADED some of my more confusing Northern Irish banknotes
in exchange for provisions at Newry, then re-entered the Republic without ceremony, the only indications of a change of country being:
1. The A1 became the N1.
2. The morning sun turned to afternoon rain.
3. The traffic got stuck behind a tractor.
   Through damp Dundalk, reassuringly disrupted by roadworks, and
unpronounceable but delightful Drogheda, busily straddling the River
Boyne, to Ireland's most famous beach, at Laytown, where horse races
are run on the sand.
   We spent the night at the eccentric little campsite at North Beach, Rush,
a few miles north of Dublin, run by a Yorkshireman from Cleckheaton
(and you can't get much more Yorkshire than that, even if you have lived
in Ireland for 33 years).
   No disrespect to Daisy, but there's something uniquely seductive about
sleeping in a tent.
   Whether it's the sense of danger produced by knowing there's only a
thin sheet of material between you and the elements or whether it's simply the cosy feeling caused by the unaccustomed accoustics, I'm not sure.
   But when I went to bed that night, there was no doubt I felt a twinge
of envy for my conspiratorially giggling neighbours as they settled snugly under canvas beside me.
   Maybe it was just that I was just missing The Chauffeur. Still, Daisy
and I were only 20 yards from the strand, and I was contentedly lulled
to sleep by the soothing sound of the gently incoming tide.
   In the morning I had work to do: My mate Brian Donaldson was flying out to join me for a couple of days' golfing, so I needed to investigate

possible venues. I'd heard there were some nice courses near Trim, about an hour's drive inland, so I set off to find them.

Tiny Trim, so small that it has a mere three betting shops, is most famous for having the castle that was invaded by Mel Gibson and his clans for the making of Braveheart.

Its other great landmark is a massive monument to that most British of heroes, the Duke of Wellington.

(The duke, Irish born but none too proud of it, once upset his fellow natives by telling them: "Just because you're born in a stable that doesn't make you a horse." Ireland's own hero, Daniel O'Connell, gave as good as he got, though, replying: "No, but you could be a donkey now.")

Trim also has a tourist office, which is where I went to find out about those golf courses. And that's when life got complicated.

The Irish tend to become a bit vague when you start asking them for directions (almost as vague as when you start asking them the time) and that happened here.

But the main problem was a different one: As the very friendly, very obliging girl in charge quickly explained, she wasn't from Trim now. And she didn't know the area now.

Twice she went into an office next door to ask for help, and the people there said they thought there might be a golf course on the Navan Road.

Then a visiting American came in to ask for information for herself (which wasn't forthcoming) and she said she thought she might have seen a course on the Longwood Road.

Daisy and I set off, without a lot of confidence, along the Longwood Road and my fellow tourist was right: I found County Meath golf club. A lovely looking course. But unfortunately booked solid for the next two days.

Next, we took the Navan Road, but here I saw no sign of any golf courses. I asked again in Navan and was directed to the Royal Tara club on the Dublin Road. But it too was fully booked.

So back to the coast passing a notice saying PICK YOUR OWN (unsure whether that was an invitation or a threat) to the Donabate and Balcarrick golf clubs, and success: Both said they could fit us in.

South to Malahide, an attractive seaside town which looked the ideal place for Brian and I to stay. I tried several guest houses but they were all full, so I ended up booking a couple of rooms at the trendy-looking Maud Plunkett's Hotel.

Then I went off to the station to enquire about trains to Dublin. I asked at the ticket office if the service was efficient, and was told: "Now it's the best in the world now."

This was good news except that, as soon as he'd said it, the man behind the counter then began to laugh uncontrollably just like Will Hay in Oh Mr Porter.

I also called at the local Paddy Power betting shop to catch up with latest developments at Royal Ascot and was intrigued by their Special Bet: What Colour Will The Queen's Hat Be Tomorrow?

The odds: Yellow 4/1, Pink 5/1, Red 5/1, Royal Blue 6/1, Green 6/1, Cream 7/1, Pale/Light Blue 8/1, Apricot, Peach 8/1, Maroon 10/1, Navy Blue 10/1, Lilac 10/1, White 12/1, Black and White 16/1, Straw 20/1, Stripes 20/1, Polka Dot 20/1.

I put a fiver on Lilac. (Well, I'm nothing if not a mug punter).

Back to Rush for another night in Daisy before meeting Brian at Dublin Airport the following morning. We picked him up and drove to Donabate, where we had an enjoyable hack round.

I knew Brian was an expert ball finder but I was grateful to him on this occasion for finding one of my clubs, which I'd managed to leave behind when it had slipped from the bag on my back as I bent down to look for a ball in the rough.

So to barge our way past the half a dozen bouncers guarding Maud Plunkett, and sleep in a real bed for the first time in over a month.

The cost: 70 punts each for two nights (about the equivalent of 10 nights in Daisy, but including a Full Irish Breakfast and with less far to walk to the bar).

The hotel was noisy throughout most of the night as hundreds of young cráic heads revelled in and then spilled out of its four bars.

In fact the only sound I didn't hear was the eight o'clock alarm call they'd agreed but forgot to give me (an uptight English concept none too readily grasped in laid-back Ireland).

We made it to Balcarrick, though, and asked the pro what the course was like as we handed over our green fees. "Now it's like a hen run," he told us. "And there's some lovely long short ones now."

Three hours' happy hacking later we returned to Malahide, left Daisy at Maud's, and set off for the station. On the way I called at Paddy Power's and (drat) the Queen had worn peach.

In the event we failed to check out the efficiency of Will Hay's trains because a bus came along, and we caught that to Dublin instead. When we got there we caught another bus, this time an open-top one, and went on a sight-seeing tour of the city.

During it we learned:
1. Dublin means Blackpool.
2. The Natural History Museum is known as the Dead Zoo.
3. Whiskey makes you well when you're sick and sick when you're well.
4. The Guinness Brewery is the holiest site in town.

We also heard of the brewery worker who drowned when he fell into a vat of Guinness. When they broke the news to his widow, she said she hoped that at least his death had been quick. Oh no, they told her, he'd had to get out four times to have a pee.

After our tour we went to check out Dublin's so-called Cultural Quarter, Temple Bar. But once again the main art we discovered was that of drinking.

And it wasn't even being done by Irish people: All our fellow pub customers, in various states of drunken disorder, seemed to be Englishmen on stag trips.

More ould bikes hung from the ceilings and the music was about as Irish as the customers, although of a different vintage: The Hollies, Gerry and the Pacemakers, the Righteous Brothers etc.

Keen to taste Ireland to the full on his two-day visit, Brian then insisted we visit a Spanish restaurant, La Paloma, where we ate:

1. Paella de la Casa ("A legend in circles of indulgence and gluttony this world famous seafood and meat dish offers a virtual orgy of oral pleasures.")

2. Macarrones con Carne ("All the passionate Latin frenzy of serrano ham and chorizo sausage dangerously liaisoned with tomato and bechamel sauciness and brought to you in glorious pasterama.")

Back on the late bus to Malahide and past the army of bouncers into Maud's heaving bosom where I sat beside a cigarette machine bearing the notice SMOKERS DIE YOUNGER (surely an irresistable challenge to any self-respecting Live-Fast-Die-Young teenager) and I got chatting with a beautiful blonde.

She told me her name was Maxine, so it was. And she came from Warrenpoint, so she did. And she'd missed her flight to Paris, so she had. And her boyfriend was 6ft 4ins, so we didn't.

AFTER breakfast Daisy and I returned Brian to the airport for his flight home, and set off to investigate Ireland's interior.

We drove directly inland to Portlaoise (best known for its high-security jail) and checked in at another campsite of character, Kirwan's, just a mile from the town centre.

It was a pretty site, hidden away behind high hedges beside the Limerick road and filled with colourful flowers and shrubs and brightly painted old school desks and benches.

It was also a God-fearing place, with many notices about church services and bible studies and an instruction telling us not to use the laundry on Sundays.

Glad again of my golfing umbrella, I walked through heavy rain into Portlaoise, its intimate little main street of old-fashioned shops well pubbed and well bookied.

I entered Ramsbottom & Sons, which sounded as if it should have been in the north of England but couldn't have been more Irish.

It was another schizophrenic anachronism of an establishment unable to decide if it was a shop or a pub, its landlord dressed in the sort of old brown coat (complete with pens in the top pocket) that used to be the uniform for grocers when Queen Elizabeth was still a princess. The wooden cupboards and shelves, in green and cream, came from the same era.

I sat at the old counter between the weighing scales and the bacon slicer, opposite the lard, the corned beef and the firelighters, and drank Guinness with the quietly-spoken locals, who seemed quite content to let the rest of the world grapple with the modern cares of a new millennium.

It was both wet and windy when I arrived, dripping umbrella in hand, but mine brown-coated host cheerfully told me how lucky we were being with the weather, which was so mild now.

It was true, of course: The weather wasn't particularly cold, but the strong winds and the torrential rain rather than the mildness were its more notable features.

There weren't many women customers, but those there were had one advantage over the men: Their lavatory was indoors, under cover. I got seriously wet when I visited the uncovered Gents in the yard.

The main topic in the bar (apart from the weather) was sport: Not football or Gaelic Football (a cross between rugby and football) but hurling (a lacrosse between rugby and hockey) and, in particular, the chances of the local teams, Laois and Offaly, in the big matches at the weekend.

All the customers were addressed, with immense politeness and courtesy, by their first names. And there were plenty of them: Needless to say, the place (like every bar in Ireland) was packed.

In the morning, Daisy and I drove through sunshine and showers between farms of green and yellow and hills of green and blue, past a sign saying NO DUMPING OF BEET (which I can honestly say I had no intention of doing).

Through a village called Horse And Jockey, then we were interrupted in our journey by the magnificent intrusion of the Rock of Cashel, which wouldn't have needed to feel inferior in Tuscany or Umbria.

I stopped to investigate its crowning glory, ruined Saint Patrick's Cathedral, and got a wonderful bonus in the Hall of the Vicars Choral: Beautiful and beautifully appropriate hymns performed live and for free, not by vicars choral but by tourists choral: A Swede-singing group of them from Gothenburg.

Into Cashel Town and John J Freeman's (GROCERY HARDWARE FUNERAL DIRECTOR BEERS WINES AND SPIRITS SELECT BAR AND LOUNGE), now just another Irish theme pub well geared up for the grocks with old bottles and lamps and tractor seats in the window, but still a handsome reminder of an unforgotten past.

Next, to a real Irish treasure: Tipperary's county town, Clonmel (which means Honey Meadow and was the birthplace of Tristram Shandy author Laurence Sterne) with wonderful old shops and houses, bars by the firkin and bookies by the furlong.

The best building, the Main Guard, more than 300 years old and topped by a weather-vaned, weather-beaten wooden tower, was submerged beneath a sea of scaffolding and plastic sheeting when I got there. And not before time: It was a wreck which appeared to be sinking fast, with a heavy list to starboard.

There was only one problem: I lost Daisy. The trouble was the place was bigger than I'd realised. I knew I'd parked her in a side street outside a pub.

But of course that didn't narrow it down very much and the result was that I spent nearly an hour walking the busy streets before I bumped into her again. (It was a very pleasant hour, though, in that delightful place).

To Caher, dominated by the sturdy castle that gave it its name (which means fortress) for a pleasantly wooded walk along the river past a golf course (with warning notice describing it as a GAME SANCTUARY and saying NO DOGS ALLOWED) to the marvellously silly Swiss Cottage, thought to have been designed by John Nash, architect of the even more marvellous and even sillier Royal Pavilion at Brighton.

Much verandahed and balconied, with tree trunk supports to the eaves and roses climbing to the thatched and dormered roof, quite without symmetry or order, it was built to appear as if it was growing out of the ground.

Upstairs, the walls and ceilings were curved, slanted, arched, bowed and angled every way but straight. It had never been lived in but had been used by Lord and Lady Caher and their toff friends to play at being peasants during days out in the country.

(Having inspected the place I am pleased to be able to confirm, as the Royal Pavilion's No 1 fan, that it was indeed daft enough to have been designed by the same person).

Beneath the slopes of the Galtee Mountains, basking reflectively in the early evening sun, to Tipperary's lovely Glen of Aherlow and the beautiful Ballinacourty House Caravan and Camping Park.

In the morning I watched a middle-aged Welsh caravanning couple's lengthy leaving procedure as they spent about 20 minutes checking their oil, water, brake lights, indicators etc. They'd virtually done an MOT by the time they'd finished.

They were so different from a carefree young tenting couple who requested a jump start from Daisy for their old banger before they were able to set off. (We campers come in all sorts).

By unsignposted winding roads to Tipperary Town, to be overtaken along the way by a speeding hearse, complete with coffin.

It must have been very late for a very important funeral because it raced past Daisy, throwing up a cloud of gravel, at a good 70mph.

It didn't have a WELL DRIVEN? sign on the back. Nor those twin bumper stickers you see saying OVERTAKING SIDE and UNDER-TAKING SIDE.

Tipperary was less attractive than Clonmel, but quainter: Geared up more towards the farmer than the tourist. Apart from the usual bars, barbers, bookies and butchers, its main street was full of old-fashioned ironmongers and haberdashers and a Wellworth store that bore a strong resemblance to stores with a similar name back home.

Next: Thurles, a monument in the centre of its broad main street saluting the memory of its Nationalist martyrs, then past two boys and a hurling stick precariously sharing a bike, and over humpy Devil's Bit Mountain to Moneygall.

So to Roscrea for a Supermac burger at Supermacs fast food restaurant (100 PER CENT GAELIC) and Birr, which not only had a fast-food restaurant called Wondermacs (although I didn't go in for a Wondermac burger) but also another claim to fame: The Leviathan of Birr Castle.

For 70 years the Leviathan was the world's biggest telescope, giant plaything of the third Earl of Rosse and a magnet for every top mathematician, scientist and astronomer.

This must have been a most inefficient location for it, though: Imagine the frustration of all the wasted nights the earl and his illustrious guests must have spent sitting up waiting for the Irish clouds to disperse so they could reap the benefits of his wonderful contraption.

The telescope was an impressive sight all right: A dozen huge wooden wine vats clasped together with metal hoops to form a giant factory chimney poking out at 45 degrees from the stonewalled battlements of its keep in the castle grounds.

And I got there at an important moment: Just as a huge new mirror was being winched into it.

Quite a crowd had gathered to witness the Big Event, including Press photographers and a film crew, and there were gasps of admiration as the man in charge of the delicate operation proudly announced the mighty mirror's unveiling.

They were an innovative lot, the Rosses: Also on view were the oldest wrought iron suspension bridge in Ireland and a turbine house from which electricity was supplied to both the castle and the town long before it became readily available elsewhere.

As ever, though, there was a price to be paid for all these scientific advances: Death. A guest at the castle became Ireland's first motor accident victim when she was knocked down by an experimental steam-powered car.

The castle wasn't open to the public but the grounds were lovely, with a well-lilied lake, wild flower meadows and walled formal and kitchen gardens containing magnificent greenhouses of geraniums and the world's biggest box hedges (as well as some pretty major beech ones).

We ended the day at the Hodson Bay Caravan and Camping Park beside choppy Lough Ree, just north of Athlone.

Next morning I parked Daisy near Athlone Castle, beside the broad, boat-filled River Shannon, and set off to explore the town, the shops and cafés in its little streets busy with young mums smoking and chatting to excess.

Athlone is right in the centre of Ireland, which is why it was famous to me half a century before I got there: Like every member of my generation I knew of it long before I'd heard of many places nearer home, because of the family wireless.

Athlone was right there on the dial along with Daventry, Hilversum, Stuttgart, Munich, Rome and the rest.

As a child, I had no idea where it was and I don't remember getting a snap, crackle or squeak out of it but it was always there for me somewhere, right from my Listen With Mother days.

I asked about Radio Athlone at the local tourist information office but they didn't know anything about it. Instead, they directed me to the library where I learned that it had been set up in the 1930s as the main transmitter to all Ireland of programmes which were originated in Dublin.

North to the fascinating Claypipe Visitors Centre and Workshop at Knockcroghery. For nearly 300 years the village was famous for making the pipes (or dudeens) as 100 people and seven kilns worked flat out to keep up with demand. They were delivered all over Ireland by the cartload in huge round baskets.

Production ceased abruptly in the 1920s when the village was burned down by the feared Black and Tans during the War of Independence.

The pipes came in all lengths, and the long-stemmed version was an essential at Irish wakes. A gross of them would be laid out for the mourners along with a gallon of whiskey, half a barrel of porter, claret, Guinness (obviously), tobacco, snuff, tea, bread and jam.

The pipes were known as Lord Ha' Mercies because that was the supplication expressed on behalf of the departed when they were smashed at the end of the wake. Before smoking, they were dipped in booze to improve their flavour and to cool them down.

As with the Red Indians' peace pipe ceremony, it would be considered rude for a mourner not to smoke one when it was offered.

Now production of the pipes has been revived in the village by Ethel Kelly (appropriately enough, as they were always smoked by women as well as men).

On to colourful Roscommon where we parked in the main square near the Bank of Ireland's most impressive branch building, in its time a court house, a market house, a Catholic church, a school, and the Roxy Cinema.

Beside it was the even more impressive Old Jail, now being converted into a shopping centre, where a plaque affirmed with accuracy: "It was here that 'Lady Betty' the last hangwoman in Ireland executed her duties."

There was also a castle (of course) and a tiny museum in the old Presbyterian church, filled with all the obvious items of interest: Ancient stones, old farm implements, thatching rods, horseshoes, flags, clothes, swords, guns, grenades etc.

But a more unusual exhibit was its wonderful collection of Melody Maker magazines from the 1950s and 1960s headlining the highs and lows in the careers of Eve Boswell, Bill Hayley, Ray Charles, Alma Cogan, Bobby Rydell, Eddie Calvert and Co.

"It's the best museum in the world," the curator assured me, before adding: "But then I've never visited any others."

He followed me round as I viewed everything on display, and talked as much as any Irishman I'd met. But he wasn't Irish at all: He was as English as me, and came from Cricklewood.

Next, to Longford where we parked beneath the ugly cathedral, its style more Roman Temple than Roman Catholic with a giant frieze atop huge columns.

Inside the entrance, a sign on a plastic barrel said: HOLY WATER PLEASE MAKE SURE TAP IS TURNED OFF.

Longford, home of the Longford Slashers Gaelic Football Club, was the biggest and busiest town in these parts. But, like its cathedral, it was no beauty.

I'D seen signs saying GOLDSMITH COUNTRY, so decided to investigate. I asked for literature about it at the Longford tourist office. And got a real ear bashing from the formidable lady of post-colleen years on the other side of the counter.

"Goldsmith Country? Goldsmith Country? Goldsmith Country haven't sent me so much as a paper bag now," she complained.

She suggested I head for the heritage centre in the village of Ardagh. And when I got there, she said, I could give them a telling off from her for their inefficiency.

(I should say that such inadequacies on the part of the the Irish tourist authorities are most unusual: Along with brewing, bookmaking and diddly-diddlying, tourism is one of the things the Irish do best).

I set off in the direction I'd been told, followed a sign to ARDAGH... and ended up back in Longford.

I tried again, and knew I was on the right track when I passed a sign which said GOLDSMITH COUNTRY DRIVE ON LEFT CONDUIRE À GAUCHE LINKS FAHREN (giving the impression that up till now we should have been driving on the right).

Ardagh didn't have any literature either. I didn't tell them off, though, because it wasn't their fault: They felt just as deprived as Longford at not having been sent any.

But they did point me in the direction of Featherston Hall, in the centre of the village, which the young Oliver is said to have mistaken for an inn, thereby giving him the central joke for his comedy She Stoops To Conquer.

(I don't know how he could have made the mistake: It looked much too grand. But far be it from me to spoil a good story).

They also attempted to direct me, in an indeterminate Irish sort of a way, to the Jolly Pigeons pub where Goldsmith is said to have done some of his (considerable) drinking:

"Now you go straight on to Carrickboy now and you turn now [a gesture to the right] and you be careful now because it's a dangerous crossing now and you turn in Ballymahon [a gesture to the left] and you'll come to it now."

They confided in me, too, that Goldsmith probably never drank there, but at a different pub which used to have the same name. (I mustn't tell the landlord they'd told me, though).

Unfortunately, when I finally found it, I didn't see the inside of the pub which Oliver probably didn't see the inside of either because it was closed. Instead, I set off on another golf recce.

I found (in the end) Mount Temple Golf Club which was hidden in a web of country lanes miles from anywhere shown on any of my maps, and asked whether I'd be able to play the following day. To be sure I would. So I said I'd be back if the weather improved. I was told it would be perfect now.

I was asked where I was staying, and said I was heading for Ballykeeran. I enquired whether anyone knew how to get there, and this sent the bar-room jury into full session with much animated argument in which place names and pub names were prominent.

Eventually, the foreman hand-signalled the members' verdict: "Now you turn [right] out of the gate and now you turn [right] at the Athlone Road. Now you turn [left] to Glasson and now you come to a crossroads [straight on] and now you'll see [right] a lovely view of Lough Ree. Now you turn [right] at the Dog and Duck now."

The verdict was a fair one, so Daisy and I were able to check in at the Lough Ree East Caravan and Camping Park, on the opposite shore from where we'd spent the night before.

Mount Temple was wonderfully situated: On high ground, with 40-mile views across the magnificent Midlands.

And it was a history lesson as well as a golf course, built on several important sites including an old castle beneath the first tee and an ancient ringfort beside the seventh green. A round cost 15 punts.

The land had been a farm until eight years before, when the owner (and golf fanatic) had realised that thanks to bountiful Aunty Europe he could afford to turn it into a golf course.

The entrance to the locker rooms was through the farmyard (now fortunately both cow and pat free).

Unusually, little oak saplings growing in the middle of the fairways served as 150-yard distance markers from the greens.

The hardest hole was the 16th, the well named Heartbreak Hill, where the hazards were: 1. Bunkers. 2. A ditch. 3. A pond. 4. More bunkers. 5. The (virtually vertical) hill.

Once again, on a rain-sodden morning, I had the course to myself. As I made my way round, I was sorry to see that many of the plastic tee notices, giving the hole numbers and distances, had been vandalised.

Some of the damage could only just have been done, because splinters of plastic still littered the grass.

Worried that as the only person out there I might get the blame for these wanton acts of destruction, I decided I'd better mention them when I got back to the clubhouse.

But I was told not to worry: The greenkeepers did it with their mowers. (With greenkeepers like that, who needs vandals?)

By now I was becoming quite proud of my burgeoning beard, which I thought was shaping up pretty well and starting to give me a rather distinguished appearance.

Unfortunately, though, my illusion was becoming threatened by all the strangers who kept seeking me out to tell me what a splendid chap that old boy was who played Uncle Albert in TV's Only Fools And Horses.

WE spent another night at Ballykeeran, and the next day I played another course, nearby Moate, getting a severe thrashing from a little schoolboy called Thomas who was half my size but hit the ball twice as far.

Afterwards, I set off for many-templed Clonmacnois, one of Ireland's holiest places (despite strong competition) overlooking a broad bend of the Shannon.

I got there just before 7pm and went to investigate, expecting I'd be far too late to be allowed in.

But not at all: I was welcome to come in now and look around for as long as I liked now. They wouldn't be able to charge me now, though.

A plaque told me: HIS HOLINESS POPE JOHN PAUL II PRAYED HERE. And alone in that tranquil place, now empty of the crowds who'd have invaded it by the coachload earlier in the day, with the song of birds and the lowing of cattle carrying for miles on the still Shannon air, there in the heart of Ireland, I felt as close to spiritual peace as I've ever felt.

Then, as silver harp strings of evening sunlight played across the wide valley, we crossed the river by 16-arched Shannonbridge and returned for a third night at Ballykeeran.

The camp was run by a big friendly guy called John who always insisted I sit in the chair across the desk from him in his office each time I checked in.

The reason: So he could chat with me for longer. And he told me some interesting things about his country's changing fortunes.

Nowadays, he received Irish visitors as well as the traditional English, French, German and Dutch. Up till a couple of years ago, this would have been most unusual. Not only that, but French youngsters were coming to work in Athlone: Unheard of previously, when it was the Irish who had to go abroad to earn a living.

Next day, we set off for Mullingar: Busy but not beautiful, an eight betting shop town. I'd heard the military museum, in the local barracks, was worth seeing and contained some interesting exhibits including Michael Collins's pistol.

There were no signs to it, so I pulled up alongside a police car at traffic lights and asked the driver how to get there. He thought for a while about whether to give me directions, then said: "Now it'll be quite hard to find. It'll be better if you follow me now."

At least it saved him from Tony Blair trouble: Trying to tell his right from his left. Not only that, but it was fine for me: I followed him through various side streets and suburbs for about 10 minutes (during which time we seemed to double back on ourselves quite frequently) until he stopped abruptly, got out and pointed towards the barracks entrance across the road. Unfortunately, it was closed.

So to cross a meadow of a thousand orchids, scale a derelict dry-stone wall and scramble through bramble to reach the eerily deserted church and overgrown graveyard at Reynella, on the Delvin Road, and marvel at the huge ivy-ravaged beehive of a tomb containing the remains of Adolphus Cooke Esq of Cookesborough, eccentric local landowner who believed he would be reincarnated as a bee.

He was also convinced that one of his turkeys was the reincarnation of his father, and threatened to sack any worker who didn't doff his cap to it. And he was keen on crows, forcing his workers to collect sticks and build nests for them.

Through Tullamore (where Paddy Power the Bookmaker was next door to Paddy Field the Oriental Restaurant) to spookily Gothic Charleville Forest Castle, panelled, vaulted, mirrored, chandeliered and staircased like a vampire movie waiting to happen.

The round library in one of its towers contained not books but hats and helmets: Police, fire, army and pith, English, American, French and German.

The place was owned by an Irish-American family whose ancestors had been cruelly evicted from their thatched cottage in these parts a couple of generations earlier.

Members of the family had recently returned, bought the castle, and only then discovered that it had been owned previously by the landlords who had evicted them. What goes around comes around.

I chatted with Bridget Vance, a member of the "crazy" family (her word, not mine) as she delved for mushrooms in a mountain of mire beside the castle forecourt with her alluring daughter (dressed in black lace negligée barely concealed beneath blue denim overalls). Bridget informed me that this was the only estate left intact in Ireland.

For the second time that afternoon I grappled with heavy undergrowth as I explored the castle's dilapidated gardens and tumbledown stables.

Next, to Athy where a pub was available to see you on your way in its additional rôles of both travel agent and funeral director, and the Forest Farm campsite where I bumped into my golf pal from Strandhill, Benny (The Skip) McDermott.

I visited him and his wife Kay in their van to share a bottle of red wine and our experiences of the golf courses and campsites of Ireland (but we never quite managed to stick to the subject when it came to discussing The Troubles).

SO to the climax of this year's travels: Irish Derby Day at The Curragh. As soft rain fell, we drove through dripping hedges of honeysuckle past a Bull Performance Testing Station (which conjured up for me images of ice-skating judges holding up score cards for artistic impression and technical merit) to Kildare Town, its little square smothered in almost as much bunting as the Shankill Road.

Here, as the prevalence of betting shops and bars soared, I set off in search of breakfast. I rejected the Jailhouse Fast Food Restaurant, which had signs in the window saying STAFF WANTED (but not what they were guilty of) and chose Jimmy Bean's (BREAKFAST LUNCH AFTERNOON TEAS).

A woman behind the counter was doing the washing up so I asked her about breakfast, but she replied: "Now I'll have to get one of the others to look after you. I'm a kleptomaniac and I'm not allowed to touch money now."

We got over that when I explained that I wasn't trying to pay, only to order. And the breakfast, when it came, was excellent.

I took a look round the town. The pubs included The Vatican, Dixie D'arcys and Silken Thomas but they were all officially closed, like every bar in Ireland on Sundays, until 12.30.

There were public lavatories in the middle of the square, so I called in for a pee before driving to the course. And it was the first time I'd been propositioned in the Gents: Not for sex, but for money. (Well, I think that's what it was).

A fellow bearded itinerant, with an obvious liking for strong lager, had been standing in the doorway as I entered, sheltering from the rain.

And as I unzipped my flies and set about my business he lurched up to me, leaned against me, breathed alcohol fumes up my nose, and began asking (as far as I could gather) for cash.

It seemed that after all the lager he'd downed that morning he was badly in need of a cup of tea now.

I did my best to help (I wasn't in much of a bargaining position) and managed to hold my own with one hand as I fished some change out of my pocket with the other.

He seemed less than impressed with what I handed over, but fortunately I was able to march off to the sanctuary of Daisy quicker than he was able to stagger after me.

It was time for me to make further charitable donations, this time to the bookies.

The Curragh was a huge area of open green space, virtually flat and more reminiscent of Newmarket Heath than Epsom Downs. You couldn't really say it was beautiful and you couldn't really say it was ugly, although in that dismal weather it tended towards the second.

I parked Daisy (for free) on the rails near the two-furlong marker. There wasn't much to see, apart from a big grandstand and a vast number of bedraggled people.

A few courageous women were well turned out in dresses and hats as if it was summer, but the only fashion winners were those with raincoats and umbrellas.

And there, blonde and beautiful in a red trouser suit, was Margo Ann Murphy from Macroom. What's more, she remembered me (despite my beard): "You backed a winner with me now," she said.

She's surely the best-looking bookie who's ever laid me.

Obviously, course cred is all important among racegoers. You've got to dress correctly for a start. The right hat is important for men as well as women: A brown trilby in the rain or a straw panama in the sun.

(A high-risk strategy, this, as a sudden change of weather can soon spoil the effect).

Binoculars also make you look the part (even if there's no longer any need for them now that every major racecourse has a giant TV screen right in front of the grandstand).

Also, it looks better if you carry just a racecard rather than bundles of smudgy, crumply newspapers.

And it's always advisable to cheer home every winner, even if you haven't backed it. This gives the impression you're a shrewdie.

(Be careful not to do this wildly or amateurishly, but in a contented, smug, I-know-what-I'm-doing sort of way, just loudly enough to be noticed by all those poor losers around you).

One thing about going racing in Ireland: You never have to queue at the tea counter because everyone else is always at the bar. And in fact it wasn't too bad getting served there either because they only supplied two drinks: Budweiser (who sponsored the racing) and Guinness (who sponsor the country).

There was much meeting of old friends in the scrum, usually with the favourite Irish greeting "How're y' doin'?" or sometimes "An' y'rsel'?" (in answer to the first question, taken for granted even if not actually asked).

There was live music, of course. At the posh end, near the winning post: A genteel brass band huddled together under a canvas shelter (apart from the conductor, whose back was getting soaked).

At the other end, beside the furlong pole: A full-scale ceilidh, as the cráic addicts of The Curragh swayed, lurched and sang to a rock band inside a massive marquee.

Another thing about the Irish: They don't know when to stop. Although there were eight races on the card (more than enough punishment for any gambler) there were as many punters in the betting ring before the last race as at any time during the afternoon. And the drinking and dancing carried on long after the bars had closed and the music had stopped.

Back to Kildare and The Vatican, its walls covered with holy pictures of its sainted heroes: Shergar, Arkle and Lester Piggott, its bars crowded with punters looking just like those same people who had seemed so gloomy as each favourite had got beaten, except that these were miraculously telling of their triumphs over the bookies which became even greater with each pint of Guinness.

In the square (now barred to traffic) a live band belted out a rock concert (complete with smoke effects) from a covered trailer to the delight of a large and none too sober audience.

Every one of them appeared to be well below drinking age apart from my friend from the Gents who was unsteadily leading the dancing, lager can in hand.

NEXT stop: Shankill, on the coast 10 miles south of Dublin, where Daisy and I checked in for two nights at the Shankill Caravan and Camping Park.

In the morning I caught the 85 bus to Dublin, through thriving suburbs full of young people and smart cars, where the property prices were soaring as quickly as the new buildings.

I got off at Eden Quay, beside the Liffey, and walked to Grafton Street, the city's stylish main shopping centre, which Brian and I hadn't seen from our bus tour because it's pedestrianised.

Past the statue of Sweet Molly Malone, wheeling her wheelbarrow, to beautiful Bewley's Café to drink morning coffee seated in a high-backed chair at a marble-topped table.

Again, I was reminded of what the Irish do so well: Retain the best of the old as well as introducing the best of the new.

The place spoke volumes of Dublin and Dubliners, Joyce, Behan and the rest, mirrored and pictured and dark with benches of deep velvet, stained glass windows too patterned to let in the light, and brown wood and walls gently decayed by decades of nicotine and hot air. (And the loveliest lavatories in the whole Republic).

Over the humpy Ha'penny Bridge and through a sea of anxiously smoked cigarette butts to enter the Four Courts, where the Irish Civil War started and where, with Mirror colleagues including legal chief Charles Collier-Wright (affectionately known as Charles Collier-Wrong) I once held the Irish record for libel damages. Against, not for. (Is this legal, Charles?)

People were sitting or standing in the domed main hall looking smug or strained, clever or stupid, at home or lost. There was an information desk, but nobody was at it.

I wandered around at will, unchallenged by officialdom as I climbed to the top floor past not four but dozens of courts off a maze of corridors. (One was No 29).

In such places are life's real gambles won or lost. I went next door for a lunchtime sandwich at the Chancery Inn, and a merry group of customers were enjoying a lively sing-song.

I wondered whether they were celebrating a vital court victory, or had merely won a few million on the Lottery.

Back on the bus to Shankill and then to Sandycove, at the southern end of Dublin Bay, and the James Joyce Tower, built by the British Army in case of invasion by Napoleon, which was never Joyce's but was once home to the poet and wit Oliver St John Gogarty.

Joyce came to stay here, but it seems there was little love lost between the two men after he had been rude about Gogarty in a poem. One night a fellow guest had a nightmare about a black panther, reached for his gun and fired it into the fireplace.

Gogarty then took the gun, shouted "Leave him to me" and shot down the saucepans from the shelf above Joyce's bed. Joyce left immediately and never returned. But Joyce's best-known novel, Ulysses, assured fame for the tower which was the setting for its opening scenes.

From the top of the tower I gazed across the Irish Sea and imagined I could see the British coast.

Beneath me was the Forty Foot Gentleman's Bathing Place, where half a dozen wrinkle-tanned members of the Sandycove Bathing Association disported their bellied bodies on and off the rocks. An official notice warned: TOGS MUST BE WORN.

I wondered how much easier relations between our two countries might have been if it wasn't for the fact that, in many ways, the Irish are more British than the British.

SO what are the Irish like? Well, they're: Friendly, generous, helpful, relaxed. And above all funny. Very funny. (No, their humour isn't unconscious. It's conscious: They're able to laugh at themselves, but you can't help laughing with them).

Their country isn't backward, it's booming: They've been clever enough to hang on to the best of the old as well as taking on board the best of the new. And (with a little financial help from Europe and us grocks) it's paid off.

Their population isn't an old one: The streets are alive with young people who, less than a generation ago, would have had to leave the country to earn a living. Now, youngsters come to Ireland from other countries to find work.

They love life's simple pleasures, and allow themselves to enjoy them: Talking, drinking, music, sport. (They don't play enough cricket of course, but you can't really blame them: They haven't got the weather for it that other parts of the Empire had).

And it's all beautiful. Nature didn't indulge in discrimination or division when she handed out good looks: The Antrim coast in the North is stunning. Just like the Kerry coast in the South.

It isn't perfect of course: To visit Ireland is to enter into an Idealisation Conspiracy with the tourist board and the postcard manufacturers. What's in it for them is that they take our money. What's in it for us is that we tell our friends back home we're not daft to go there because everything is blissful all the time. And it hardly ever rains.

Next day I left with regret, boarding the Stena Explorer with Daisy and sailing from Dun Laoghaire to Holyhead. Then I drove home, took The Chauffeur in my arms and tried to give her a kiss.

But she took one look at my beard, and suddenly remembered it was time to watch Only Fools And Horses.